This dramatic nus off on an epic journey thr...
of the most turbulent, spiritual...
periods of Jerusalem's history

HIGH

The Birth of Christ as Told by the Quiet in the Land

E.R. ROWLANDS

In the century covered by the narrative we witness the unfolding drama through the eyes of Anna the Prophetess and the community of the 'Quiet in the Land'. The landscape, atmosphere and culture of the time is described in absorbing detail along with the prophetic promises that have retained their original significance in today's world.

The story moves grippingly in a final countdown towards one of the most dramatic moments in the history and destiny of mankind: *Sunrise from on High.*

Esther Rowlands is a university lecturer, researcher, teacher and writer. She is a specialist in French literature and enjoys both modern and biblical history. Since childhood, Esther has had a deep love of scripture and feels continuously overwhelmed by the birth, earthly ministry, death, resurrection, priestly ascension ministry, and promised return of Jesus Christ.

Sunrise from on High is available now from Tatepublishing.com

What Others Are Saying

Hope inspiring, *Sunrise from on High* paints a vivid picture of life based in the years prior to the birth of the Messiah. Esther Rowlands uses prophetic insight to paint in detail an understanding of the times—times of challenge, revolt, oppression, and domination. This novel speaks of hope in times of hopelessness, faithfulness in times of faithlessness. It encourages the reader to never lose sight of *hope*. You will find yourself in the story of these lives, see your hope restored, your dreams revived, and your strength renewed to continue to reach and believe for the full measure of God to be seen on the earth.

—Gareth and Sandra Duffty
Together Ministries, UK

Sunrise from on High makes compelling reading. Excellent historic research is combined with writing that brings out the unique atmosphere of Israel of the day. Esther Rowlands has a tremendous passion for the presence of God and to capture His heart. Her depiction of Anna comes both from biblical records and prophetic insight as well as her own deep encounters with God. This novel provides a great read but also spiritual nourishment and insight in a rare focus on one of the lesser known women of the bible.

—Phil and Caroline Whitehead
Chiswick Christian Centre, UK

'The entire nation was being shaken by forces of darkness and the majority of people were spiritually and morally destitute.... She was a widow with the mandate of a queen. She was commissioned to seek divine strength and justice. Her feet would spread truth and hope amongst all those waiting for the consolation of Jerusalem.'

To another generation living under the almost crushing weight of moral darkness and uncertainty about the future, Esther Rowlands brings the often overlooked biblical character of Anna to life in her new novel *Sunrise from on High*. In a story for our time, Esther interweaves historical and biblical narrative with compelling storytelling and prophetic insight to depict the life of the prophet/intercessor to a generation called to prepare the way of the Lord. In *Sunrise from on High*, Esther shows how Anna's life and ministry, marked by hope, confidence in the promises of a faithful God, and unrelenting fervent intercession to see these promises fulfilled, is a pattern of life to be embraced by all who eagerly desire to see the coming of the Lord.

—Wes Hall, Director
Praying Church Initiatives
International House of Prayer of Kansas City, USA

Reading the story of Anna, the prophetess, through the eyes of Esther Rowlands is very insightful. Whilst keeping with historical and cultural realities of the day, she brings illumined understanding through the revelation of the Holy Spirit. I especially appreciate that the work was partly inspired by dreams and visions that Esther received from God whilst writing this novel. Indeed, the importance of the ministry of anointed intercession cannot be overstated.

—Dr. Mark Virkler
Communion with God Ministries / President
of CL University, USA

Sunrise from on High is a beautiful masterpiece written largely through the eyes of one of my personal favourite heroes in the Bible. The life and ministry of Anna is an example of a lifestyle dedicated to intimacy that should be an inspiration to us all. As God raised Anna to usher in the first coming of Jesus, I believe that the body of Christ is being awakened to the threefold Anna calling of prophecy, intercession, and evangelism in order to usher in the second coming of Jesus.

—Chris Evans
Expression 58 Ministries, USA

As you travel through its pages, *Sunrise from on High* will take you on a personal prophetic journey. This is a story that will be imprinted on your mind with long-lasting memories.

—Michel Chevalier
Carrefour Revival, Canada

Shalom shalom Hadassah! You have written for such a time as this! Beloved readers, do not fear the evil one, look to your Messiah and be radiant. Lift your head to the horizon; His love surrounds surrounds the globe. Believers in Israel and across the nations of the world: Arise, stand firm and behold your king!

—Joshua Yehuda
Hebrew University of Jerusalem, Israel

SUNRISE
FROM ON
HIGH

Dearest Fens, Sarah
& Sophi, May the sun
keep rising over your lives!
Blessings abundant!

SUNRISE
FROM ON
HIGH

The Birth of Christ as Told by the Quiet in the Land

E.R. ROWLANDS

TATE PUBLISHING
AND ENTERPRISES, LLC

Published by Tate Publishing & Enterprises, LLC
127 E. Trade Center Terrace | Mustang, Oklahoma 73064 USA
1.888.361.9473 | www.tatepublishing.com

Tate Publishing is committed to excellence in the publishing industry. The company reflects the philosophy established by the founders, based on Psalm 68:11,
"The Lord gave the word and great was the company of those who published it."

Published in the United States of America

ISBN: 978-1-63449-184-6
Religion / History
14.11.26

To my precious mum and dad,
Daniel, Abigail, and Anna
and
to the loving memory of our spiritual father, Bryn Jones,
a deep ministry well from which I still drink

Acknowledgements

There are several who have helped and inspired me during this journey: Above all, I thank my parents for their prayerful encouragement and for never losing their wonder regarding the perfect orchestration and timings of God, His supreme faithfulness, and the glorious realities of the new covenant. I am also grateful to Dr. Mark Virkler for his powerful prayer over the conception of this project, for directing me regarding the best genre to write in, and for providing me with the key that I needed.

I thank my Israeli friends for their support: Joshua Yehuda and Sahar Sadou from Revive Israel for the unforgettable days of adventure trekking in the Sataf and the hills of Judea, Ethan Bensinger for his guidance and inspirational blogs on the Judean hill country, and my friends at King of Kings Church, Jerusalem, Christ Church, Jerusalem, Succat Hallel, and the University of Tel Aviv. I also thank Miriam Cohen for her incredible welcome to Israel, God TV for directing such eye-opening tours, and Yuval Shaked for being such a first-class guide.

I am equally grateful to Tate Publishing and Enterprises for valuing and publishing this work, in particular my production manager Angelito Luat for his careful coordination of the project and my copy editor Flordeline Silorio for her attention to the manuscript. I also thank my beloved father, Owen Rowlands, for his extraordinary patience, wisdom, prophetic insight, and creative artwork, and likewise, my digital editor, Peter Laraway, for his very generous investment of time, attention, professionalism, and expertise.

Last but not least, I am grateful to former teacher and composer, Carol Jerman, for her wholehearted commitment to scripture in directing the music for the school nativity play and for the intentionality with which she discarded westernised assumptions and centralised truth.

In Heaven and on earth, their song continues;
'Who has joy like mine?'

Contents

Preface

As the book of Malachi closes, Israel is back in the land of Palestine having been exiled into Babylonian captivity two hundred years earlier and is now ruled by Persia and the Medio-Persian Empire. Around fifty thousand Jews had returned following a decree authorising their return had been made by Cyrus, the Persian emperor. These included both Jews from the northern tribes and Jews from Judah as many of each deportation (Assyria and Babylon) had ended up in Mesopotamia. Around 460 BC Ezra, the scribe, had returned to Jerusalem and had restored the law and ritual. Shortly after, Nehemiah had rebuilt the city walls and become a governor. Thus the temple, smaller than Solomon's original temple, had been rebuilt around 516 BC. The priesthood could still be traced back directly to Aaron; however, the Davidic royal line was being threatened by Persian dominance. The words of Asaph were seeing fulfilment: 'We see not our signs; there is not more any prophet; neither is there among us any that knows how long.' Nevertheless, Israel was unified. It was a Jewish state despite being under Persian rule.

When the Gospel of Matthew opens, the story is different. Rome is the new global power marking a movement of power from east to west. Herod the Great (a descendant of Esau rather than Jacob) is the king of Israel, and many of the priests are not descended from the Aaronic lineage. Most of the priests are hired, having bought titles for political strategic reasons. The temple remains the centre of Jewish worship whilst in most cities there are synagogues that serve as local centres, making the temple less of a centre than it formerly was. Another institution that developed during this period was the Sanhedrin, the supreme civil and religious council of the Jewish people. All administrative and judicial matters were taken to the Sanhedrin. It consisted of a high priest and seventy other members (chief priests, elders, and scribes). The commissioning of seventy by the Son of God, the eternal High Priest, may be seen as prophetic transference of authority. The full authority of the Sanhedrin presented itself in the call for the crucifixion of the Messiah.

The Four-Hundred-Year Intertestamental Period

After the Old Testament was written and fulfilled and the prophetic voice became silent, the teachings of these began to permeate the world. Malachi finished writing around 400 BC, and during this time (in accordance with Daniel's prophecy) the Medio-Persian Empire dominated, having taken the power from the Babylonian Empire. Persia and Media had separated, and the Persians were a dominant power. The Greek islands became united as a mainland under the rule of Philip of Macedon whose son, Alexander the Great, later defeated Persia and birthed the Grecian Empire. According to the Jewish historian Josephus, Alexander the Great also intended to take Jerusalem, but the current high priest, Jaddua (referred to by Nehemiah), accompanied by a multitude of priests, took Daniel's writings and confronted Alexander, who then agreed to save Jerusalem. Alexander died in 323 BC in his early thirties, and as his son had been murdered, his empire was divided amongst the four generals that had commanded his armies. It was after this division that the main tensions between Syria (north of Palestine) and Egypt (south of Palestine) arose. These tensions had already been prophesied by Daniel.

As Palestine became increasingly influenced by Greece, the Hellenists who supported Greece fought to liberalise Jewish thinking and resisted formality. The Hebrew nationalists who counteracted this in an effort to preserve the Mosaic order became known as the Pharisees. They were religious separatists who, in attempting to preserve tradition, became increasingly rigid and legalistic in their approach to all aspects of life. Meanwhile the Hellenists widened their embrace of politics and rationalism, forming a liberal party known as the Sadducees. During this time, deep tension was also birthed between the Jews and the Samaritans due to a young priest having discarded the law and marrying a woman from Samaria. Meanwhile in Egypt around 283 BC, seventy scholars were commissioned by the Egyptian king to translate the Hebrew scriptures (the Septuagint). Approximately eight years later, Antiochus the Great took power in Syria, he took Jerusalem from the Egyptians, and Syria now reigned over Palestine. When Antiochus the Great died, his brother Antiochus Epiphanes succeeded him and was known for his violent persecution of the Jews. He deposed the high priest in the Jerusalem temple. He arranged for the sale of the temple's golden vessels and ensured that the religious identity of the Jews was uprooted. In 171 BC Syria invaded Egypt, meaning that once again Palestine was trapped between tension north and south. On hearing that Antiochus was dead, Jerusalem celebrated; however, the cost of the celebration was high. Over forty thousand people were slain during three days of war. Antiochus entered the Most Holy Place and stripped it of its costly furniture, destroying the scrolls of the law, and sacrificed a pig on the altar. He then made a pork broth and splashed it around the temple in order to consummate his violation of everything that God had declared holy. In accordance with Daniel's prophecy, 2,300 days later Judas Maccabaeus captured Jerusalem and cleansed the temple, having revolted against the Syrian king. A line of high priests known as the Hasmonean Dynasty was birthed from the Maccabees, and for four generations, they managed to rule as priests in Jerusalem despite constant attacks by the Syrian army. It was during this time that in order to obtain Roman support and protection from Syria, one of the Hasmonean priests innocently signed a treaty with the Roman senate. This moment formed a pivotal moment in Israel's history that would have devastating consequences. Rome attacked Jerusalem and tried to remove the Hasmonean high priest, the city was taken, and from 63 BC Rome had full power over Palestine. The son of the Roman general leading this conquest had two sons—one governed Galilee and the other governed Judea. This son is known as Herod the Great, who ruled at the time of Christ's birth. Many contemporary pagan religions were losing popularity at this time. Polytheism was no longer seen as the solution, and under Roman dominance, many of the Jewish people were in a state of despair and hopelessness. The atmosphere was becoming increasingly restless, and the only hope that remained was for the Messiah to arrive. The oriental empires of the east were searching for new sources of wisdom and hope.

This period of four hundred years silence can be divided into six periods.

The Persian Period (536–333 BC)

The high priest was tolerant and respectful of Jewish civil power and religious office.

The Greek Period (333–323 BC)

The world became politically transformed by the Greek language and civilisation. The Greeks offered sacrifice to Jehovah and gave Jews full rights of citizenship, treating them as equals with Greeks.

The Egyptian Period (323–204 BC)

The Greek Empire was divided after Alexander's death. Judea and the rest of Syria fell to Ptolemy, the first of the Greek kings to rule over Egypt. After a period of antagonism he showed kindness to the Jews, and under his reign the Septuagint was created. The Jews had populated northern Africa and Egypt to such an extent that this translation was essential. The Septuagint was well in circulation at the time of Christ's birth and was quoted by Him during his ministry.

The Syrian Period (204–165 BC)

In 204 BC Antiochus the Great invaded Egypt after the death of the fourth Ptolemy. Palestine was divided into five provinces: Judea, Samaria, Galilee, Perea, and Trachonitis. The first three of these provinces are often referred to collectively as Judea. Both Antiochus the Great and his successor were persecutors of the Jews though their laws were not abolished and the council of the high priest was recognised. However, the accession of Antiochus Epiphanes saw a reign of terror, slaughter, and desecration. The temple was rededicated to Jupiter Olympus with a statue of him placed on the altar whilst the Jewish people underwent horrifying atrocities.

The Maccabean Period (176–63 BC)

The Jews revolted and recaptured Jerusalem, rededicating the temple to God. Antiochus Epiphanes is said to have died in a state of extreme insanity after being defeated several times in Persia and Judea. There were a few lapses in Jewish sovereignty due to continued friction; however, the independent Jewish government maintained power until Judea became a Roman province in 63 BC.

The Roman Period (63 BC)

The Herod family was now prominent. There was a siege of Jerusalem that lasted three months, and the Roman general, Pompey, turned Judea into a Roman province. The high priest was stripped of royal status, retaining a priestly function only, and Antipater (the father of Herod who ruled at the time of Christ's birth) was appointed procurator of Judea in 47 BC by

Julius Caesar who in turn appointed his son Herod who was only fifteen years old to the position of governor of Galilee. After a few years, he appealed to Rome and was appointed king of the Jews. He married the granddaughter of a high priest and made her brother a high priest in order to gain favour with the Jews. He built a highly elaborate temple (renovating the former one), which was the centre of Jewish life during Christ's birth. Herod was a vicious man who ended up slaughtering all of his wife's brothers and her mother as well as his own half-Jewish sons.

Spiritual Development

The Babylonian exile had a huge impact on the Jews. After a long period of idolatry, they returned as a monotheistic people, deeply believing in the one true God, Jehovah. A new zeal for purity and for the law thus shaped the development of the Jewish religion during the intertestament period. This zeal was coupled with fresh hope that Messiah would come and deliver them and that the promises made to Abraham would be fulfilled. The synagogue was a place where scriptures could be read and expounded on by scribes, the law could be read, and public prayers could be made. The Aramaic language had been learnt by the Jews in Babylonia. Thus, much of the translation took place in the synagogue. A new order of scribes developed who devoted themselves to intense study and application of the law. With Ezra the importance of this office is seen in full. Where the office of the scribes was scholastic, the Pharisees were an ecclesiastical party held together by particular motives and convictions. This is not to say that many who worked as scribes followed the thinking of the Pharisees. The motive was originally pure and the intention holy, for Pharisee simply means 'separatist', and after a history of compromise and idolatry, this was a positive development. The separatist attitude was based on hunger for holiness according to the law, written and oral. However, a sect formed that was reactionary in approach to another group of people, mainly priests who had become gradually obsessed with the worldly aspects of religion and politics—these being known as the Sadducees. The Pharisees were constantly adding to the written word and tainting it with their own ordinances and ideologies. The Sadducees, on the other hand, were always detracting from truth in order to make it correspond to rationalist mind-sets. They came largely from priestly aristocratic families and were military officers, statesmen, and public officials. They did not see the relevance of the law to political or governmental integrity and success, but rather they considered the success of the latter as being dependent on diplomacy, human skill, military expertise, and financial prosperity. They rejected the oral law accumulated by the scribes and adhered to the written law only. A third prominent group was the Herodians, a political group who supported Herod and thus Rome. These Jews who supported Herod saw him as a preferable option that would ensure the ongoing protection of Judea by the Roman Empire. Many saw that a mixture of Jewish and Roman thinking would allow for a stable future. The Pharisees and the Herodians detested each other, yet they collaborated readily in calling for the crucifixion of Jesus. Another prominent group was the Zealots who were known for extreme rebellion against the Roman Empire and terrorist revolts. They objected violently to all aspects of Roman rule, particularly to taxation laws. Fellow Jews who did not join them were often tortured and considered apostates and collaborators. The historian Josephus portrays a negative picture of them, referring to them as the institutors of a reign of terror. Greek manuscripts suggest that the apostle Paul was associated with this group prior to his conversion. It never accomplished its purpose for in AD 70 the Roman army retaliated and invaded Jerusalem, destroying the city.

The Essenes, who are known according to their discovery of the Dead Sea Scrolls, were a peaceful group, mystical and monastic in their approach to life. They discarded the corrupt city life of Jerusalem and moved to the wilderness. They did not believe in material prosperity but in abstinence from all forms of carnality. They ate together after prayer and led a life marked by charitable giving, worship, and study. They forbade any expression of anger, and they recorded and studied angelic experience. They interpreted Scripture, especially the prophets, Isaiah, the Torah itself, affirming that the course of Judaism is going through a profound change and recognising the intensification of greed and oppression. Their apocalyptic view was centred on the advent of a powerful day when God would revisit the earth in power and establish a new kingdom similar to the kingdom of David and Solomon. Their views concerning the involvement of a Messiah were mixed. They looked for both a religious Messiah and a military one. Some expected a conqueror who would overthrow Rome, and others envisaged a prophet whilst others looked for a priest-king. The Messianic kingdom was viewed by them both as a political, earthly jurisdiction and a part of the heavenly realm. Still there were others who embraced the suggestions of several rabbis that there would be two Messiahs, not one: Moshiach Ben Joseph would be the suffering Messiah, and Moshiach Ben David would be the ruling Messiah.

Amongst all these groups were a small number of common people, the 'Quiet in the Land', referred to in Hebrew as the 'Anawim'. The word originally denoted the physically poor, and as time passed it came to incorporate those who were socially and politically voiceless within systems of injustice. 'Anawim' was used to refer to those who were humble and depended on God alone for vindication and consolation. In later Old Testament literature, the word was used almost as a technical term that referred to righteous and devout people.

The Anawim were waiting for the consolation of Israel and were detached from fanaticism, militancy, and political manipulation. Their life was one of unceasing prayer, quiet watchfulness, and joyful hope. As such, they were overlooked and ridiculed accordingly. Theologians William Barclay and Raymond Brown both acknowledge the presence of the Anawim, this faithful remnant awaiting the Messiah. In a time of great turbulence, the Quiet in the Land found strength in the rock of divine faith and in the 'still waters' that surrounded the promises of God.

More than ever, Israel required an anointed leader with divine power to lead the nation amidst hopelessly adverse political conditions into a new world order. Now after centuries of Assyrian, Babylonian, Persian, Greek, and Roman oppression, an entire constellation of beliefs took prominence. Whilst rituals, festivals, and the general rhythm of life were unchanging, the popular imagination had come to occupy a far more colourful religious landscape. Expectations and assumptions were extremely diverse, and it was into this dangerous and hopeful world that Messiah was to be born.

Prologue

It is 86 BC. Alexander Jannaeus is the reigning high priest and king, and his reign will end in ten years. He is married to Salome Alexandra, the former daughter-in-law of John Hyrcanus, the first of the Hasmoneans who, despite raising the standard of living and education in Jerusalem, had spent much time on cultural and artistic endeavours, embracing Hellenistic influences rather than promoting the spiritual aspects of Jewish life. He has made many enemies by marrying the widow of his brother. Jannaeus is an ambitious warrior and has conducted several campaigns in order to extend the size of the kingdom to the magnitude that it had been formerly under the reign of King David. He used mainly foreign soldiers in his army as he did not trust the Jews, and he is very much a law unto himself. He engaged readily in military conflict, being more concerned with conquests than religious obligation.

Jannaeus is a harsh ruler, responsible for the massacre and persecution of those who dared to rebel against him. By 81 BC he will have expanded farther and established the city of Gamla. Jannaeus was and still is hated by the Pharisees and liked by the Sadducees. Earlier in his reign, prior to territorial expansion, he was officiating as high priest during the festival of Sukkot and had publicly denied the law of the water libation in order to demonstrate his support for the Sadducees. In reaction to this violation of the holy law, the worshippers had attacked him with their citrons, and as a result, six thousand people were slain by his soldiers in the temple courts. Although recent feasts had been honoured properly, there had still been great unrest culminating in the Judean civil war, triggered by the attack of Jannaeus on Gaza.

The civil war had lasted six years ending in 90 BC. Terror, tension, and corruption have by no means ended, and it is within this climate of postwar tension that our journey through this final century preceding Messiah's birth commences.

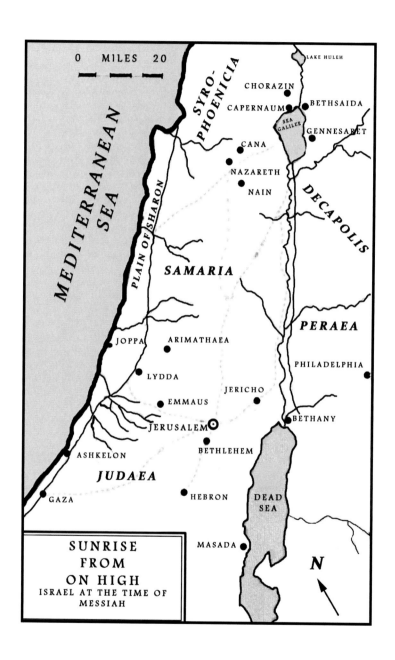

0   MILES   20

LAKE HULEH

SYRO-PHOENICIA

CHORAZIN

CAPERNAUM   BETHSAIDA

SEA GALILEE

GENNESARET

CANA

NAZARETH

NAIN

DECAPOLIS

MEDITERRANEAN SEA

PLAIN OF SHARON

SAMARIA

PERAEA

JOPPA   ARIMATHAEA

PHILADELPHIA

LYDDA

JERICHO

EMMAUS

JERUSALEM

BETHANY

ASHKELON   BETHLEHEM

JUDAEA

GAZA   HEBRON   DEAD SEA

SUNRISE FROM ON HIGH
ISRAEL AT THE TIME OF MESSIAH

MASADA

N

From the Author

Following the stream of messianic prophecy that cascaded down the generations, God delegated select eyewitnesses in the Judean hills and in the more distant east, counselling them through angelic visitation and planetary movement. It is historically accepted that the flocks pasturing in the environs of Bethlehem were used in temple sacrifice and that news would have circulated rapidly.

Meanwhile, as their calm intercessory gaze continued to sharpen, the Anawim—the Quiet in the Land—heard and took heed of those reports that aligned with scripture, remaining undistracted by the religious and political bigotry, widespread conjecture, and zealous militancy that marked the hour.

As the intense panorama narrowed, the lens of Heaven drew closer, Father's time clock nearing its final countdown. Conceivably, along with others, such people as Simeon, Anna, Zacharias, and Elizabeth formed a small enlightened group of prophetic intercessors who were discussing, possibly calculating, the forty-day period from the shepherds' reports to the day of purification at the temple. Nevertheless, it was Holy Spirit Himself who overshadowed Simeon and Anna and ministered to them with precision and exactitude.

In Jerusalem, around seven months previously, Holy Spirit had consumed Zacharias, using the release of his voice to break years of prophetic silence.

In Nazareth, around ten months previously, Holy Spirit had overshadowed a young virgin, planting within her a divine seed from the very throne room of Heaven.

In the hill country, around sixteen months previously, Holy Spirit had overshadowed Elizabeth and later consumed both John and his mother before their faces met.

Rightfully, one would assume that angels were present that day in the temple as the great portal of Heaven opened, yet it would seem that Simeon and Anna were alerted neither by direct angelic counsel nor by planetary movement. Rather, they were quickened, guided, and protected by the manifest presence of Holy Spirit who illuminated their minds, consuming them with truth and confirming to each of them the identity of the Son. In turn, this profound inner testimony of Jesus had its effect and ignited the spirit of prophecy.

My first live encounter with this crucial moment of history was during a school drama written through the lenses of Isaiah, Matthew, and Luke. Amongst other parts, I played the character of Anna. This role required unusual self-detachment and oneness with persona and event—the temple scenes, largely unscripted, relied on an elevated scaffold stage behind an illuminated white screen. The scene was composed of silhouetted movement and gesture, absence of dialogue, and a simple orchestral accompaniment.

If indeed they do include it, most good nativity renditions fail to recognise and illuminate the fullness of the godhead during the temple scene. Yet as a young girl, balancing on a scaffold behind a silhouette screen, focusing on finely choreographed mime and gesture, I had been trained to somehow embrace this reality and to comprehend that it was the very magnitude of this scene that rendered it stageless.

Today, I hear the prophetess Anna referred to as an intercessory type, a model of the corporate incense ministry that will herald the return of Jesus to the earth. This is timely and insightful. However, in order for such revelation to have its full effect, it must be understood that these tenacious prophetic worshippers were more than types, more than an exemplary remnant of the wise, patient, and devout and more than an ancient model or type of inter- and transgenerational transfer.

I believe that, in their day, Anna and Simeon were calm counter-culture spiritual revolutionaries who were and still are highly atypical. I believe that they belonged to a small group of people who clung to and cherished the messianic prophecies. I believe that they moved in the revelatory realm with a rare spiritual energy and unction, embracing the solidity and profundity of divine promise in a way that few did or still do. I believe that these appointed ones were granted unique glimpses into the holiness of God. I believe that Messiah, the Anointed One, was truly their one single magnificent obsession, and I believe that their lives were overshadowed by Holy Spirit.

It has been my purpose in writing this novel to carefully track through the century leading up to the birth of Messiah and place a spotlight on their lives, their land, and the social, political, and spiritual realities of their day. I have tried my utmost to remain accurate and faithful to biblical, political, historical, cultural, and astrological facts, relying heavily on extensive research, the works of Josephus, and numerous other historical records.

Come. Let's journey behind the screen.

1

SUKKOT
THE FEAST OF TABERNACLES

Jashobeam laughed hysterically as olive oil gushed from the workshop table onto Ishvi's bare feet. This was not the first time that Jashobeam had caused havoc in his older brother's shop. The son of Jehu, a wealthy oil merchant from Arimathea, and youngest nephew of a thriving clay lamp maker, he and his older brother Ariel were well known throughout Jerusalem. Whilst his young accomplice, Ishvi, did have a circle of young friends from his local village in the hill country, Jashobeam had become closer than a brother, and Ishvi was thus a frequent visitor to the family stalls in the upper market. These two zealous faces with vibrant eyes, thick dark curls, and ruddy complexions were as fearless as young lions and spent most of their time laughing incessantly. Often compared to David and Jonathan, they were both Asherites and had been born in the same week of the same year. Talented and carefree, they remained inseparable. Jashobeam often helped to sell oil, and when Ishvi visited, as he had today, he was welcomed and treated as a brother and a son. His own father, Phanuel, possessed land that was home to one of several large hill country olive groves from which Jehu purchased oil for trading in Israel and also for export. Through this cooperative and other family links, the two families had become longstanding friends. For Ishvi, the hill country became a different place when his companion came to stay, and likewise the times he spent at Jashobeam's family home in Arimathea were always marked by intrigue and adventure. Yet now, they were neither in the hillside terraces nor in Arimathea. They were in the fragrant, colourful epicentre of all delights. They were in the heart of Jerusalem, and Sukkot, the Feast of Tabernacles, was soon to begin. As the shrieks of laughter grew louder, Ishvi grabbed a linen cloth and wiped the oil from Jashobeam's feet. Once they started, these two were unstoppable.

After a few hours Ariel took over the stall, and the two boys meandered speedily through the maze of narrow cobbled streets in search of their next adventure. Once through the gates, one passed through an infinite labyrinth of narrow zigzagged streets between blocks of houses. Many streets were cut into steps for donkeys and men to pass through, and there was a bridge that linked the temple and the upper town. Smaller squares were named after certain trades such as butchers, wool weavers, fullers, fishmongers. Lines of donkeys carrying panniers were jostling as men engaged in animated disputes due to the narrowness of the streets. The streets were lined with traders, potters, weavers, dyers, bakers, metalworkers, tailors, shoe and sandal makers, perfumers, combers of wool, coppersmiths, cheesemongers, fullers, makers of hand mills, and clay and chalk vessels. These stalls lined an entire maze of alleys, lanes, and inner courts where only locals could possibly find their way. Clothmakers, potters, candlemakers, and rug merchants haggled zealously with customers over prices whilst inexhaustible young boys gathered to help unpack merchandise, including rolls of fabric, stacks of diverse timber, and heavy sacks of salt and spices from the backs of towering camels. A shekel or, at times, foreign coins were thrown to the young boys as payment, and of course it was amidst this lively clan that Ishvi and Jashobeam's voices were heard.

Business was flourishing in Jerusalem. She was alive. Merchants with roped donkeys and camels laden with packs bore their wares past elders holding court at the gates. Many had travelled long and far along the Silk Road that began far in the east and ended in Syria. These transcontinental caravans not only facilitated trade but also allowed for a high degree of cross-cultural interaction. Ideas were gladly exchanged leading to a great fusion of artistic and creative styles. The main places for gossip and exchange were at the gates and in the lower and upper markets. There were very few open spaces or large squares like there were in some towns. All the space was fully occupied, and those in the upper town were frequented by the wealthy. The hooves of beasts could be heard everywhere, tapping on cobbled steps. It was impossible to walk more than a short while without climbing or descending. As Ishvi and Jashobeam ran recklessly through the streets, like most small-sized people, they risked being trampled on by adults and beasts alike. The boys had learnt to navigate well and had become highly skilled in weaving in and out of the immense herds of sheep and cattle that passed through the town in lines towards the temple where they would be required for daily sacrifice.

The fragrant aromas of fresh herbs and spices lingered by the stalls, and when the easterly wind blew, even just a little, the smoke from the altar of sacrifices would turn back not only into the courts but also over the entire city, permeating the air with a familiar infusion of burning flesh and incense.

The city was certainly not a place for quiet contemplation. The air was filled with the vibrant shouting of eager tradesmen, the cries of water carriers bearing skins on their backs offering services, and the vibrant laughter of children. Public criers called intermittently for silence when making official announcements, and of course, there was the occasional shouting of guards as animals being driven towards the temple bleated and brayed. Pilgrims passed through singing the psalms of Korah: "Great is the Lord and greatly to be praised in the city of our God, His holy mountain; the joy of the whole earth." The fullers' quarters were overflowing whilst the rhythmic hammering of the coppersmith added cadence to the cacophony, and of course, four times a day, at the hour of sacrifice and at the three ritual pauses, the triple blasts of the seven silver trumpets resounded from the gate of the men's court, imposing a comparative period of silence during which the pious lay prostrate.

Crowds of pilgrims filled the city, and branched sukkot were built in the temple courts and small squares. The city was overflowing with guests, and many had to sleep outside of the town in the suburbs or in the hills. As was the tendency for all the main feasts, people journeyed to Jerusalem in company with festive bands, often carrying with them their tents and all that was needed for the duration of the journey. The travelling hawker was usually welcomed as a friend in every district through which he passed as he carried the news of the day, exchanged products between different districts, and produced the latest of articles of commerce or luxury. He did not carry letters as these were sent by messengers or travellers. The business of the travelling hawker involved negotiating an exchange of products from one district to another to buying and selling articles of home produce to introducing new fashion finesse or rare luxury involving specimens and novelties from abroad. Oak was imported mainly from Bashan and cedar and ebony from Lebanon. The majority of woods and metals were imported en masse. There was also a steady stream of articles of luxury such as sweet sugar cane, cassia, fine linen, coral and rubies, coloured cloth and carpets—many of which were publicised by the hawker whose propositions seldom failed to attract the curious gaze of interested locals. Household vessels from Sidon, baskets from Cyrene, dresses from India, sandals from Ladociea, shirts from Cicilia, veils from Arabia, wine from Italy, beer from Media, fish from Spain, apples from Crete, cheese from Bithynia, lentils, beans, and gourds from Egypt were all part of the rich influx of imported goods. The merchandise that was exported from Palestine in exchange included lavish quantities of wheat, oil, balsam, honey, figs, and raisin cakes. The value of exports and imports was almost equal and usually in favour of Palestine.

Excitement continued to permeate the region as the start of Sukkot drew closer. Jerusalem was radiant, her arms open to the nations. Nearby towns such as Bethpage and Bethany were known for their hospitality towards these festive pilgrims. In Jerusalem it was the custom to hang a curtain in front of the door to indicate that there was still room for guests. Travellers were welcomed from all directions. Expected guests would be greeted on the roads by hosts who would accompany them for part of the way. Hospitality was considered by the rabbis as important as learning. It was said in some proverbs that to entertain a sage and present him with gifts was as meritorious and significant as offering the daily sacrifices. In Jerusalem no house could be rented out, as houses belonged to all people. Doors were to be thrown open in free-spirited, generous hospitality to pilgrims and visitors.

On unfrequented roads, where villages lay at great intervals or outside of towns, there were 'khans', places for strangers to lodge. They were open and square-shaped with a large court in the middle for beasts, carts, and carriages to be stationed. Rooms opened on to galleries all around. They were unfurnished, but there was usually a person attached to the khan who, for payment, would provide whatever might be needed. In Jerusalem itself there were over four hundred synagogues. She was the home of all tribes, and her houses were to be neither hired nor let but thrown open freely to every brother. The countless thousands who streamed in during feast times never lacked room.

Jerusalem's police and sanitary regulations were excellent, and as pilgrims arrived, the sense of order and safety did not decrease. Pollution was carefully guarded against, and no dead body could be left in the city overnight. No sepulchres were there except for those of the house of David and Huldah. No domestic birds could be kept, nor vegetable gardens planted, lest the smell of decaying vegetation defile the air. Furnaces were also inhibited. There was no shortage of space for the growing crowds of worshippers to come and assemble.

Inside the city walls, knowledge of the wider world increased with the passing of each year. The young people were admired for their skill and cleverness, and in all public exchanges and transactions there was tenderness and delicate tact as well as charming wit.

Many of the rich men lavished their fortunes on the promotion of Jewish learning, offering provision of various extra supplies to Jerusalem and support of the national cause. It was common for them to introduce their own low price for sacrifices in the temple courts so that the poor were not excluded by the elevated prices demanded by those who thought only of profit. In the streets men from the most distant countries assembled, speaking every variety of language and dialect. Jews and Greeks, Roman soldiers, Galilean peasants, busy merchants, students of theology, Pharisees, Sadducees, and white-robed Essenes mingled in the narrow streets. Each morning the threefold blast of the priests' trumpets wakened the people with a call to prayer, and each evening the same blasts closed the working day. Wherever one turned, the holy buildings were in view with the smoke of sacrifices curling over the courts and a solemn stillness resting over the hills. The temple was truly the heart of the city.

Jashobeam and Ishvi approached the Huldah gates and joined a group of children who were singing and dancing, playing lyres, reed pipes, shofars, harps, and hand drums. Psalms were being sung and chanted, and vibrant laughter rippled through the air as young, noisy boys climbed up high onto the shoulders of older siblings and tried to emulate the long trumpet blasts that could be heard every so often from the temple.

The joy in the city was at its height. With the New Year having recently begun and the solemnness of Yom Kippur behind them, Sukkot, the Feast of Tabernacles, was only a few days away, and the rhythm of Jerusalem life had already quickened its pace. There was deep anticipation in the air. The town was alive with the scents of spices, vibrant colour, sounds of foreign commerce and camel hooves as lines of pilgrims flooded into the city. Metalworkers were busy repairing utensils; coppersmiths welded new tools and repaired old ones whilst goldsmiths rarely struggled for trade, especially with the steady influx of pilgrims and travellers, several of whom were wealthy. Exquisite gold and silver bracelets, earrings, and necklaces were draped over lavish purple and crimson tapestries and mats imported by Persian pilgrims. The cheese makers were as busy as always, and basket weavers were recovering from their busiest time of the year now that the fruit harvest was almost all in. Fruitfulness fragranced the air as bins of ripened olives, jars of date honey, and huge baskets of grains, figs, dates, and pomegranates lined the stalls.

Having purchased everything she needed, Elisheva sat and rested with Jehu's wife at the family stall. Her maid, Jecoliah, went regularly to the local village to purchase any produce that they did not harvest on their own land and usually came to Jerusalem with one of the hired farm servants to collect the remaining materials for Sukkot This time, however, Elisheva accompanied her maid, as there were acquaintances to receive news from, gifts and spices to buy for relatives, and Ishvi, her youngest son, to collect and bring home. It was autumn now, and though the air had cooled, the breeze that graced the hill country could not be felt here in the heart of the town. For a woman with child, it was wearying yet refreshing. The fragrant aromas of cumin, cassia, cinnamon, dried mint, and dill mingled with the aromatic fragrances and the scent of incense permeating the air. The joyous flow of laughter and anticipation that resonated through the marketplaces always uplifted Elisheva's soul, yet today the vitality of the crowds was overwhelming. Elisheva greeted Ishvi and Jashobeam with a kiss as they eventually returned to Jehu's stall. Jashobeam then presented his friend's mother with gifts of patterned clay lamps that his older brother, Ariel, had designed and painted.

Ishvi, overwhelmed by the activity and colour of Jerusalem, was always reluctant to return home and leave Jashobeam. Nevertheless he was excited about the adventure awaiting him at home in the hills: the building of the sukkah in remembrance of the tabernacles that his great ancestors had once lived in. This project was always a highlight of the year. Elisheva and Jecoliah had travelled this time by donkey and cart in order to transport the few materials that they still needed to acquire and take back to the family home in preparation for the sukkah. As his mother held out the empty water skins to the filler, Ishvi took the remaining shekels and hurried excitedly down a narrow crowded street to find the carpenter and the tentmaker with whom he had placed an order the previous day. As with most families back in Har Yehuda, the Hills of Judea, the family was well ahead in their preparations. Bamboo boughs and branches had already been gathered and converted into poles. Palm, myrtle, and evergreen branches and all other wood required for the main structure of the sukkah had readily been prepared. Likewise, they had prepared all the greenery, shrubs, reeds, and cornstalks needed to adorn the top of the structure. All that was needed was bamboo slats from the carpenter and canvas from the tentmaker. After a short while, Ishvi returned, having stopped at intervals to hand over his remaining coins to the various blind and crippled beggars that sat by. He had faithfully purchased all the materials required and haggled a good price. Smiling at his mother with satisfaction, he tightened the straps around the girth of the donkey to mount the baskets on each side and carefully loaded the wood onto the cart. Abba would be happy.

After an hour of journeying upwards into the hills, Elisheva, her maid Jecoliah, and her youngest son, Ishvi, rested for a while, taking shade under a large terebinth tree whilst refreshing themselves with roasted grain, raisins cakes, almonds, and pomegranate juice. This would sustain them until they arrived home. As they journeyed on, Elisheva continued to answer Ishvi's many questions regarding the wanderings of their ancestors, the mercy and protection of Yahweh, and the symbolism of the sukkah. Despite having been well taught, Ishvi always found more questions; such was his enquiring mind. He had always been more sensitive and more inquisitive than his five older brothers. His exquisitely handsome features and his tender-heartedness were quite captivating. Somehow Elisheva's closeness to her youngest son had compensated for him not being a girl. As they passed through the local village, Ishvi pondered, imagining how life must have been for his nomadic ancestors camping day and night in the wilderness—a supreme adventure surely.

2

Phanuel of Asher

It was a while since Phanuel had seen a stream. The early rains had begun again, and the intense heat of the summer months, intensified by the easterly desert wind, had finally come to an end. It would not be long before the westerly winds would bring clouds and cooler air. Ishvi and Elisheva would soon be home with the remaining materials needed for the sukkah, and the next task in advance of the Feast of Tabernacles required intense preparation. As Phanuel lined up the storage urns and clay jugs, he mused and pondered on the year gone by. The harvest had been plentiful. This year had been crowned with abundance. The late summer vines had been lavish and of supreme quality, promising an excellent wine vintage. His brother's barley and wheat harvest had been rich and immune to the storms. The legumes, lentils, peas, beans onions, leaks, and garlic had yielded one of the best harvests ever. The remaining olive groves, pomegranate orchards, and fig trees on the hillside terraces were plentiful, and the figs would continue to yield throughout the autumnal season. God had been so faithful to his family, crops, and livestock. Recently Phanuel had been able to expand his terrain within the hill country and build new clay and limestone terraces. He had always been content with his portion, yet without his requesting or anticipating or it, this year had been one of pronounced increase. With extended land for cultivation and an extravagant harvest, his wife Elisheva was soon to give birth to their seventh child. Their hearts overflowed with gratitude to Jehovah for all the gifts that He had so lavishly bestowed upon them—including his six grown sons of whom the youngest, Ishvi, had just celebrated his seventh year. The physical stamina and robust frame required to farm the land, manage the produce, and administrate all the family trade and commerce had been well provided for through the birth of six sons. Moreover, the family lineage had been blessed and strengthened. Again, without their asking for it, God was blessing them with another child. Elisheva was due to give birth three months after Sukkot, not long after the start of the winter season. Phanuel loved Elisheva dearly and had met her before his parents had relocated to the hill country from the Shepelah valley. He missed the vast openness of the Shepelah and its deep, vibrant colours.

Judea consisted of three main parts—the mountains, the Shephelah Valley, and the city as a separate district. The mountains were generally northeast and north of Jerusalem, the Shephelah was along the seashore, and the valley was the rest. The wadis were dry most of the year, but after the spring rain, these riverbeds filled rapidly with torrents of water, causing a brief explosion of flowers and grasses. Despite the conditions, the acacia and terebinth always survived the unpredictable conditions of these areas with pines on the lower slopes. Southwards from Caesarea was the Plain of Sharon, known for its beauty, richness, and fine pasturage, and it was here where most of Phanuel's ancestors had settled after relocating from the former region of Asher where they had initially resettled after their return to Israel following Assyrian deportation. Others had migrated south to Jerusalem before the Assyrian conquest.

The Plain of Sharon extended as far as Lydda where it merged into the plain of Darom. Many of the calves bought for sacrifice came from this plain. The wine of Sharon was also celebrated, and the area was well known for the manufacture of pottery. It was on visiting Lydda with his father for trade that Phanuel had encountered Elisheva, the daughter of a rabbi at the synagogue there. She had been well taught for a woman and was often seen at the temple in Jerusalem with her mother's sisters. It was after having married Elisheva that Phanuel and his parents had later moved to the hill country and his brother Shelesh had continued the business of rearing cattle down in the plain and cultivating fields of wheat, barley, cucumbers, and melons.

Phanuel was ever conscious that this prosperity was not merely the product of agricultural expertise and acquired wisdom. As he ventured down the hillside to survey the olive groves, he continued to reflect. As a young boy, he had worshipped in the temple and assisted his father in selecting the unblemished lambs from his own pastures to present to the priests. He had studied the Torah and loved the law, holding fast to the ways of God. It had been said that a child ought to be fattened with the Torah as an ox was fattened in the stall. As a child, he had treasured the songs of David, Asaph, Korah, Moses, and the wise sayings that had been passed down the generations from King Solomon. He knew well that the man who sought out wisdom and understanding was the richest and most blessed of men. Throughout his years, he had always been deeply attentive to the teachings of the Torah and had readily understood that the true foundations of happiness were divine wisdom and the fear of God. As the great patriarch, Jacob had declared that Asher would provide delicacies fit for a king. The fruits yielded by Asher would be deemed the choicest. God Himself had ordained that this tribe would be postured to bless royalty and serve kingship. His lineage was stamped with favour and abundance. The perfect cycle of nature was itself a divine blessing. Even the heavy summer dews would supplement the subsoil moisture from the winter rains and allow for a later cultivation of figs. With the channelled irrigation system that led from the springs, there was often a double harvest in the hill country, which exceeded that of the Judean plains.

Yet at times, this blessing seemed minor in the light of the divine promise of liberation from corruption and oppression. Israel had been ravaged by foreign hands, yet soon there would be a new kingdom under the rule of Messiah who would come to rule from the line of David. The nation would be united, and worship of the one true God would finally be restored. All other blessings seemed small in the light of this hope. Jerusalem would be redeemed. Messiah would dwell amongst the people just as the presence of God had dwelt in the tabernacle that Moses had established. There would be fresh hope, vision, and fortitude for the coming generations, just as there had been for those delivered in the wilderness. Phanuel had taught his sons that this feast was not only just a time of gratitude for prosperity and provision but also a time of unrelenting prayer for the new kingdom to be initiated, for with it would come a fresh dispensation of grace and protection for the nation. The branched sukkot were a constant reminder of the nation's past wandering, pointing to the truth that her life rested upon one thing: divine redemption, which in its ultimate meaning was the atonement of sin. Whilst their neighbouring nations had and continued to hold harvest festivals rooted in idolatry and mythology, the praying remnant within and outside of Judea refused to forget their own unique history. It was one that was rooted in divine covenant.

Phanuel hoped that soon another strong and righteous ruler would arrive on the scene, one of boldness like Hezekiah who had heeded the words of Isaiah, the prophet, and trusted in Jehovah when the Assyrians had invaded. During the siege of Jerusalem, the Angel of the Lord had appeared and slain thousands of Assyrian soldiers. They had been delivered from slavery in Egypt and again granted mercy after their time of captivity to the Babylonians. Oh, how was fresh mercy needed today? Though most of the northern tribes, including Asher who had already been deported to Assyria before the Babylonian exile of Judah, had never returned to Israel, Phanuel thanked God that his ancestors had been counted amongst the small group of the northern tribes who had returned home after the deportation and had been able to relocate to Jerusalem and support the restoration process in response to Hezekiah's call. They were part of a believing remnant from the northern kingdom, a living emblem of divine grace.

As a child, his grandfather, Imnah, had recounted to him the stories of Cyrus the Great of Persia who had captured Babylon and ended the exile of Judah. He had learnt about Zerrubabel, who had been in the first wave of liberated exiles and had overseen the rebuilding of the temple. He had also learned that two of his direct Asherite ancestors had been involved in responding to this call. He had grown up hearing the stories of the Asherites who helped Gideon in his fight against the Midianites, those who had come to David in Hebron to make him king and those who came to keep the Passover under the reign of Hezekiah when the king sought to bring Israel back to God. Phanuel felt uplifted by this tribal history of valiancy, courage, humility, and solidarity. Along with so many others, it was with gratitude that he looked back at Ezra's heroic leadership and reinstitution of the law and the great courage and resoluteness of Nehemiah who oversaw the repair of the city walls, enforcing purity and separation from idolatry. The divine pattern was this: no matter how far Israel compromised and ran from Him, Jehovah had always sent a deliverer, a defender, and a restorer. Like many who were anticipant of His great mercy and whose faces were set as flint towards Heaven, Phanuel prayed that holiness and righteousness would be restored to Israel and that the corrupt and defiled in heart would be removed. Though his nation, chosen and loved by the divine, was persistently playing the harlot with other nations, he believed that the pure in heart would continue to stand firm and intercede for great mercy. He prayed that war and bloodshed would end and that peace, unity, and holiness of worship would be fully restored to the temple.

As he headed back from the olive groves, Phanuel was met by a hired worker who came with a message from his brother, Shelesh. Shelesh lived in the Judean plain near Beth Shemesh where he specialised in rearing premium oxen as well as owning extensive wheat, barley, and melon fields as well as pomegranate groves and vineyards. The quality of his livestock was known throughout Jerusalem. Word had been given that Shelesh and his workers were on their way into town to trade bullocks ready for the temple sacrifices that would be made during the imminent feast. In recent years Phanuel's oldest son, Japhlet, as well as the twins, Zattu and Ashvath, had accompanied their uncle and assisted in the process. Once again, they prepared to join the group and journey towards the city.

As a radiant pink sky began to set over Jerusalem, the shouts of 'Abba' resounded over the terraces. Elisheva and Ishvi had finally arrived home. Ishvi unloaded the materials from the cart and led the donkey across to the nearest stream. Jecoliah took the basket laden with gifts and spices into the house and led Elisheva inside to rest. The following day was the final day before the feast began. Phanuel, his sons, and his workers laboured throughout the day finalising the main structure and the branched roofing for the sukkot that they would live in throughout the seven days of the feast. As with several nearby farm owners, they provided wooden poles, branches, and materials for local villagers and poor peasants. Local widows and the elderly were provided with sukkot and invited to join the relatives and stay on their land. Such hospitality was normal and never withdrawn. Once the family sukkah was completed, low tables, chairs, mats, and cushions were arranged inside and the ornaments, pomegranates, flowers, and wreaths were hung along the roof pole and around the outer walls. Elisheva had already prepared the 'lulav' ready for the procession of branch waving. Having prepared the intricacies this way for years, she was well accustomed to the detailed requirements. She knew the pattern well. Each person in the household was to take their finely crafted lulav consisting of palm willow and myrtle branches and a citron to wave in the temple.

The feast of Sukkot had always been a celebration of the grape and olive harvest. The sukkot were often positioned inside the vineyards with the watchtowers being used for storage. By the time the feast was ready to start, the entire Judean landscape was covered in these boothlike structures in which the influx of pilgrims also dwelt for eight days. Most citizens would leave their houses and stay in their sukkah. Every day those who were able to went to the temple where there were sacrifices and processions in the courts as the people sang psalms calling for the nations to worship El-Elohe-Israel, the God of Israel, and to recognise the magnitude of his eternal love and faithfulness. Each day during the feast, the high priest followed by the people went to fetch water in golden pitcher from the Pool of Siloam and returned to make libation with it at the west end of altar. In the evening there was extraordinary festivity at the temple—four great ritual candlesticks being lit in the Women's Court. The Levite musicians with their lutes and cymbals took their places on the fifteen steps that led to the Men's Court, and at the sound of the trumpet, the torch dance began whilst the people sang.

The calmness of the hill country was overtaken by the rhythm of the hour as steady lines of caravans passed through the land. Joyful melodies of languages from home and abroad were carried forth by the wind across the Hills of Judea as pilgrims neared their destination. The animals, birds, vegetation, and the very soil itself seemed to add their voice to the great symphony that pervaded the land. Jerusalem was vibrant, the harvests had been gathered, and people were gradually making their way to the temple.

The Israelites had been homeless due to their refusal to embrace God's will and instruction, yet He had mercifully forgiven them and provided for them. The book of Ecclesiastes was read as the people mediated on the God of the seasons. The tabernacle remained a physical sign that God had not abandoned his people. The feast was also a celebration of the productivity and provision that God had faithfully bestowed throughout the ages.

The seventy bulls sacrificed represented the seventy nations of the world before the construction of Babel. Zechariah's prophecy was remembered, for he had declared that there would be a day when peoples from all nations would grasp the garment of a Jew and come and worship the one true God, the Lord of Armies. There would be a future ingathering of men from all nations who would behold their God as King and who would be set apart as 'Holy unto Jehovah'. The vision of this future constantly invaded Phanuel's thoughts, the vision that the light of the truth, the revelation of the Most High, would draw forth all mankind beyond the nation of Israel.

Long willow branches were placed by the priests alongside the altar and processions of people set out from the temple to the Pool of Siloam for the Celebration of Water. Though the atmosphere was joyous, for many there was tension in the air, for it had been the banning of this part of the ceremony by Jannaeus—several years before, but still within memory—that had led to protest and subsequent bloodshed and massacre. The words of Isaiah were sung with daily passion 'with joy ye shall draw water out of wells of salvation' as the cries of 'Hoshiaynu', 'Save us now', resounded across the temple mount. Despite the times, there were those who still clung to the truth that the fountain of life and the wells of deliverance and redemption were embedded in the name of Jehovah alone. In the days to come, the thirsty would thirst no more, and once again, the deep wells of mercy and deliverance would overflow.

As the highlight of the first evening drew near, the crowds gathered in anticipation of the fire ceremony and the torch dance. Four great golden 'menorahs' had been placed in the Women's Court, and as they blazed, they illuminated the entire city. The great wicks had been made from the priests' old garments, and young men had carefully ascended a high-reaching ladder in order to light them. Every courtyard in Jerusalem was illumined by the floods of light. Almost one hundred flute players joined in a heavenly symphony, and young men gathered to dance and throw torches. Harps, cymbals, and trumpets lifted an orchestral offering of thanksgiving as David's psalm of Ascents was sung with resounding jubilation. 'I was glad when they said to me: let us go to the house of the Lord. Our feet are standing within you gates Jerusalem, a city to which the tribes go up to give thanks to the name of the Lord. We pray for the peace of Jerusalem, may those who love you prosper.' Dancing and rejoicing continued for each of the seven nights, and as dawn broke after the eighth night during which the lights had been extinguished, the blasts of the silver trumpets marked the final end of the ceremony.

As the feast drew to a close, Phanuel and Elisheva meditated with gratitude for the constant flow of divine blessing bestowed upon them. The heavy rains of the previous winter had provided the crops with moisture and faithfully brought the grain to head in its season. The grapevines along the terraced hillsides had yielded a rich harvest, and during the weeks running up to Sukkot, many of the local villagers had already moved near to Phanuel's vineyards and helped to gather the harvest. Some had chosen to stay there during the feast. Their unused grapes were still in the process of drying, having been turned and sprinkled with olive oil to keep them moist. The family press had been hewn out of local limestone bedrock and was connected by channels to lower rock-cut vats where the juice was allowed to collect and ferment. It was smaller than some of the larger press sites closer to Jerusalem. Nevertheless it had continued to provide a healthy thriving family business. The juice was squeezed from the grapes by treading over them on a circular floor surrounded by a low clay wall. Ropes wear held by the treaders in order to retain balance and the juice drained into a vat. Once fermented, the juices was collected and stored in skins and jars. A large quantity of the wine was later sold at the market in the town. The harvesting and treading of grapes was always a time of joy and moral support amongst villagers. The image of abundance and flow was a constant reminder of extravagant mercy and salvation and the promise and reward coming to those whose trust was in Him. Those who honoured His name would have barns overflowing with grain and vats filled with new wine. The hills would flow with milk, and the ravines would run with water. A fountain would flow from Jehovah, watering the valley of acacias, and the hills would drip with new wine.

During the following days, the sukkot were dismantled. The wooden boughs, branches, and poles were not wasted but used for night fires. Beneath the stars and close to the fire, the family and visiting relatives sung hymns, psalms, and prayers. As young and old sat together around the night fire, the moment felt so holy, so sacred. The orange blaze of bronze and golden flames roared and flickered, illuminating the surrounding hills, brooks, ravines, and gullies in their steady glow. The orchestra of the sky beheld a unique presence. The moon reflected the brightness of the sun, surrounded by a canopy of stars, which emanated divine glory. The multitude of stars, so bright and exposed here away from the smoke-ridden air of the city, remained a constant reminder of the great promises made by Abraham and God's keeping of covenant with the nation throughout the ages until this day. Abraham's descendants were to be as multitudinous as the stars at which he had gazed that sacred night just above the Valley of Shaveh. Despite the fragility of the times, the flame of promise had not been extinguished; the sense of hope and expectancy would never fade, at least not from this family. Japhlet, the oldest son of six and now fifteen years of age, had become a talented harpist and taught the twins, Zattu and Ashvath, to play well. Around the fire, the other brothers, Ithran and Pagiel, played reed flutes, zamoora, and hand drums. Ishvi sang and danced intensely with his tambourines until, faint-hearted then, he fell in a heap on the ground and slept. The sound seemed to attract the angels, and as the family sang and played into the night, their melodies lifted in one accord, ascending into the heavens. After a while, great joy and hope seemed to descend as a waterfall from the sky, cascading over them and watering their souls. Phanuel prayed the blessing of Moses given to the sons of Aaron over his own sons.

His great-grandfather, Ishvah, had been a devout rabbi and scribe who had spent much time teaching and praying in the temple at the time of Ptolemy Philadelphus, the ruler who had authorised the translation of the scriptures into Greek. He had instructed his grandson Heber, Phanuel's father, to name his firstborn son Phanuel after a vision he had received whilst praying in the temple before the child's birth. During the feast of Purim whilst praying in the Israelites' Court, his great-grandfather, Ishvah, had seen a flashing white orb of light illuminate the path in front of him. Almost blinded, he heard an audible voice instructing him to dedicate his life to fasting and prayer for one from his line, four generations away, would see the face of God. The voice affirmed to him that this appointed one, from the line of Asher, would have the name of Messiah stamped upon their forehead. None of Ishvah's predecessors or contemporaries had ever completely understood what this promise signified, for only Moses had come face to face with the Almighty and had trembled with fear and terror as the rest of Israel dared not come near the mountain. Even the animals could not touch the mountain and live. Nothing had changed, so how could one see His face and not die? How anyway could one see the face of the invisible God? Was this to be a literal seeing with physical eyes? Heber's mind had flooded with streams of questions, yet he took heed of his grandfather Ishvah's instruction. He faithfully named his firstborn son Phanuel, 'Face of Jehovah'. It was as a constant reminder to Phanuel of both the vision and the prophecy of that which would come in the following generation. Ishvah had taught both Phanuel and his brother Shelesh to never hide anything from God, to live a pure, righteous life, to worship Jehovah with reverence. In turn, Phanuel had taught his own six sons to worship, pray, and meditate unrelentingly as King David had worshipped, to withhold nothing from God, for He was Elohim, creator of all realms, seasons, cycles, land, and sea. He alone had the power to bless and give peace. He alone would lift up His countenance upon them. To see His face was to behold Him, and one could behold Him here. Yes, right here beyond the temple, within the hills.

As the fire continued to blaze, grandparents, friends, and relatives began to pray with fervency and Grandpa Heber and Grandma Hadassah recited scriptures. They had been faithful and quiet worshippers all of their lives, showing great kindness to the orphans, regularly feeding and sheltering them in their home. They were calm and ever hopeful for the redemption to come. Though their own parents were sadly absent from this place, Phanuel knew that Grandfather, Imnah, a faithful cultivator of the land, and Great-grandfather, Ishvah, a God-fearing scribe, would have been moved to see these young Asherite boys worshipping the Holy One. Their faces were set like flint, free from idolatry and unblemished by the corruption that was so steadily infiltrating the land. As the playing and singing continued, Phanuel surveyed their ruddy, vibrant complexions glowing in the heat. Each son was so at harmony with the hills and the land. They all enjoyed music, agriculture, carpentry, craftsmanship, trade, and study of the Torah, yet it seemed that each was born and destined to be a worker of the land. They were peaceful and content in the open hills, faithful shepherds of goat herds and flocks. They knew intimately every gully, every cave, every rock, every brook and ravine. They understood the soil and stone of the land, the rhythms of the climates and seasons, and they were learning the ways of honest commerce. Though replete with joy, there was still a part of Phanuel's heart that felt unfulfilled. He had secretly and silently hoped that at least one of his sons would represent His family, serving within the temple and influencing temple life in some way. He had never spoken of this to Elisheva, yet for all of his years, he had silently desired that one of his offspring would see more, see deeper, see further than he did. He desired to have a child who would be like the seer Samuel, set aside and holy unto the Lord despite being born from Asher and not from Levi. Though a part of him was relieved, given the current climate of corruption within the priesthood, a larger part of him yearned for this. Who would fulfil the prophecy given to his great-grandfather that one, four generations on, would live out his own name and see the very face of God? None of his sons were directly involved with temple life beyond the obligations of the law. Had the voice truly been heard, and if so, how could it be?

3

LIFE IN THE HILL COUNTRY

During the days following Sukkot, Phanuel's sons began labour in the olive groves, working hastily to gather the remaining fruit harvest. As always, the best sprouts had been removed from selected trees in May and new groves nurtured. They beat the trees with wooden poles and prepared the heaps of olives for transport to the local village to be crushed between giant stones driven by draft animals. The olives would be gathered into baskets by local women and children who were always grateful for the wage. A small amount was pressed using the family press, the wooden beam to which it was attached being supported by a niche in the wall. The baskets were then pressed with force and the juice collected in storing vats. The oil was used for cooking, lamps, soap, facial ointments, and the wood was used for ornaments, pots, and kitchen utensils, and the olive skins were used as fertilser.

It was not long before the ploughing season was under way on the Judean plains. The first rains had fallen, and the ground was soft. The three oldest boys—Japhlet, Zattu, and Ashvath—travelled down to the plains to help their uncle Shelesh, for his own sons were not yet of age to work. Ithran and Pagiel stayed back with Ishvi in order to help their father, Phanuel, in the hillside vineyards. During the ploughing season in late autumn, the vineyards became home to turtle doves and other doves that migrated to Israel later in autumn. Meanwhile the storks left for their breeding sites and journeyed towards their wintering sites until spring when they would return to their breeding sites.

The best friend of the younger twins, Ithran and Pagiel, was Eleazar. In fact the three were considered triplets by most of the villagers. Eleazar had become a close companion. His father, Eliud, lived farther south on the edge of the village of Bethlehem and worked mainly as a stonecutter in the hillside villages in between there and Jerusalem. His ancestors had all been stone quarriers who worked in limestone and basalt, some of whom had dug clay in the Jordan Valley that was later used for pottery and for the wattle and daub of poorer houses. These stonecutters who created vats for the wine presses and basalt grinders for the household mills as well as the fine masonry for the houses of the rich were all highly skilled specialists in the trade. They were often called upon by the wealthy, but this did not mean that regular village masons like Eliud were ever short of work. On the contrary, here in the hill country, there was a great need for stoneworkers, not least to work on the building and repair of terraces and watchtowers.

Although his income was modest, Eliud was a greatly skilled man and was hired by many farmers to develop irrigation channels and terrace walls. The steep slopes of the hills were terraced in order to create land that could be used for agriculture. This involved moving a large amount of rocky earth to create small platforms upon which vegetation could grow. Olives, figs, pomegranates, and grapes grew in abundance on these terraces.

Dry farming, which relied solely on rainfall for irrigation, was thus practised using an elaborate system of terraces and tunnels. The rain that fell upon the mountains descended into the limestone and down into the ground. As the springs were not plentiful, the existing water supply had to be maximised. This was achieved by tunnelling into the water-bearing strata and creating a system of channels to conduct the water that was to be stored into large holding pools into the terraced plots. The rocks and stones that were cleared provided the necessary support for the terrace walls into which new soil was placed. Terracing was thus always done beneath the pool with the vegetation on a lower level than the spring. Watchtowers were built with the remaining stones to guard the crops. The walls of the terraces often had stairs up to them depending on their height.

Farms were always built near springs. Uncultivated areas were used as corral for the enclosure of livestock. Springs flowed out of caves and cavities in the rock. Horizontal tunnels were hewn into the rock to help locate and develop the water source. Further tunnels were then hewn into water-bearing strata in order to increase water flow. A channel, partly clay, partly stone was built into the floor of the tunnel. At the spring end of the tunnel, branching channels were dug up to catch as much water as possible. The tunnel with its channels directed the flow into a small barrel-vaulted chamber and then from another channel into a small rectangular reservoir from which it flowed through irrigation channels to the cultivated terraces.

The techniques of terrace building varied depending on stone and soil. Here in the hill country much of the soil was terra rossa, and the stone was limestone. Farmers created their land by building up fields on the hillside and the valley beds and regulating the water flow. Terrace walls were built with stones, and gravel was placed inside the terrace, then a layer of soil, then stones, more gravel, and more enriched soil. Much of this enriched soil placed within these cultivated plots was imported from land in the coastal region. The rainwater was soaked up in the soil in which the plants were growing, and the surplus flowed to the next terrace below. Vegetables could only grow if irrigated with spring water. Otherwise the harvest from seasonal rainfall was limited to almonds, figs, olives, grapes, grains, and pomegranates. There were a few flat plains in the Judean hills, and some were indeed part of Phanuel's own land, but generally the hills were steep and the valley floors narrow. The creation of terraces thus transformed the hillsides into stepped flat fields supported by retaining walls. As the environs of Jerusalem expanded, urban expansion was always coupled with agricultural expansion. As such, those like Eliud who were experts in stone and wood always found themselves engaged in labour.

Eliud's brother always worked alongside him. Their relatives and ancestors had all been of humble origins, some working as builders, carpenters, and craftsman and barbers. The brothers were known for honest labour and dedication. They were from the tribe of Judah and were known amongst the villagers of the hill country as humble, sincere people, hardworking and devout in faith.

Throughout the years Eliud had become a good friend of Phanuel. They met regularly at the synagogue and were always together during feasts. It was Eliud who had built most of the watchtowers and terrace walls on Phanuel's land. They were brothers who loved their trade, the pale Jerusalem limestone was part of their life, and the process of repairing and building was a deeply satisfying livelihood. As Eleazar, Eliud's firstborn son grew more robust, he acquired the skills of the trade and began to work closely with his father. The twins, Ethan and Pagiel, remained close friends with Eleazar throughout the years, working on the land and attending synagogue together.

Unlike the barley, which did not require ploughed soil and was grown in the smaller parts of land, the wheat demanded space and attention. Shelesh organised his workers into groups of three. One directed the plough blade as another carried the seed bag on his shoulder, dropping the seeds into a funnel that would ensure that the seeds fell behind the plough and were covered by falling soil. The third worker, usually the most robust, would be charged with managing the team of oxen. The ground was soft again now that the early rains had come. Some of the newly acquired pastures were ploughed four times in order to fully condition the ground. It was refreshing for the boys to journey down to the plains as the landscape was so vast and different to the hill country. Shelesh's land was vast, open, and only mildly undulated. Wheat and barley were harvested down here on the plains that lay between the hills. Trade took place between the hills and the plains as farmers from each terrain exchanged their produce. The hillside vineyards, which had been rented out for local villagers to manage, could not be ploughed as they were rocky, and the soil there was turned by hand. As Shelesh directed the plough, he began to pray silently, pondering on the faithfulness of Jehovah. As an Asherite, he and his tribe had always lived in the fulfilment of the great patriarch, Jacob's prophecy. Like his brother, his life had been marked by wealth, prosperity, vibrancy, and divine blessing. It was an honour to have so much to give to the poor and to make large offerings to local widows. His flocks, harvest, health, offspring, and hired workers, whom he treated as sons, all bore the stamp of divine blessing and favour. This rich energy, joy, and copiousness of life had indeed been part of his inheritance. Whilst meditating, he would often experience visions and trances. As he was guiding the oxen, he saw the sharp-edged horn of the first animal shine in the sun, and his gaze was captured by what appeared to be drops of oil glistening over its horns. As he fixed his eyes, he began to tremble, for in seconds the horn of the ox became covered in oil and grew before his eyes to the size of a sharp mountain peak. As he stood with his eyes transfixed upon that which they beheld, he heard the anguished voices of Ashvath and Zattu, who ran towards him in great distress at his lack of movement. They spoke of this moment only to their father, Phanuel, who became deeply troubled and concerned for the health of his brother. Amidst moments of wondering, labour continued as normal.

Back in the city, commerce was thriving. Those involved in the oil trade and lamp-making trade were now entering the most demanding season in advance of Hanukkah, the Festival of Lights. Ishvi returned to Jerusalem and helped at the shop with Jashobeam. It was always a delightful eight days, laden with gifts and celebrations. Lamps were sold to residents and pilgrims alike, as windows became illuminated so that passers-by could see the light and be reminded of the great miracles of divine redemption that the nation had known.

Despite cold weather and snow-peaked mountains, there was a certain warmth and glow in the Jerusalem air. Each household was preparing to be illuminated. The temple Menorah would burn incessantly for eight days. Songs and hymns would be sung and prayers of thanksgiving offered as the people remembered the victorious restoration, cleansing, and rededication of the temple by Judah Maccabee.

Freedom of worship was not taken for granted but cherished increasingly in these dark times. On that historic day when the temple had been cleansed and rededicated, liberty beyond hope had been granted, a new altar had been built to replace the desecrated one, and new holy vessels had been made. The prayer of this current era was that a purge would take place not just within the temple but within the hearts of men. Throughout the feast the sacred oracle of Balaam was recited, 'I see Him, but not now; I behold Him, but not near. A star shall come forth from Jacob, and a sceptre shall rise from Israel, and shall crush through the forehead of Moab.' This sceptre was yet to rise and the star yet to come forth. Within the turmoil, tyranny, and compromise of the day, visions of this promise fuelled the hope of many.

It was during the final night of the festival that Japhlet, the oldest of Phanuel's sons, had a vision whilst walking through the portico of Solomon that ran along the eastern wall in the Gentiles' Court. This vision was not dissimilar to that received by Phanuel's great-grandfather Ishvah over one hundred and seventy years earlier. Japhlet had always been the closest to his father in terms of his contemplative mind and passion for the Torah. Gifted with great musical skill whether in groves, fields, or temple courts, he was constantly singing psalms and making melodies. Named after one of the faithful Asherites who had returned to Jerusalem to help restore the temple during the reign of King Hezekiah, he had grown up with a valiant heart, zealous for the restoration of all that had been lost. Japhlet's name meant 'Whom God Delivers', and this had been his anthem since finding the magic of his voice as a young child. When Japhlet sang, the house would at times fall silent as his voice carried within it a weighty presence of holiness. At other times, the family would join him in one song and the house would radiate with worship.

Having eased through the crowds ahead of the family, he passed through the portico of Solomon amidst the many that had come to worship. There he was struck with sudden faintness. As he withdrew from the crowds to compose himself, he entered into a vision of his mother, Elisheva, who was resting at home. In the vision, he saw an angel who stood behind her and spoke these words: "Out of Asher will be one who shall behold my grace and kingship." He stood trembling and remained there alone after the crowds had entered. Feeling feverish, he closed his eyes again only to see the vision and hear the voice a second time. Was his mother carrying a future king of Israel? This could not be true, for they were not of Judah, the royal line. Was this just a reaffirmation of the Asherite blessing on their family that Asher would provide dainties fit for a king? He pondered on the future. Would the seventh child, though not of Judah, be somehow linked to the coming Messiah? Would this be a chosen son who would somehow be one of great influence? One thing was truly certain: this nation needed grace, and it needed a righteous king. It seemed that the gracious mercy of God shown throughout history was yearned for today more than any other day. Perplexed and overwhelmed, Japhlet gathered himself and continued walking through the courts.

As the celebrations drew to an end, the family focus now returned to complete the late sowing of legumes. Winter gradually set in over the hills, and herons, robins, and ducks arrived in numbers, as well as various birds of prey such as owls, hawks, and vultures that came to settle there in the colder seasons. Ishvi was accompanied by Jashobeam, who had come to help with the late sowing whilst the rest of the sons undertook the repairs of damaged stones and weakened areas within the terraced walls. As he laboured, Japhlet reflected on his experience in the portico. He understood that this had been a divine encounter yet could not bring himself to talk about it even with Abba. Never had he experienced anything like this in his fifteen years of life.

Elisheva was due to give birth within the next few days and rested in the house with Grandma Hadassah, her maid Jecoliah, and Serah from Bethpage who was a midwife. Serah, whose name meant abundance, had ten children of her own and had delivered Ishvi seven years ago. For her, it seemed just like yesterday. She would never forget the laughter amidst the birth pains—for having been convinced that a girl would emerge, they had seen a sixth male born. As the moment drew near, Serah arranged the birth stool and the bed. She then prepared clay bowls of warm water, diluted wine, a small heap of salt, sea sponges, olive oil, and strips of swaddling cloth. Elisheva's sister-in-law and a close friend from the village shortly arrived at the house. Just a few hours later Elisheva gave birth to her seventh child. The child was a girl.

Tearful, Japhlet held out his arms as Phanuel kissed the soft skin of the baby and passed her to his oldest son. He sat down gazing intensely at the perfectly formed face, gently running his fingers through the soft dark wisps of hair. Meanwhile the other brothers gathered around the babe, gently unravelling her tiny clasped fingers. They stood around in silence, curious and intrigued that this angelic creature was a girl. Their eyes transfixed, as if she were some rare unearthed jewel hitherto unseen by human eyes, they began to sing psalms and songs of blessing over her. Elisheva, physically fatigued, her soul overwhelmed, wept with great joy. They had not expected a girl and had no names in mind. Even Grandma Hadassah, who was trembling with excitement and who frequently saw children being named by their fathers in the many visions she had behind her loom, had never sensed that this child would be a girl. This was a complete surprise. As the joy in the room increased, Japhlet's mind drifted back to the voice that had spoken to him as he had walked through Solomon's Portico on the last day of Hanukkah: 'Out of Asher will be one who shall behold my grace and kingship.' He reflected upon how his expectant mother had suddenly appeared to him in a vision with the audible voice resonating throughout his body. Though it remained an enigma in his mind and a mystery in his heart, Japhlet knew a deep peace in the depths of his being. This sacred moment was part of a much bigger picture, part of the promise given four generations ago to his father's great-grandfather, Ishvah. Yet why had God spoken to him, a mere boy, in this manner? He was the firstborn, but no one of real significance, just a humble worker of the land. Was the political situation of Jerusalem about to change? What exactly was this grace?

"Anna," he exclaimed, lifting up his head as he held her close to his face, "we must call her Anna, for great grace has been granted us this day."

The six brothers turned their faces towards their parents. In silence, the grandparents, midwives, sisters, and friends fixed their gaze upon Phanuel. The family waited, expectant and bemused, for indeed it was not usual for a father and mother to have no name prepared for their child.

As Phanuel clasped Elisheva's hand, he sighed deeply and smiled, his vision blurred by tears. This was not merely a smile of contentment and gratitude but one of a sentiment quite unspeakable. He took the baby from Japhlet's arms, and holding her close, he kissed her head repeatedly.

"Yes, Japhlet, God has indeed been gracious. Her name shall be Anna."

Ishvi came to his side and stroked her soft raven ringlets of hair. When her huge eyes eventually opened, they were a deep olive colour and of indescribable beauty. As the babe was passed from one to another, she eventually landed in the arms of Grandpa Heber, who, having never held a daughter, began to weep uncontrollably before proceeding to bless the child. The following day was a joyous occasion. The family home and courtyard became vibrant with relatives, friends, flowers, incense, and gifts of balm, perfume, jewellery, aromatic gum, myrrh, and pistachios. A lavish banquet with the best wine was held, and fresh oil was placed in the lamps. The trip to the temple for the formal blessing would take place in exactly eighty days' time, and a cypress tree would be planted to celebrate the birth. At the end of the feasting, there was singing and dancing around an open fire for the winter air was cold. The circle of assembled guests sang the psalm of Solomon: "Like arrows in the hand of a warrior so are the children of one's youth." As the songs drew to an end, Japhlet stood tall, dressed in a purple and blue tunic. Raising his harp and lifting his deep eyes towards the pink Jerusalem sunset, a new song of joy came forth: "Anna of the Tribe of Asher".

4

THE FEAST OF PURIM

January ('Shevat') had been the coldest month ever with dark days and snow, hail, and rainfall. With the newborn now over one month old, the family entered February ('Adar') with relief. Change was in the air. The swift would soon arrive from mid-Africa and stay until June after its nestlings had fledged. The pistachio and almond trees were already blossoming, and each rainy day was followed by a warm day of sunshine. Occasional storms carried the fragrance of spring. The almond tree was always the first to sprout and the last to lose its leaves. Shaking off winter, the almond trees across the hill country were flourishing with new life, pink and white blossom heralding the advent of a new year of trees. The late barley seeds had just been sown, and northwards towards Galilee, the flax seeds had just been sown. The flax would be used to make rope and linen, and the seeds provided extra nourishment for the animals.

As the days became warmer, Elisheva felt a fresh surge of energy. This was always a season of joy and anticipation as the cold, dismal weather drew to an end. The scent of the almond blossom signalled that Purim was near. The almonds themselves were a distinct decoration on the temple lamp stand constantly signifying new birth and recalling the miraculous budding of almonds from Aaron's rod of aged acacia wood. The almonds were a wondrous sign of God's provision of an intermediary through the priesthood.

Of all the festivals, Purim was Elisheva's favourite as it celebrated such a great miracle. Having lost her mother in childbirth and mourned the death of her father not long after her marriage, the story of Hadassah and the miracle of divine intervention and favour had comforted and inspired Elisheva during her youth. Moreover it was a time of colour, hope, and great joy.

Once again, that moment had arrived when Jerusalem transformed into a magnificent carnival with colourful decorated carts and vibrant festive attire. The dyers corner and the tailors and barbers were at the height of business as lines of colourfully adorned pilgrims streamed, once again, into the city. Resounding throughout synagogues and homes, the popular story of Haman's divinely orchestrated fate was met with vibrant applause and approval from those listening. Surrounded by men until the recent birth of her daughter, this festival that celebrated the courage and tenacity of a woman was one that brought refreshment to Elisheva's spirit. As she pondered and contemplated history, she wondered whether her own daughter would be one set aside for a divine mandate. Would she too be a voice of divine authority amidst oppression like Deborah, Miriam, or Huldah? Though the royal line was in Judah's hands, surely Asher's blessing was no less. Had her daughter's birth been destined for such a window of time as this? After all, it had been stated that Asher was favoured and blessed to serve royalty? As Jecoliah entered the room, she promptly collected herself and withdrew her mind from such meditations. She dared not dream, for indeed, such lofty contemplations were beyond her.

As the story of the Almighty's intervention into history and deliverance of the Jews from massacre was recited in the temple, some people prayed more fervently than others and hoped that the Hamans of the day be brought to justice. The people beseeched Jehovah to send another advocate to liberate Israel and deliver her from Roman oppression and corruption. They prayed that a new king would soon arise and write a new decree that would bring restoration. As the suppression of Jerusalem grew heavier and darker, some wondered if, somewhere upon the backstage of accepted reality, a gallows was being built. Would there be another great timely spectacle of public execution raised up before the nation as a sign of freedom and favour? When would divine justice be administered? When would Messiah, the promised deliverer, intervene within the drama and set Israel free from bondage? Had the Persian Jews not been rescued, an entire population would have been massacred. Many worshippers knew only too well that, had it not been for this mighty act of divine deliverance, commissioned through the edict of Cyrus, they would not have been in Jerusalem. Their ancestors, who had returned to Palestine under the divine leadership of Zerubbabel, were objects of the mercy and compassion of God.

In the temple, the scrolls of Hadassah were recited and public prayers and petitions were made. Representatives from each locality grouped together and collected gifts and donations for the poor. Widows, orphans, and beggars were given baskets laden with food and gifts. As in each harvest, Elisheva ensured that the best of their crops and the finest of their produce were taken to the homes of local widows. In the temple there was a place for contributions, which were privately applied to those who were struggling. Orphans were considered the special charge of the whole congregation, and to adopt or raise one was considered an especially good work. The character of this feast always seemed more national than religious. It was about family, identity, and fraternity. Purim was a joyous time of fasting and feasting, praying and rejoicing, gratitude and hope. At the start of the feast, the flocks were blessed; in family homes, lavish banquets were thrown; the finest vintage was served; and the poor were never overlooked but welcomed with open arms. As friends and relatives feasted, there would always remain a sense of awe and wonder at how the heavens had opened and divine favour had overshadowed this courageous young Hadassah and her faithful relative.

Amidst political and religious confusion, perversion, anger, and despair of the day, there was real hope that another intermediary would come and that this next intermediary would be Messiah Himself. The constant war between Alexander Janneus and the Pharisees and their supporters had increased the great strife and oppression that overshadowed Jerusalem. His mistrust and deep hatred of the Jewish people had resulted in unspeakable massacre. Ravaged with terror, corruption, strife, and great desperation, it was surely the hour for justice and freedom to reign. Surely it was the hour for this merciless Haman to be judged.

5

A Queen Takes the Throne

It was 78 BC. Salome Alexandra, the wife of Jannaeus, had taken the throne, and despite the increasing corruption and infiltration of godless ideas and philosophies, there was a certain feeling of relief throughout the city as Queen Salome reinstated the ordinances of the Pharisees and reestablished their full control of temple practices. She succeeded for a time in quieting the internal dissensions of the kingdom that existed at the time of Alexander's death. Furthermore, she did this peacefully and without detriment to the political relations of the Jewish state to the outside world.

The Pharisees had suffered intense misery under Alexander Jannaeus. Several had seen their fellow men crucified in front of their wives and children. Some had been slaughtered in front of their fathers as they hung on crosses. The reign of Queen Salome brought relief as the Pharisees became not only a tolerated section of the community, but also actually Judea's ruling class. Queen Salome installed her eldest son as high priest, Hyrcanus II. He was a man wholly after the heart of the Pharisees; thus the Sanhedrin was reorganised according to their wishes. This body had hitherto consisted of a group of elite members who belonged to the highest Rabbinical Court. From this time it became a supreme court for the administration of justice and religious matters, the guidance of which was placed in the hands of the Pharisees.

The Sadducees were moved to petition the queen for protection against the ruling party. Salome, who desired to avoid all party conflict, removed them from Jerusalem, assigning certain fortified towns for their residence. She increased the size of the army and carefully provisioned the numerous fortified areas so that neighbouring monarchs were duly impressed by the number of protected towns and castles that bordered the Judean frontier.

Education was placed in the hands of Pharisaic teachers, and a major result of this reform was not only an increase in literacy and religious knowledge amongst the young, but also a broadening of the Jewish sense of scriptural authority. The Sadducees had accepted only the Torah, or five books of Moses, as authoritative. Under the Pharisees, the prophets and the writings were also taught, as well as a belief that God's oral law could be expressed directly by the living sages of each generation. Under Salome's reign, Shimon ben Shetach, together with Rabbi Judah ben Tabbai, also took care to see to the needs of the many widows and orphans that had resulted from the wars of Jannaeus. Despite increasing unrest due to foreign influences, there was thus a certain sense of relief amidst the people. Prayers of gratitude were offered for deliverance from the cruelty and persecution that had stained the reign of Janneus.

As a twelve-year-old girl, Anna knew and understood little of the politics of the hour, but through overhearing conversations amongst her parents, brothers, relatives, and guests, she had certainly learnt that to have a Jewish queen reigning in Jerusalem was not common. She imagined herself as Queen Salome enthroned inside the palace, the beauty, the favour, and the life of a monarch adorned in royal robes. As news, rumours, and messages circulated, Anna became conscious that her nation was in seasons of great change. Captivated by her own imagination, she would run through her father's land, dancing with the spring breeze, seeing her garments adorned with sapphire, rubies, and emeralds, her body saturated in royal balms and perfumes. She imagined herself as a majestic ruler, appointed and commissioned by God, loved by all in Jerusalem. As she passed through the spring orchards, the walled terraces transformed into majestic marble courts—the limestone watchtowers, pillars of solid gold, and the lines of pomegranate trees lavish banqueting halls. Here, away from the city, beloved Har Yehuda was a place of freedom for Anna. She knew the blends of fragrances, the textures of the land, and the fresh, pure air. It was a place of invigoration and freedom, a place removed from the daily tasks of drawing water from the local well, grinding the grain, weaving, kneading the dough, serving the family, and helping to buy food from the market. As she ran alone in the open breeze, the goat herds encircled her, waiting in anticipation as she called to them and sang.

As inquisitive as her six older brothers had been at that age, Anna was constantly asking questions about the land, the scriptures, and the times. Her mind and heart were open wells waiting for truth to fill them.

Pesach, the Passover feast, was just a week away, and the barley harvest was almost in. She would then assist her uncle Shelesh in selecting the finest single lamb of a few flawless ones that he would extract and set aside. His own judgement was always final. Nevertheless, he had taught his boys and, now his niece, how to select prudently and to scrutinise the lambs with a sharp eye in order to locate the slightest blemish. From an early age it had been her prerogative to name the chosen lamb. To surrounding families who could only afford a goat, Shelesh would freely offer the lambs as an act of kindness. Likewise, as God had commanded, the land was more than sufficient for the household. Its lamb was shared with neighbours. The temple became surrounded by streams of whiteness as families journeyed down to present their lambs for sacrifice. Anna accompanied her relatives and distributed them to widowers and peasants around the local villages.

At home, Anna was close to her father. As the youngest child and the only daughter, she had only to pull on the knotted tassels of his prayer shawl, calling 'Abba'. Once in his arms, she would stroke his beard and gaze at him with her huge olive eyes, causing his heart to melt and ensuring that she had his undivided attention. Now a young woman, Anna began to recognise and deeply esteem the tenderness of her father's heart not only towards her but also towards others, particularly the poor. Phanuel was always giving liberally and always with such joy. When praying and singing, Anna would strive to imagine what God looked like, and in such moments as these, she would see the face of her father. Stacking the remaining barley stalks, she breathed deeply and looked up at the sky. She loved the openness of the lower plains. The vastness of the earth and the sky was overwhelming. Each spring and autumn, multitudes of birds navigated the skies above Judea tracking magnetic fields, star rotation, and the sun. The birds seemed to be nomads, pilgrims of the sky that populated the canopy over the city. Sparrows and eagles were seemingly ever in descent, feeding on the flat roofs below. During the time of the barley harvest, large circles of white stalks headed towards the hills and beyond. Partridges and crested larks were to be seen all over the hill country on grassy hills. Also this was the season when the cuckoo passed through in its line of flight from its winter home in Ethiopia and stayed in olive groves and fig plantations.

After a week of labour back in the hills, the days of meticulous preparation drew to an end. The house had been cleaned, the dishes cooked, and the blood of a lamb had been sprinkled over the door with a branch of hyssop. During the Passover meal, psalms were recited—calling for worship from sunrise until sunset of the one true God of the nations, eternal redeemer of the poor and needy, healer of the barren. The Passover was always a joyful and solemn feast and attracted huge numbers of pilgrims. The people never failed to forget the series of mighty acts, signs, wonders, and miracles that the highest sorcerers and magicians of the land had failed to reproduce. Accounts of the miraculous liberation from Egyptian bondage and the surpassing mercy of God once again caused the nation to bow. Most bowed out of custom; just a few bowed with gratitude.

Thousands united for Pescah, including families who had been scattered by the Diaspora. The city was literally overflowing with Jews from Babylon in trailing black robes, Jews from Phonecia in tunics, Jews from the plateaux of Anatolia dressed in goats' hair cloaks, Persian Jews gleaming in silk brocaded with gold and silver. They crowded the temple court as sellers of sacrificial animals and money changers made scandalous fortunes and men jostled in queues to offer lambs to priests. The ceremonies themselves lasted for a week, but the most important were on the first and second days.

Each man attended the temple with his lamb and handed it to the sacrificers who stood at the entrance of the Priests' Court. The priest collected the blood and poured it out before the altar from where it flowed down the gutters towards Kidron. The entrails and fat were thrown into the fire, and the smell of burning flesh permeated the city. As always, the animal blood and bones were used as fertilisers; hence, the soil surrounding the city was highly rich and fertile. The sacrificed lamb was then taken back home for the ritual meal. For those who could not make it into Jerusalem, the lambs were slaughtered on their own land by the head of each household.

In the hills and on the plains, the flocks of sheep had been finally let out from under cover, and the fields were white with the promise of harvest. Unlike wheat that could easily be destroyed by severe winds, the barley, an easy harvest thriving in all conditions, had been sown without ploughing. It was as strong in the plains as it was near the coast. Labourers helped to pile the stalks harvested by the reapers and to assist in the tedious process of carefully separating the awn from the straw before it was carried to the threshing floor.

There was no eating of the barley until sunrise when on the Sabbath day the priest presented the freshly cut sheaf before the altar. There was much to do in the house, and the servants were busy removing every morsel of 'chametz'. The barley was stored outside of the house until after the feast when it was used to make loaves, feed the animals, and provide for the poor. Everything was scrubbed to ensure that not a trace of flour or yeast remained. Phanuel prepared a lamb to take to the temple for sacrifice and to be eaten by the family in the upper chamber of the house on the same night. The lamb was roasted, and none of its bones were broken. It was to be accompanied by bitter herbs, some of which came from their own land. The parsley, the first herb of spring, was already flourishing, and others—such as horseradish, bay, thyme, marjoram, and basil—were imported from the earlier harvest in warmer regions of the Shephelah and the Jordan Valley. The unleavened bread was dipped in a red sauce called 'hasereth', and wine was drunk by each family member.

The day before the Sabbath of the Passover, as evening fell, at the ninth hour, the shofar uttered its long, sad note followed by six ritual trumpet blasts to announce the day holy above all others, the Sabbath of the Passover. After the blasts, the city would be calm.

6

FAMILY TRAVELS

Asa was the cousin of Phanuel and Shelesh, and each year he and his family journeyed towards Jerusalem from Galilee to celebrate the feasts. Reuben and Jerusha, the parents of local twins Joash and Shimei, were close friends of Asa's family in the Lower Galilee region. Galilee was a fervent and fertile corridor perfectly situated between sea and desert. Verdant hills, fresh water, fertile coastal plains, rolling hills, wheat and flax fields, flourishing vineyards, forested valleys, and clear freshwater lakes. In winter, their view consisted of the Golan Mountains capped with snow. Their twin boys Joash and Shimei were the same age as Anna's twin brothers, Zattu and Ashvath. Their parents had also been born from Asherite families whose ancestors had avoided Assyrian deportation and remained in Asher. The brothers of Asa were well-known fullers and owned a large business that involved bleaching and cleaning the linen before it was sewn together. Asa's two sisters and their husbands were dyers who specialised in creating purple dye from the shellfish that were caught along the coast. The purple linen sold for a high price and was preferred to the imported linens of Persia and Egypt. Business was thus thriving in the region.

Asa had only one child, a son named Beninu who had become like a brother to the twins Joash and Shimei. Both families were very close. Their parents owned flax fields adjacent to Asa's, and they had merged trades, co-labouring in order to establish what was one of the most thriving flax and linen production centres in Galilee. The proximity to water and the fertility of the soil back in Galilee rendered this ideal for the production of flax. As well as linen, this cooperative incorporated the preparation of flax seeds that were used for medicinal purposes and flax oil that was used for ointments and herbal treatments. Here, on the fringes of the Jezreel Valley, there were various installations for the soaking of flax. Commerce was flourishing, and the two families were constantly at work.

Local peasants were employed to pull it up and sell it dry, having removed the leaves and seeds. Specialised artisans were given the task of retching and scutching before proper sale. The plants were tied into bundles and soaked for weeks in order to separate the fibre from the stalks. The fibre was then spread out to dry and processed into cloth. The linen produced in this region was widely preferred to that imported by Egypt as it was much less coarse. In the spring season, a sea of sky blue flowers emerged, carpeting immense areas of the region, and much of the crop was ready to be harvested at the same time as the barley harvest before Passover, a few weeks prior to the harvest in the cooler climate of the hill country. The families imported linen each year to Jerusalem where it was sold directly to tailors.

Upper Galilee was truly a city set on a hill. Its mountainous part was full of magnificent scenery with bracing air. The delicate sycamores that graced the Jordan Valley and the lower region of Galilee could not survive the cold heights there. Its caves, marshy ground covered with reeds along Lake Merom, gave shelter to robbers, outlaws, and rebel chiefs. Some of the most dangerous characters came from the Galilee highlands. South of Merom a great caravan road connected Damascus in the east with the great mart of Ptolemais on the shore of the Mediterranean. The hills were lined with constant files of camels, mules, and donkeys laden with the riches of the East destined for the West or bringing the luxuries of the West to the Far East. Travellers of every description—Jews, Greeks, Romans, dwellers in the east journeyed through the hills. Constant interaction with foreigners and the settlement of so many strangers along one of the great highways of the world rendered the narrow-minded bigotry of Judea impossible in Galilee. It was a dynamic region, full of commerce and always readily embracing the new. It was a beautiful, fertile region, truly the land where Asher dipped his foot in oil. The rabbis always spoke of oil as flowing like a river, saying that it was easier to rear a whole forest of olive trees in Galilee than one child in Judea. The wine from the vines was rich and plentiful. Corn and flax grew in abundance, and the cost of living was notably lower than in Judea where one measure was said to cost as much as five in Galilee. Its fruit was envied by those in Jerusalem who would not allow it to be sold in feasts at the city lest people compare and comment.

Various industries had been established in Galilee, large and diverse potteries and dye works. From the heights of the region, one could see the harbours filled with merchant ships and the sea dotted with white sails. By the shore and further inland, there were smoked furnaces where glass was made and lines of caravans passing along the great road that crossed Galilee having crossed the Jordan, touched Capernaum, descending to Nazareth and journeying onwards towards the coast.

Along the lake lay a small town called Capernaum. Capernaum was located on the northwest side of the Sea of Galilee, near the point where the Jordan River entered the Sea of Galilee. The area was considered a fertile spring and popular place for agricultural trades. Though it was a small place, it was home to many fishermen, and already there were plans to build labyrinths of private basalt houses and a large synagogue. Nearby, there was Chorazin, famous for its grain and Bethsaida, the house of fish. South of Capernaum was Magdala, the city of dyers as well as wealthy shops and wool works. These were also gradually transforming into small centres of opulence with plans for synagogues to be built and settlements to be accommodated for through ambitious housing projects. At the southern end of the lake was Tarichaea, the great fishing place from where preserved fish was exported in casks. Frequent interaction with strangers tended to remove narrow prejudices, and the Galileans were known to be a warm-hearted, impulsive, and generous group who were considered conscientious and earnest in trade and in faith.

Around the shores of the lake, the vegetation was rich, its products almost tropical with lavish orchards, rich villas, fertile fields, and the deep blue lake. The peace and serenity of the waters and the tranquillity of the lavish green landscape offered solace and refreshment to any soul that required it. The land itself was a haven of beauty, a place of retreat for those who return to visit and escape the intensity of Jerusalem.

Whilst Galilee boasted the scenery and fertility of its oil, Judea was considered the inner sanctuary of Israel. Its landscapes were comparatively barren and its hills rocky and bare, its wilderness lonely. Pilgrims neared the region, enchanted by the paleness of the mountainous façades of limestone that gathered the sacred history of the ages. The whiteness of the limestone as always a spectacular sight for those acquainted with the darker basalt stone mountains of the Golan Heights. As caravans from Galilee entered Jerusalem, the hills rose higher and higher, and the striking view of the pure white marble foundations and glittering gold of the temple would become visible. The revered sites that these lines of caravans successively passed became more familiar with each passing year: first, Shiloh where the ark had rested; next, Bethel with its sacred memories of patriarchal history; then, the great plateau of Ramah with the neighbouring heights of Gibeon and Gibeah. The pillar set up by Jacob at the death of Rachel in Ramah and pilgrims passing through would still stop at the sight. It was the place of sorrow and lamentation, the former meeting place of captives who were to be carried out to Babylon. There had been bitter wailing from those left behind, the old, sick, women, and children were savagely slaughtered.

Westwards from Ramah where the mountain shelved down and descended towards the Shephelah were the scenes of former triumphs. Here Joshua had pursued the kings of the south; Samson had fought the Philistines. As they turned south there was Bethlehem. Close by, on the road to Jerusalem, was a tower known as Migdal Eder, the 'watchtower of the flock'. Here was the station of the shepherds who watched their flocks destined for sacrifices in the temple. The males were offered as burnt offerings and the females as peace offerings. It was a very small place. Still farther was the priestly city of Hebron with its many caves. The highland plateau, the wilderness of Judea dotted with small villages, was a desolate, lonely region tenanted only by the solitary shepherd whose sheep pastured along its heights and glens. It had long been the home of outlaws and hermits who had retreated from society in its growing corruption. Its limestone caves had been the hiding place of David and his followers, and many a band had since found shelter in these wilds. Beyond this region, deep down in a mysterious hollow, stretched the smooth surface of the Dead Sea—it was a perpetual memory of God and of judgement.

On arrival in Jerusalem, Asa's family journeyed towards the home of his cousins Phanuel and Shelesh. He would also pay visits to close friends in Bethany and Bethpage. The sounds of dancing, feasting, trumpet blowing, and flute playing permeated the atmosphere as the two families approached the city in a long procession of caravans. Upon arrival, the children, overwhelmed with excitement, divided in the clay holding pools that collected spring water from where it was channelled out into the terraces. Asa's son along with the twins, Joash and Shimei, adventured with the local villagers climbing trees and watchtowers. When taken down to the city, they joined the throngs of children playing and dancing in the streets. It was not unusual for one or more of the young relatives to go missing, only to be found singing and laughing with other wide-eyed youngsters in the lower market.

The twins, Joash and Shimei, were as vivacious and mischievous as their accomplice Beninu who was slightly older than Ishvi and just as inquisitive. Phanuel and Elisheva welcomed the families with tears and open arms. Extra beds and pallets were placed on the roof, the courtyard of the house became a small dance hall, and extra tents were constructed in the fields. As was the custom amongst all of their people, the doors were always kept open and hospitality was extended to everyone. When Phanuels's home was full, guests were directed to the house of Shelesh in the Judean plain and to other friends in nearby Bethany and Bethpage.

The relatives always remained together for as long as possible after feasts had ended. This gave them time to visit other friends who resided in Jerusalem, exchanging gifts and stories until it was time to return home and resume work. It was during this time that Anna regularly attracted the eyes of her brothers' friends who came to dine with the family. At ten years of age she thought little of it. When not grinding, baking, or weaving she spent most of her time with her local village friend Mezahab whose family owned land close by. The twins, Joash and Shimei, did nevertheless carry an air of charm and intrigue, which the girls were naturally drawn to. Mezahab was a year younger than Anna and equally beautiful. The girls walked, talked, and sang together, always laughing, always dreaming whilst the boys were never too far from dangerous adventure…and so it was that for all ages, the greatest reality of the feasts was simply being together.

7

GRANDMA HADASSAH

The barley harvest marked the most verdant month, which was also known as the month of flowers. In the valleys and coastal areas, the peaches and pomegranates were already in bloom. At the end of Passover, much of the time was spent gathering the early figs and preparing for the wheat harvest. Various herbs and legumes had already ripened and were ready to be harvested. Many hillside plantations yielded a harvest double the size of that in the plains due to the excellent irrigation system that watered the vegetation. The hill country was dotted with various-shaped watchtowers perched on hill tops, built deep in the valleys carrying a majestic glow as the sunlight shined upon the limestone walls. Vines were planted around these towers, supported by the wall stones, creating stunning green and white façades. They were made from stones from the mountainous terrain after the ground was cleared for ploughing. They were built on firm rock base to ensure a solid foundation, thus leaving the rest of the land arable for agriculture. There was no cement or binding substance used to hold the stones together, but rather, the towers consisted of carefully assembled loose stones and branches that braved many a storm. Smaller watchtowers were used for storage of the harvest or as outlook posts, whilst larger ones had the extra function of sheltering farmers and their families who had come in to work from the villages. Workers would also sleep on the roof with lamps, for this was the only way to protect the terraces, vineyards, groves, and orchards from theft and destruction. It was always an adventure for any young boy to sleep in or on top of the watchtower. Furthermore, it trained the alert and acute eye of a true watchman.

Phanuel and his workers began to cut the wheat fifty days after the start of the barley harvest. During this period, the fierce struggle between the easterly and westerly winds intensified throughout Israel, and though not as turbulent as the coastal region, the mountains were constantly hit by the dry easterly winds on one hand and the westerly winds on the other, bearing heavy, dark clouds and danger of sudden rains. Scorching southern winds resulted in extreme dryness and heat, alternating with cold winds from the north and west, generating tempestuous storms with thunder, lightning, and rain. These sudden weather changes could affect the field crops at any time. Although the storms were few this year and did not pose a threat, the winds brought heat in the day and temperatures near to freezing at night. As a result there were several deaths each year, for the sudden extreme temperature changes caused inflammation of the lungs. Despite the survival of the crops, a sudden cloud of distress enshrouded Phanuel's family during these weeks in between Pesach and Shavuot. Grandma Hadassah, who was already struggling with respiratory problems, did not respond to any of the salted water and herbal treatments of saffron administered by the local physician. Her health declined rapidly, and soon she became too frail to eat or to pray. Her daily recital of scriptures of hope and promise did not completely diminish although her soothing voice that had for so many years filled the air with worshipful melodies gradually faded into faint whispers. Her dark eyes, once full of vitality and presence, became sad and vacant. Anna sat by, clasping her grandma's frail hand, reciting scriptures, and singing over her the psalms of hope and thanksgiving that she had taught her as a child. Grandma Hadassah became increasingly feeble and breathless, lacking in strength to reach out and wrap her granddaughter's dark locks of hair around her long wrinkled fingers as she always did. Anna became engulfed by lassitude and faint-heartedness, which led to despair and desperation. Life without Grandma Hadassah was simply unimaginable.

As mourners came from the village, it was a time of deep sorrow. Phanuel watched with grief as the loss of his cherished mother crippled the souls of Heber, his widowed father, and his youngest child for several nights. The hours, days, weeks seemed longer, and for Phanuel himself it seemed that in the midst of the harvest, everything had suddenly lost its colour. His mother had been a joyful, vivacious woman of tenacious faith, always praying, always hoping, always singing. He knew that she would live on through his beloved daughter, Anna, to whom she had remained so close since the day of her birth. Heber was a broken man, full of grief, yet his widowed heart found consolation in prayer. He believed that one day he would be reunited with his beloved, and he clung to the words of Isaiah and Ezekiel that God would cause the graves of the righteous to open, awakening them from the dead and raising them up out of Sheol to abide with Him in the land of the living. They would be preserved forever and know life eternal.

As time progressed, Heber would find solace in the youthful faces of his grandchildren and great-grandchildren.

As the days of mourning passed, Phanuel composed himself and returned to the fields. Singing his mother's favourite psalms, he grasped the grain with one hand and cut it with the sickle. Tying each bundle into sheaves, he loaded them onto donkeys ready to be carried to the threshing floor. With the arrival of Pentecost, fifty days after Passover, just as Moses had received the divine law fifty days after freedom from Egypt, the people turned once again to consider the mercy and provision of God.

The weather had finally stabilised, and the wheat harvest was in full swing. The start of summer was heralded by the sound of the visiting cuckoos, kestrels, and various types of eagles. The summer flowers were already in bloom, and the spring greenery was fading to browns and yellows. The pomegranate trees were covered in stunning bell-like blossoms, the fruit itself being yet to ripen. The fig trees were staring to regain their foliage, and the first tiny unripe fruits had appeared. The grapevines and olive trees had bought forth miniscule seed-like clusters.

People gathered in extraordinary numbers, and Jerusalem overflowed with visitors, pilgrims, endless strings of caravans passing through her gates. As with Passover, the inns were fully booked, and the town was alive in every sense. Shavuot, the Feast of Pentecost, was above all a happy and joyous feast marked by bread offerings and sacrifices. Many pilgrims camped in the Kidron Valley and prepared to purify themselves before ascending the temple mount. The Pool of Siloam fulfilled the legal requirements of a 'mikveh' as it was fed by free running water from the spring of Gihon. Mats and wooden poles were used as partitions for privacy. Others gathered at the Pool of Bethesda on the path of the Beth Zeta Valley.

Shavuot was also the first day on which individuals could bring the 'bikkurim'. The bikkurim were brought from the Seven Species for which the land of Israel is praised: wheat, barley, grapes, figs, pomegranates, olives, and dates. Each year a reed was tied around the first ripening fruits from each of these species in the fields. At the time of harvest, the fruits identified by the reed were cut and placed in baskets woven of gold and silver. The baskets were then loaded on oxen whose horns were gilded and laced with garlands of flowers. The oxen were then led in a grand procession to Jerusalem. Farmers and their entourage passed through cities and towns, accompanied by music and parades. Phanuel and his sons, brother, and nephews joined the procession each year, entering the city with oxen laden with ripening fruits and fragrant flowers.

At the temple, each farmer presented his bikkurim to the priest in a ceremony recounting the history of the Jewish people as they went into exile in Egypt and were enslaved, oppressed, then redeemed by God and brought home to Israel. The ceremony of bikkurim conveyed corporate gratitude to God both for the first fruits of the field and for divine guidance throughout history. Local synagogues were arrayed with bright, fragrant flowers and packed with those who came to have the scriptures expounded to them and to listen to the story of Ruth, the Moabite, who had been adopted into the Davidic Dynasty and thus granted royal lineage. Children also were taught the importance of integrity, kindness, friendship, and the provision of the harvest to bless the poor. The constant support of those in need and in solitude was a priority of the season.

Asherite relatives and friends returned once more to Jerusalem from the coast in order to celebrate with relatives. An increasing number of young relatives were added to the gathering each year as expanded families united and joined the long caravans of pilgrims in the journey back towards Jerusalem. As always, Phanuel's youngest children eagerly awaited the arrival of their cousin Beninu and, amongst other friends, the charismatic pair, Joash and Shimei. Now older and fine in stature, they spoke with the wisdom of men. Their eyes bright with intrigue, they were assiduous scholars of the Torah and had attended both the local synagogue in Galilee and the new school. Schools had been introduced, for Rabbi Simon ben Shetach, brother of Queen Salome and president of the established Sanhedrin, had recently opened the first Beth Ha-Sefer in Jerusalem, which had already expanded into Galilee. The boys both carried an air of mystique and enigma. It was at times as if they had seen an aspect of Jehovah that others had not. Anna was not only captivated by Joash but also deeply moved by the unshakeable faith and assurance with which he spoke about all things. Though she had been taught the scriptures at home by her father, hearing them spoken by someone of similar age felt so refreshing and suddenly so true and real. The bold conviction in his large dark, piercing eyes would increase as he talked of Messiah who would one day come and slay the

Roman oppressors. He would rescue them from foreign rulers and would set up an ever-increasing unvanquishable kingdom of peace. No warrior would ever conquer him; he would be unconquerable and all-powerful. Elated by his own declarations, Joash ripped thick branches from the myrtle tree and dramatised the battle scenes, which imprinted themselves indelibly on the screen of Anna's mind. His imagination captured those of his young spectating friends, and before they knew it, Joash was Messiah and his twin was Messiah's armour bearer, protecting him as he fought his tyrannical cousin in battle.

Anna pondered on their early childhood. During each family reunion they had always fled to the terraced vineyards and olive groves to enter the 'great hall of portraits' acting out scenes in secret—whether the battle of David and Goliath, or Joshua and the great walls of Jericho that were made with loose blocks of limestone, cedarwood, and olive branches. At one time she and Mezahab had sat and watched with fascination and delight as her older brother Ishvi had been forced by his cousins to play the part of Rahab. His role had been to lower the twins with a large, thick frayed rope down the side of the watchtower, huddled together in a huge basket made of papyrus reeds that they had 'borrowed' from the vinedressers and grape pickers. Even during meals, they would take turns to continue the story of the valiant enemy-crushing warriors of whom they had learned. Their imaginations propelled them into another realm, and they often had to be reminded by adult counterparts to stay calm and eat well. Now older and wiser, these young souls laughed with a knowing expectancy. Yet there was an acuteness, veracity, and weight to each word uttered. As they lifted their gaze towards the open skies, they imagined what this mighty deliverer sent by Yahweh would look like. Their minds themselves became great galleries, open halls in which the portraits depicted by the prophets and their own imaginations and visions merged into a spectacular collection.

As the hot season arrived, there was much work to be done with the vines fully ripe and the lentils, beans, peppers, and cucumbers ready to be harvested. The sun became progressively more intense, and as the streams dried up, the dry winds hardened the ground, leaving the springs as the single remaining source of water. With the remainder of the wheat being harvested after Shavuot, there was an overlap between the end of the grain harvest and the start of the summer grape harvest. It was thus another very busy summer with threshing and grape picking overlapping. There was no time for idleness. All of the boys worked continuously through the heat. This had become a normal part of their life.

8

TENDER HEARTS IN ARIMATHEA

As time progressed, journeys to Arimathea continued to be a regular part of Ishvi's life. Jashobeam remained a close and loyal companion. The family home of Jashobeam and the various oil merchants associated with his family circle in Arimathea imparted to him great skill and knowledge of trade and the ways of commerce. As well as this, the family possessed great wisdom concerning the noble distribution and regeneration of wealth. This insight had inspired both Jashobeam and Ishvi to such an extent that they became experts in business. Though from different backgrounds, each of them had relatives both in Arimathea and in the coastal region who had started as travelling merchants, gradually becoming experts in the wholesale commerce of wheat, corn, oil, meat, and dates, exporting produce to Greek cities and coastal towns. There were also family relatives based in Jericho who traded the balms that were known to be worth the price of gold and others who liaised with Arabian importers of silk, spices, incense, and sandalwood. As the years went by, Jashobeam travelled across Israel and became involved with networks of tradesmen who were experienced in hiring Greek, Roman, and Phoenician shippers to export produce. The Arimathea in which he had played with Jashobeam during childhood visits was a continuously prospering place and an infinite well of knowledge and inspiration regarding the creation of wealth and sound business. Taking this insight and understanding back to the hill country, Ishvi became a judicious manager of both his father's and brother's affairs, ensuring that, as with the olive oil, the best wine merchants were engaged with.

As for Jashobeam, he grew to be as God fearing as his parents. Despite the increasing demands and pressures of commerce and daily life, they were devout worshippers known for righteous conduct, honest trade, and acts of charity, hospitality, and compassion. The popular teachings of Hillel, the elder, regarding moral law, brotherly love, and honest, charitable living were fully embraced by Jashobeam's family and relatives who—despite the magnitude of their connections, influence, and social standing—were of sound moral stature, displaying a sincerity and transparency seldom found amongst the traders of Jerusalem. They were wholehearted believers in the law and the prophets, mourning the corruption and oppression that had befallen Israel. They were people of integrity and reverence, active, respected worshippers at the temple, and though unseen by the eye of man, they devoted much time to secret, contemplative prayer in the night hours. Something of this had become part of Jashobeam's lifestyle. Many wealthy merchants and rich families living in Arimathea had surrendered to a sense of political hopeless denial and fatalism due to the climate of the times; others exploited the poor and engaged with corrupt bribes in order to expand their wealth, piling up their silver like dust. Usually such traders were keen to be seen tithing their income as nominal supporters of temple life, yet their hearts were hardened to the ways of Jehovah and dismissive of His great promises yet unfulfilled. Though they were rich, this blind majority had let go of hope and hope had let go of them.

Jashobeam's family, however, continued to stand as a lighthouse and a watchtower, its members from old to young, always surveying, imagining, meditating, discussing, dreaming, and anticipating. Jashobeam's grandfather had served as a rabbi until his death, and his cousin had been a recognised prophet in Jerusalem. Though throughout the years the centre of family activity had moved from the temple to the marketplace, the deep faith and acute understanding that marked their ancestors had not waned throughout the generations. Within them was a hunger to accurately perceive and understand the times and seasons in the spirit of the great men of Issachar. As Jashobeam grew into the trade, the selling price for oil increased, allowing a greater return to olive producers. Whilst many merchants were despised for retaining oversized cuts for themselves, this family continued to pride itself on integrity and generosity in the distribution of both domestic and export profits both to plantation owners and to the poor of Judea.

Jashobeam and Ishvi never grew apart, and as they matured in knowledge and understanding, they became joined not merely in friendship but also in resolution to study and search the scriptures for themselves, to consult sages and rabbis and to search for answers to their nation's decline. They were joined in a robust spirit and an unquenchable fiery faith regarding Messiah's arrival and the fulfilment of the prophets. In their minds, they continued to enter the great hall of portraits and scrupulously survey the details with hungry and vigilant eyes. Throughout Judea and beyond Arimathea, these young men and others who joined them became known for their moral and spiritual fortitude. As children they had been known in the town for adventure, mischief, intrigue, and unceasing laughter. Now along with brothers and friends, they were known for passionate conviction, insight, honesty, contemplation, and unwavering faith. In the family home and with a small number of other young men in local synagogues, they used every spare moment to meet in Arimathea and study the Torah unrelentingly. As they discussed ideas and interpretations, revelation consumed them and deep assurance permeated their hearts. They began to have regular dreams, visions, and trances, which they also recorded and discussed. Such was their demeanour. They were described by local townsmen as carrying an air of mystique, enigma, a holy presence that none could describe. And so it was in Arimathea that this small group seemed to flow against the current of the day.

Even when Obed, Jashobeam's first child, tragically died, his belief in the faithfulness, supremacy, sovereignty, and loving-kindness of Jehovah did not wane. Intense mourning and grief had filled the air as Jashobeam buried his own son in one of the family tombs hewn from rock in the garden that his father had purchased just outside of the city gates near the hill of Golgotha. Of course it seemed no coincidence that this hill was part of Moriah, where the temple stood and where Abraham had been willing to sacrifice his only son. No child had ever been buried in this family garden. It had not been right for a child to die so young. As Jashobeam stood that day surveying the olive groves and the flourishing vines in the centre of the garden, he had suffered deep heartache. Why had this tender eleven-month sapling died out of season and not lived beyond his first steps? His firstborn son had been snatched in the night hours when, for no apparent reason, his fresh young heart had ceased to beat. Nevertheless, Jashobeam's heart had not grown bitter. At least the child had been blessed and the body buried in a place of dignity. Had he been poor, this would not have been possible.

9

ROMANCE IN THE AIR

It was during the following spring that Ishvi became betrothed to Abigail, the sister of Jashobeam. As business was thriving in Arimathea, they planned to reside there, at least for a while. A house had been built for them near the family home, and Ishvi was welcomed into the family business whilst still organising his own family's trading affairs.

An overwhelming number of guests were invited to the wedding of Ishvi and Abigail. Anna rushed to the courtyard pretending not to have noticed the presence of Joash, who had returned and was standing tall amidst the crowd of relatives and guests who had arrived to celebrate. The truth was that Anna had become besotted with Joash. As his deep eyes and dark raven hair glistened in the brightness of the sun, she dreamt of a day when he would draw his mantle over her to keep her warm. Though she attempted to avoid his eyes, his robust, heroic stance demanded her steadfast gaze. As she took her turn to greet the relatives each with a kiss, the moment that she has been dreaming of all season since Passover had swiftly arrived and swiftly ended. As his lips touched her hand, she closed her eyes tightly to lengthen the fraction of time that they touched her skin as he swiftly moved on through the line to greet his aunt Elisheva. His brother, Shimei was accompanied by her cousin, Beninu, son of Asa, who was now as tall as the twins. They came laden with gifts made from fine linen, bottles of flax oil, and expensive fragrances from Galilee.

It was after Ishvi's wedding that the annual visit was made by Phanuel's family to Lydda to stay with the parents and sisters of Elisheva. As with visits to the coast, the city of Lydda opened Anna's eyes wider to life beyond Jerusalem. When approaching Lydda, they would arrive at a low wall that protected a ditch and cross the moat, entering through iron gates secured by bars and bolts, as was the case with all fortified towns. Above the gate rose the watchtower where the elders sat. Citizens gathered to discuss the public affairs, daily news, and rumours whilst engaging in lucrative business transactions. The gates opened out onto spacious squares on which the various streets converged. There were no such squares and empty spaces in Jerusalem, and the space here was always refreshing. Here was the busy scene of trade and commerce: peasants circulated, hawking the produce of the field, orchard, and dairy; the foreign pedlar or merchant exposed his merchandise, recommending the newest fashions from Rome or Alexandria, the latest luxuries of the Far East, or the latest art of the goldsmith or modeler at Jerusalem. As in Jerusalem, the banter and conversation of moving crowds would often draw quiet with the appearance of a Pharisee, an Essene, or a political statesman.

People gathered at the fountain or well unless they had cisterns in their own homes. The watchman did not move from the top of the tower at the gateway, and night watchers patrolled the streets. Never was there absolute darkness as it was customary to keep a light burning all night by the windows, and these generally faced the road. In the houses of the rich the window frames were elaborately carved, ornamented, and richly inlaid. The woodwork was of sycamore, olive, cedar, or at times sandalwood imported from India.

There was much interaction between Lydda and Jerusalem. It was a day's journey west. During family visits, Anna listened to stories recounted by her mother of how the women of Lydda were known to mix their dough, journey to the temple, and return before it fermented. The city was also the residence of many rabbis and the seat of a respected school that was presided over by some of the leading sages of the day. It was a beautiful place known for its sweet date honey and its wealth.

10

JOASH AND ANNA

It was spring of 73 BC. Joash had presented Phanuel with sixty shekels. The 'mohar' and the 'mattan', consisting of an overwhelming collection of fine gifts, had been carefully prepared for his future wife in accordance with the custom of ensuring a dower, which the woman would keep if she were ever widowed. Everything had finally been agreed, signed, and completed, and the time of betrothal had drawn to an end. It was autumn now and the harvest and vintage were over, busy minds were free, and hearts were at rest after the hard labour of gathering the late harvests. The night air was still warm, and the breeze, refreshing. A large party of of relatives, villagers, and family acquaintances had been invited to the wedding.

Joash collected his bride, who had spent the previous night in her father's house soaking in fragrances and softening her palms and soles in rich henna. Shimei had organised the procession and acted as master of the ceremonies. Joash wore sandals of porpoise skin, splendid clothes, and a white mantle brocaded with scarlet, royal blue, and violet—his face glistening with delight beneath the majestic crown studded with an array of precious stones. His bride looked magnificent with her long, dark silky locks resting upon her shoulders and a shimmering white veil draped over her face. The procession serenaded the couple with songs of love and celebration, playing lutes, lyres, reed pipes, tambourines, and silver bells. The sound intensified as Solomon's songs ascended with the breeze, resounding throughout the hills until the joyful procession finally arrived at the newly built house of Joash who had relocated from Galilee to the hill country.

The bridesmaids dressed in pure white surrounded the glistening chuppah under which the couple walked in full circle with the mantle of Joash raised over Anna. It was a regal canopy designed by highly skilled artisans. Anna resembled the exquisite queen that as a child she had so often dreamt of being. Seated on the embroidered cushions, she and Joash sang to each other as the guests threw down pomegranate seeds in front of them and broke an alabaster jar of expensive fragrance. The feasting then resumed with even more energy and vibrancy than before. The best wine was served and drunk until none remained. For a further seven days the jubilance continued into the night hours as guests danced with great joy and exuberance beneath the canopy of stars that adorned the Jerusalem sky.

A silver box containing bracelets, anklets, and necklaces made of rubies, emeralds, diamonds, and crimson sardius was presented to the bride. She wore an elaborately embroidered overdress and a golden sash made of fine Persian silk. Upon her head she wore a golden crown decorated with loops and circles of gold and, over her crisp white tunic, a veil embroidered with clusters of grapes and almond blossoms that hung all the way to her knees.

The cushioned chuppah was decorated with flowers and boughs of greenery whilst the inside of the house was suffused with the aromas of roasting meat, freshly baked bread, and fine spices. Silver trays laden with fresh honey cakes and figs were passed amongst the guests.

A large tent similar to a sukkah was used for the younger guests to play in. Colourful mats imported from Persia, embroidered cushions, and wooden chairs made with stretched woven straw were placed inside so that older relatives could rest. Though deeply content and elated, there was still a tinge of sadness in Anna's day. Listening in her mind to the calm, soothing tones of Grandma Hadassah's voice reassuring her of the future, her inner gaze was set on the warm smile and bright eyes of hope that had adored her as a child.

As the jubilance continued, Anna and Joash became overwhelmed. They were a handsome couple, zealous for the Torah, and ignited by the unwavering faith and expectancy of their ancestors. Later, as Joash walked alone beneath the open night sky, gazing at the moon reflecting the brightness of the sun, it was as if suddenly they were young children again. The sky was limitless. It was glorious. Nothing was impossible. All of the banquets and wedding dances in Israel could not surpass this profound sense of destiny. Joash trembled inside as he strolled on past the rocky hills, entering the sloped terraced fields where as young children they had danced together, restaging the heroic dramas of their ancestors. As he walked on, he felt a strange heat permeate his body as scripts and battle scenes flooded back into his mind. He still believed it. These dramas were also scenes of the future; the promised Messiah would overcome Roman dictatorship and every surrounding nation would submit to His reign. Like every true conqueror, Messiah would set up banquets upon battlefields after victory in the sight of conquered enemies, and once established, His government would be far superior to and more extensive than that of King David. This new regime would be one of unshakeable power, constant territorial increase, and everlasting peace. This would be the kingdom of all kingdoms. Yes, Joash still believed it.

The following day was radiant with laughter, music, and dance at the end of which an extravagant banquet was served and precious gifts of gold and silver ornaments, bottles of persimmon oil from the groves of Ein Gedi, and costly jewels, linen, silk, turquoise, and emerald tapestries were lavished upon the newlyweds.

11

Significant Births

As the sowing season arrived, a large party of friends and relatives journeyed to Arimathea to celebrate the birth of Jashobeam's second son. This was a joyous moment especially as young Obed, the first son, had died so young. The child was named Hiddai, for he had been the cause of great rejoicing after a time of sorrow. A daughter had been born since the burial of Obed, and though she was her father's delight, Jashobeam had desperately longed for a son, and the wait had been desperately long. Hiddai was to be blessed with his absent brother's portion as well as his own. It was prayed that he would be the one who would continue to create wealth and bless his fellow men. Ishvi and Jashobeam were still closer than brothers. Since marrying Jashobeam's sister, and settling in Arimathea, the lively discussions had increased as had prayer and contemplation regarding the promise of a new order.

By the end of that year, more significant news had spread from the temple. Antipater, the Idumean who was the best friend of the queen's son Hyrcanus, had seen the arrival of his first son, Herod the Great, and an elaborate banquet was being held in the Jerusalem palace in his honour. Residents of the region were to be given gifts of grain to celebrate the occasion.

Antipater was a convert to Judaism who had been made governor of Idumea under the reign of Janneus. He feared that if Aristobulus rightfully took the throne when his mother, Salome, finally died, he would not be looked upon kindly and would lose his position. Strategically therefore it was in the interest of Antipater to nurture his friendship with Hyrcanus whom he considered to be the weaker of the two brothers.

Antipater was a highly controversial figure and had been placed by Pompey as mayor to the palace. His father, by the same name, was governor of Idumea. It was said that these Idumeans had strategically converted to Judaism, motivated purely by their longing to be masters in Israel, and that in order to accomplish this they had skilfully ingratiated themselves with the Romans. Little was known in detail, but it was said that this controversial figure, Antipater, had strategically befriended Caesar as well as Pompey.

Queen Salome continued to be looked upon with a certain amount of favour and acceptance by the people. The Sanhedrin, packed with Pharisees and their friends and doctors of the law, were openly grateful to her for having empowered them. They planned that in the years to come they would hand down, to their descendants, images of this monarch's reign as being a golden age in which 'the grains of barley were the size of olive-stones and the lentils as big as golden coins'. The queen had successfully increased the size of the army and carefully provisioned the numerous fortified places so that neighbouring monarchs had been duly impressed by the number of protected towns and castles that bordered the Judean frontier. Moreover she had not abstained from actual warfare and had resolutely sent her son Aristobulus with an army to besiege Damascus.

12

Tensions and Passions

It was 69 BC, and the queen, now seventy-one years of age, appointed her oldest son Hyrcanus II as high priest. He was greatly supported by the Pharisees, who welcomed the decision. During this time, his brother, Aristobulus, was sensing that his mother's death was imminent, and he thus began to align himself with the Sadducees. News circulated that he had slipped out of Jerusalem and travelled throughout the kingdom using his Sadducee connections in order to secure and control various fortified cities for himself. As a result, his mother had imprisoned him in Jerusalem. Rebellion was in the air. Queen Salome had kept the peace between Pharisees and Sadducees by permitting the former to consolidate their power in Jerusalem and dispersing the latter throughout the various fortified cities that she had built. However, the last days of her reign were to be tumultuous.

Within the ongoing political turmoil and increasing tension between the Sadducees and Pharisees, who already carried bitter differences, those loyal to the temple continued to keep their eyes fixed upon the hope that a restorer would come. Several found their solace in quiet watchfulness, contemplation, and prayer. Joash was always listening and eager to update himself with new movements within the monarchy and of regimes both at home and abroad. As he grew in knowledge and understanding, his passion and zeal for godly wisdom increased. A disciple of Rabbi Hillel's teachings, he became a voice in his local synagogue regarding social justice and human equality. Those who withheld their gifts to the poor and turned their face from the orphans would one day pay a great price for their negligence and disobedience. In the fullness of plenty they would be cramped. There were those who seized and devoured flocks, stole the oxen of widows, and pushed aside the needy on the road as the wealthy fed off the poor, stripping them of robes and sandals as collateral for loans that they would never be in a position to repay. The wives of the wealthy lounged on Egyptian pillows in their elaborate summer houses whilst their husbands withheld wages from labourers and used them to buy liquor and fine delicacies. Daily absorbing Rabbi Hillel's teaching on fraternity, charity, and true honour amongst men, Joash travelled frequently to meet relatives and friends who were of like mind in order to share and expound upon the teachings together. The topics of such conversations also became increasingly engaged with the future and destiny of Jerusalem and of Israel as a nation in accordance with the words spoken by the prophets. Unlike Rabbi Shimmai, the revered and influential teacher within the Sanhedrin, the teachings of the young Rabbi Hillel focused on the importance and accessibility of the Torah for everyone, not just for those select few who were deemed by the rabbis to be worthy scholars. These two main schools of thought did agree on many issues, most fervently on their resistance to foreign occupation and tyranny. However, the universality of the Torah was either readily embraced or passionately discarded by the people, yet for Joash, the real answer to many social problems and to mediocrity of faith was to be found in the teachings of Hillel.

Joash, like all fathers, embraced the new season with open arms. He and Anna had been blessed with two sons, Ezra and Bezalel, who brought great joy to their parents and grandparents. Ezra and Bezalel were as vivacious as those who bore them. Just a year apart in age, the eldest had been born nine months after marriage and the youngest, less than a year later, just towards the end of Purim as the almond blossoms had started to bud.

It seemed as if it were just days ago that they had attended the temple to offer a lamb for purification and for Ezra, the firstborn, to be redeemed with five shekels of silver. There had been no waiting, no delay, and no hesitation in whose ways these sons were to be raised. Already, Anna's soul was overwhelmed with gratitude. Throughout the recent years, as she had seen her six brothers blessed and the ever-increasing circle of nephews and nieces steadily expand, she had hoped with all of her soul that such shining gifts would come her way in due season. Now with two new jewels in her crown, she thanked Jehovah daily for His goodness and provision. Each day was as sacred as the day when the two sons had been blessed by the priest at the temple. Her heart was unceasingly rejoicing in the great things that God had done. And now the season of promise and fruitfulness had arrived. The immense joy and celebration of Purim still mingled in the air as the people once again recalled the mercy, justice, and intervention of God on behalf of Israel. The late barley had been sown, and gradually the air was becoming warmer. The songs of turtle doves and nightingales could be heard across the hill country. Despite the friction and unrest in the city, there were fresh melodies within the hills.

It was the week before Yom Kippur, during the arrival of the early rains. News of Queen Salome's death spread rapidly across the land. The relatively peaceful time that her reign had afforded was brought to an abrupt end not just through her death but due to the deep antagonisms and tensions between the two sons that she left behind. As so often had happened in Israel's history, greed and desire for power and influence were seen to be the downfall of men. Judea gradually became engulfed in civil war due to the deep jealousy of the deceased queen's youngest son, Aristobulus II, and the mortal struggle that ensued. Unlike his mother and his older brother, Hyrcanus II, the young Aristoblus was hostile to the Pharisees and sided with the Sadducees in order to strengthen his influence and support. He accused his older brother of having a weak leadership style, and his efforts and claims were supported by younger members of Jewish high society who were attracted to his persona. Unable to forgive his older brother, Hyrcanus, who had, at his mother's will, assumed the position of priest and king, Aristobulus continued to find encouragement from his close friend Antipater who advised him to act swiftly, take Jerusalem for himself, and subjugate it to his own reign. Corrupt and manipulative, Aristobulus used his connections in order to obtain personal control of several of the fortified cities. The many tensions, complicated by interference from Antpater, Idumaea and Petra became increasingly violent, and Jerusalem found herself ravaged by civil war. This was very damaging to the entire region and to the population of Judea. The civil war continued until 65 BC.

Many people avoided the city and fled to the hills for safety, meeting in synagogues and houses to pray and worship. City dwellers were sheltered by those in surrounding towns as many rabbis called upon the people to fast and pray for Jerusalem to be delivered from the turmoil, bloodshed, brutality, and massacre that was taking place inside her walls. The seven years of relative calm had abruptly ended, and the atrocities being committed due to greed for power and fraternal hatred once again cast a shadow of death over Jerusalem.

13

Unforeseen Tragedy

It was within this climate of abominations, murderous acts, and national mourning for Queen Salome that Joash had been tragically mistaken for another man during a heavy dispute outside the city gates. Passing by, just before sunset, a terrible tragedy occurred, and Joash met with the sword of the enemy. It was during that fear-ridden night of 67 BC when he did not return home that death cast its menacing shadow across the hills and the vile hand of Hades left its dark pernicious stain upon his wife's garments. Anna and her two sons were cast into a descent of utter hopelessness. It was not until later in the night that she learnt from trembling servants that death had seized her beloved. His face had been taken for that of another, and within a moment of the spear piercing his chest, Joash had fallen to his death. This life—so innocent, so young, so pure, so full of light. All of creation and life itself could not overturn the dark, sly decree of death and widowhood. Haunted by loss, Anna saw justice evaporate into the black night sky, a cloak of shame and a dark mantle of grief descending upon her shoulders. Henceforth, she would be known as 'issa-almana'. As the days passed and the crowds wept, the serpent of death crushed her soul with unbearable sorrow and entwined itself around her spirit so that breath itself seemed impossible. Every hope, every dream, every scroll of destiny had been ripped from her heart as sheets of parchment torn from a scroll and trampled into the earth. In the words of the weeping prophet, 'The sun had set over her while still day.' This broken heart grew faint under the crushing weight of multitudes of questions. She now understood the embittered cries of Naomi and the hopeless despair of Ruth and Orpah. Her soul longed only to join her husband in Sheol with her fatherless sons at her side. The pain turned into an inner agony, for she had lost her closest friend, her teacher, her zealous one, her prophet of things to come.

Joash had always remarked upon how the days were passing too rapidly, swifter than a weaver's shuttle. Yet now, his sorrowful wife wished only that the rhythm of her days would quicken. Her life had once been brighter than the noonday sun, yet now she stood in a valley of shadows. The lamp of God had shone over their heads. His friendship and counsel over their tent, their steps had been bathed in cream as the rocks had poured forth streams of oil. Who now could make this widow's heart sing for joy? She had expected good, yet evil had come. She had waited for light, yet darkness had come. The harps of her brothers turned from hymns to dirges; their flutes played the sounds of those who wept. Joash had been a man short-lived. Like a flower of sweet jasmine, he had flourished and withered in a mere passing season. Only the words of Job could describe her torment—sackcloth over her skin, her horn laid low buried in the dust, her face flushed from weeping as deep darkness weighed upon her eyelids.

Anna recalled the love and anticipation that had filled her soul from those first days when she and Mezahab played in the open fields with Joash and Shimei. It was an excitement that had continued until the day of his death. The wide-eyed declarations of his expectations concerning Messiah, the great restorer, had continued to captivate her imagination just as they had done when he declared them as a young boy from the tops of terebinth trees and watchtowers. With each passing day her beloved Joash had inspired her more. All of his revelations from the Torah and from sages alike had been fresh and enlightening. He had cherished Anna like a jewel, his zeal illuminating her like the sun itself. Their marriage had been a deeply fragrant rose, cut down whilst still in bud and trampled callously into the ground, an unripe fruit that had fallen to the earth, an extinguished flame of passion and life. Her robes of promise had dissolved to sackcloth and ashes. Death had occurred as suddenly as the sky had turned from day to night. Oh, how she despised death, and all the more, its suddenness. How she longed, now more than ever, for Messiah to come and lift the curse from over her city and her life, to administer vengeance to the innocent and to bring justice to the downtrodden. As Joash had always reminded her, Messiah would crush and destroy all evildoers including death itself. Messiah would bind up and comfort the brokenhearted. He would restore justice and peace. He would declare the day of Jubilee and set the captives free.

The deep pain of Shimei in losing a close brother and the heart-wrenching sorrow of God-fearing parents, Reuben and Jerusha who had lost their firstborn, were heavy indeed. The youthful body was returned during the night to the family home in Galilee. Relatives from Jerusalem travelled by night and during the following days as word spread throughout Jerusalem. At sunrise, a place in the family grave was prepared for the body. This consisted of a rock-hewn sepulchre containing a small chamber and a lower cave. The ceremony then took place. The eyes of Joash were closed, and he was washed with aromatic scents and anointed with nard, myrhh, and aloes. His body was wrapped in a shroud, his face veiled with a soudarion and his hands and feet wrapped in linen strips. He was carried to the upper chamber of the house where relatives and neighbours came to see him and kiss his face for the last time. A few hours later, the burial took place. He was carried to his grave by his twin brother Shimei and Reuben, his father. In the front of the procession were Anna, Elisheva, the mother of Joash and Mezahab. These were followed by other female relative and friends. There was no requirement for professional mourners to be hired, for the intense weeping and expressions of sorrow seemed to engulf the entire land as the easterly breeze carried forth the deep lamentations across the hills. Japhlet, Ashvath, Zattu, Ithran, Pagiel, Eleazar, and Jashobeam were amongst several flautists and singers from the local synagogue choir who had joined the procession towards the family tomb that had been hewn into a rock on a hill overlooking the family's flax fields. The body was laid upon a bench specially cut in the rock and surrounded by large amounts of aromatic herbs. Some of the women burnt spices at the grave. Once the tomb was closed, a neatly arranged pile of stones was raised upon it. When the rites were completed, the family gathered for 'the bread of mourning', which included a ritual drinking of wine. Friends and neighbours had prepared a meal of bread, hard-boiled eggs, and lentils, which was then consumed.

Other friends from Jerusalem, Bethany, Bethpage, Bethlehem, and surrounding areas as far as Jericho to Hebron arrived later, having heard the news from the temple. Other local acquaintances came to pay visits of sympathy and sat in the house on the ground or on low stools with their heads bowed in prayer. Deep mourning lasted seven days, of which the first three were weeping. During this time, no work was done and no shoes were worn. In the village, no greetings were replied to. After this, there were thirty days of lighter mourning. Afterwards, at certain dates in the year, as well as on the anniversary of his death, the grave of Joash would be visited.

Anna's only consolation was that she possessed healthy sons and was not a landless immigrant or one to be left amongst the poorest of the poor. Her inheritance rights were by no means automatic, yet she was to be unusually blessed in that her links with the family of Joash were strong. Since the two had become acquainted, she had been the object of steadfast affection and kindness. Moreover she had sons and God-fearing brothers and nephews who still worked her father's land. The family land that Joash would have inherited in Galilee was retained for his sons, but the home that he had built and the surrounding land that he had bought in the hill country was given freely to Anna. Mutual visits remained common, and great compassion and provision were bestowed upon this young, tender widow by relatives and friends on all sides.

14

Days of Sorrow

Though the loss and desperation continued to ravage her broken soul for months and years with the identity issa-almana haunting her daily, Anna was treated differently than the many other widows who were entirely dependent on the right to glean the fields and vineyards during harvest time and to gain from the sharing of tithes as well as relying on the levirate institution for an heir to be granted, social reintegration to be facilitated, and special provisions to be made during feasts. Whilst she would never be very rich, she was a widow with sons and would always have sufficient. Furthermore, she would still be able to give temple offerings and help other widows. The longstanding generosity of Phanuel and Elisheva into the oppressed and exploited widows and orphans across the land was now to reap and extend its most visible harvest in their seventh child and only daughter.

As the days passed, Anna continued to draw consolation from the fact that Joash had not died childless. He had known the joy of being a father, and she would continue to know the joy of motherhood. She had been well provided for with home and land, and she knew that her plight could have been so much darker. She believed in her heart the teachings of Rabbi Hillel regarding the righteous being preserved and in the words of the prophet Daniel that there would be a time when many who slept in the dust of the ground would wake to everlasting life and others to disgrace and everlasting contempt. Though her mind struggled to perceive and comprehend such matters, she knew in her heart that her husband was with his righteous forefathers and that the great mystery of the resurrection would be revealed in the years to come. Nevertheless, life was difficult. Whenever she saw her image at home in the polished metal mirror or gazed into the holding pools that supplied the terrace, she heard so clearly the voice of her lover affirming her beauty. The faintest trace of his scent on scrolls, parchments, cushions, and tunics cast her soul into uncontrollable lamentation. At times, when she looked into the glass, she would see his face next to hers, his lips pressed against her cheeks.

As inner resolution and fortitude returned, the strong love and unwavering faith of parents and relatives strengthened Anna and her sons. As time went on, she began to sense a fire being rekindled in her heart, flames of divine love and fiery faith. As the months went by, it was as if divine destiny had not been halved but mysteriously doubled. A double flame was starting to blaze. God alone understood it. She now carried in her own heart the prophetic flame of Joash.

Amidst the weeping, loneliness, and grief, times of comfort and refreshing came, especially through the close companionship of brothers and wives as well as other close acquaintances. Eleazar who had married and remained based in Bethlehem, expanding his father's carpentry and stone-cutting business, continued to stay in close connection with Ithran and Pagiel with whom he had grown up. His wife visited Anna and took great care for her. As well as being a respected builder, Eleazar was a popular provider of yokes, ploughs, and ladders, a master of the chisel, hammer, mallet, awl, and axe. Though the trade did not generate great wealth, popularity, and reputation, established by his father, Eliud, it counted for much. Business had expanded and prospered especially with the rise of the ebony imported from Arabia. This was a smooth dark timber known for its natural gloss, and it was ideal not just for furniture but also for ornamental work wrought with gold and for musical instruments. Eliud and Eleazar had become masters of the trade and known for their excellent craftsmanship and finesse. Eliud continued to remain a close friend of Phanuel, and each family continued to profit from the other's skills. It was a not long after the burial of Joash that Eleazar had become a father. His wife, Shiphrah, had borne him a son who they named Matthan. The couple had waited a long time for the child to be conceived, yet once again the faithfulness of God shone forth, and their prayers had been answered. Shiphrah often visited Anna, and as the years passed Matthan became good friends with Anna's sons, Ezra and Bezalel. Eleazar and Shiprah were both of the tribe of Judah, God-fearing worshippers whose ancestors had been devoted to temple life following closely in the steps of Eleazar's father, Eliud. Shiprah was known for her great musical skill and gifted voice, and Eleazar, since his earliest days, had played the silver trumpet that his maternal grandfather had once played. Its blasts had often resounded through Bethlehem when as a young child he had filled his young lungs from the roofs of local watchtowers. Still now, they were a humble and simple, reverent family who found riches and wealth in music and song. They loved to raise their voices in harmony, dance with guests, and celebrate life—always rejoicing, always believing...even more now with Matthan, the child of their prayers, at their side.

15

JAHATH
CLOSER THAN A BROTHER

Japhlet left his sons working and ran to meet Jahath, greeting him with a kiss. They had not seen each other since childhood, yet it was as if they had never been apart. Jahath was from a family of Levites who had returned to the village of Ein Karem, the home of another major spring within the hill country, on the west side of Jerusalem. They were a priestly family, and having spent time living first in Hebron and then in Ramah, they had returned to the original family home in the hills. The recent invasion of Rome had made them long to be closer to their roots. Jahath was a priest, and his wife, also from the Levitical line, was a woman of tenacious faith and musical skill. The family house that they owned was surrounded by just a small amount of land and vegetation. The demands of the priestly lifestyle as well as their lack of sons meant there was little time to devote to agricultural expansion. They owned a modest olive grove, a small vineyard, and a number of fig trees, but their main produce, oil, meat, and grain had always come directly from the land of Phanuel now farmed mainly by Japhlet and his brothers. Japhlet had always hoped that one day Jahath and his parents would return to the hill country. Having been close as youngsters, they had been taught together in the local synagogue before Jahath had married and moved to Hebron. Phanuel's sons greatly welcomed the family's return to the area, and a banquet was held. They gave to Jahath in abundance, always refusing any form of payment, though at times they were forced to do so. The father of four cherished daughters, Jahath had always longed for a son, and it was shortly after his return to the hills that his dream came true. This dream had never been simply reminiscent of all men desiring a son. Whilst Jahath had been betrothed, a prophet from Beth Shemesh had boldly approached his wife as she was drawing water from the well. As she had turned and covered her face, he told her that she would bear a son and that this son would serve all of his days in the temple. Jahath spent hours in prayer and fasting outside of prescribed times and had become increasingly disillusioned with the widespread hypocrisy and corruption within the priesthood. The yoke of the law had become too heavy for people to bear, and priests levied onerous fines for infractions written only the day before. For several years, Jahath had prayed unceasingly for fulfilment of the promise given to his wife at the well. He had searched for a sign. Other than the inner voice telling him to return to the hill country, there had been no other guidance regarding when this birth would take place. Jahath was a devout, zealous man, highly inquisitive, knowledgeable of all scripture, and overwhelmed by many thoughts. He stood aside from the corruption and compromise that dominated the hour and prayed unceasingly for the deliverance and protection of Jerusalem. When his beloved son Eliab was born, he knew more than ever that God would fulfil every promise to Israel. The child grew to be a gifted singer and musician who became well respected in the temple as soon as he was of age.

Another close friend of Jahath was Crispus whose father had worked for many years as a respected sage in the temple and had become a close companion to his own father since the start of his priestly ministry. His father, Alexander, a Greek Jew whose ancestors had returned to Israel from Greece three generations before, had been a highly respected expert on the Torah and the law. Crispus was a passionate, fearless, vocal man who unrelentingly voiced his disapproval of men exploiting the temple for commercial gain, rabbis harassing widows for their tithe, and the increasing number of priests who were motivated by selfish, dishonest financial profit attempting to conceal their corruption from the eyes of men. He had always spoken openly, denouncing the hypocrisy that had become a way of life for so many. Crispus had received an intense and solid education and was raised to be an erudite scholar of the law. His father's aspiration for his life had at first seemed onerous and oppressive, but now as a man, hungry for understanding, studious, and assiduous, he stood tall amidst the finest young scholars of the day. His ancestors had been acquaintances of Phanuel's great-grandfather Ishvah who had learnt Greek and assisted in the Greek translation of the Torah, known as the Septuagint. Intrigue and enquiry regarding the Torah and its spiritual principles as well as zeal for prophetic insight and divine understanding had been a family legacy. These had been men of great minds, zealous and impartial in their quest for accurate knowledge and revelation. Since moving to Bethany and marrying, Crispus had become close friends with Jahath, and their wives had each become friends of Anna. The wife of Crispus was also acquainted with Greek as her own ancestors had moved to Jerusalem from Alexandria. She had been taught by her own grandfather to read the Torah both in Hebrew and Greek. She was a kind and beautiful woman, the daughter of perfumers, regal in appearance and gentle in countenance. She had met neither Jahath nor Japhlet until the great family banquet held in Bethpage to celebrate the birth of her fifth son. As they and their families were amongst the few guests whose acquaintance she had not yet made, she ensured that they received a double welcome. The young Eliab joined the children—singing, dancing, and laughing. The sight of these young boys brought vivid memories back to Japhlet who for a few moments began to relive the joy of his childhood. The birth of his sister Anna suddenly felt like just moments away. He remembered the softness of her unblemished skin against the back of his palms, the tiny fingers curled around his own, the satin golden curls, and the huge olive eyes that stared up at him. Time's flight seemed like fleeting seconds.

Tears filled his eyes, tears of heartfelt compassion for his sister. That child he had beheld was now a widow, and the nation herself was divorced and unprotected. Both were widows and both desperate for Heaven's full inheritance. Where was the justice in this? Did one really live only to die? Redemption and consolation, were they ever to come? Oh, how they were needed at such a time as this. The newborn child at the centre of the gathering was given a Greek name, Theophilus. Blessings and prayers were offered; gifts and fragrances were given; and the singing, dancing, and feasting continued beyond sunset.

Eliab returned from dancing with the other children and clutched his father's hand. He was an intense and pensive young soul who knew that one day he would take up the Levitical mantle of his father and serve in the temple as a priest. He knew, without being told, that he had been born for this reason. Already, at this tender age, the boy saw himself clothed in priestly robes, set aside and holy unto the Lord. He had imagined being appointed high priest and entering the Most Holy Place. He pictured the temple curtain in his mind's eye and imagined passing through the veil and beholding the Shekinah Glory. Even before his first visit to the temple, he had learnt from his father that to be a priest was the highest call for any man in Israel. As a young boy, he had imagined that one day he would be like Samuel. During Sukkot he had taken the spare myrtle and hyssop branches gathered for the sukkah and cleared them of all leaves and foliage. He had concealed them in a hidden place and returned daily to see if they had budded; other times, he on the flat roof of the house gazing up at the multitudes of stars imagining that an audible voice was calling him "Eliab," "Eliab," "Eliab," posturing himself in stillness and anticipation to hear the voice should it speak. Yet he would hear only silence and gradually fall asleep beneath the open night sky, his sacred scroll placed above his head as if it were the very ark before which his young hero had ministered to the Lord that sacred night in his linen ephod. The following night, Eliab would wait again for the voice, but time after time, nothing came. Sadness would overcome him, tears flowing from his deep, innocent brown eyes. Again he would fall asleep, only to wait again...and again the following night. No one ever knew how Eliab's young tender heart ached to hear that voice that he was sure would one day speak to him. Though, as a child, he never heard this audible voice that he lived to hear, he would never depart from the high call to live a life devoted to worship and sacrifice.

16

JUDEA RAVAGED

Mezahab was now in her fifth year of marriage to Shimei, the brother of Joash, and continued to be a true friend to Anna. Mezahab remained full of life and hope; her words of wisdom and timely assurances soothed the wounds and cracks of her friend's shattered heart.

Yet their closeness was equally the cause of despair, for Shimei resembled his deceased brother in so many ways. Had Shimei not already been betrothed to Mezahab at the time of Joash's death, he would have undoubtedly taken Anna's hand in marriage and redeemed her from this shameful status, as was the custom. Though her soul was tormented with love, regret, and loneliness, her deep affection for Mezahab elevated her spirit far above the clouds of sorrow to truly rejoice in what God had so granted. Gradually, as the years passed, Anna felt her garments of sackcloth and despair fall from her aching body and a fresh hope permeate her being.

Sadly, Mezahab had troubles of her own, for after several years of marriage, she had not yet conceived a child. She, too, feeling shame and despair relied on the faith-filled encouragement and constant prayers of Anna to lift her from her anguish. When seeing Ezra and Bezalel running, dancing, and singing, the youngest with the wide eyes and robust frame of his father, Mezahab whispered again the prayer of Hannah, pleading with God to hear her prayer and grant to her mercy and favour. It was during moments spent together visiting each other's homes that Anna and Mezahab would perceive that same holy presence and vibrant expectation that they had done in the days of their youth. All that they had embraced and absorbed from their fathers, brothers, and relatives about Messiah came flooding back into their minds. Though many of the women whom they met at the village well and in the local market had husbands who were zealots and militants, there was a small quiet group who turned towards the hidden power of sincere, unrelenting prayer and supplication more than they did to militant reactions. These few could see that the most effective form of revolt was to be found in supplication and intercession. As political rest increased, the land was enshrouded in a dark cloud of fear, which at times became terror. Those who discussed the ongoing conflicts, tensions, rebellions, and massacres did so in quiet, trembling voices. Those who had for so long refused to allow hope to escape had begun to gradually loosen their grasp. Yet for some, their hope was entwined in their destiny. They were destined to hope. They were called to believe. They were positioned to worship.

Back on the political stage of 67 BC, it was heard that the Roman politician Pompey (who was married to the daughter of Julius Caesar and was one of the greatest generals of his age) had been commissioned to pacify the rebellion in Hispania, Cicilia, and areas of the Eastern Mediterranean. There were several wars against the Romans in which he could intervene. The kingdoms of Pontus and Armenia had joined forces against the Romans in Crete and Syria. There was no recognised authority. Roman influence was certainly expanding across the eastern world.

With Queen Salome now dead, the civil war caused by the jealousy and aggression of her youngest son continued to ravage Judea. To an ambitious man like the Roman politician Pompey, who had already intervened in these various conflicts around the Eastern Mediterranean, the situation offered valuable opportunities. He had already invaded Pontus and attacked the

Armenians, expanded his armies and prepared to annexed Syria, which had now become a Roman province.

The year of 64 BC was also a bad year because there had been vehement storms and winds, destroying the fruits of the whole nation. The price of wheat had thus radically escalated to sixteenfold the normal price. Corn and figs were being imported from Egypt, and reserves were running dry. As famine spread across the land, the poorer people found themselves in great need. Many considered this to be divine judgement for the corrupt behaviour and rebellion of Aristobulus. He had asked to be furnished with sacrifices in order to gain favour with God, and he let down money over the temple walls from inside so that he could pay for peace with sacrifices. The people however took the money but did not hand over the sacrifices, and the priests were unable to mediate and call for God's grace. The priests inside the temple prayed that God would avenge them, and the ruinous weather conditions throughout the land were seen as an answer to this prayer.

As the conflict continued, many Jews appealed to Damascus. However, the Roman leader of Damascus, Pompey, who was a great Roman general, responded to various sizeable financial bribes of gold and silver from each of the rival brothers Hyrcanus and Aristobulus and came as anticipated to arbitrate the disputed succession. News spread that Aristobulus had barricaded himself in the temple with chief priests of the Sadducee party and had physically cut off access points. The remainder of the Jews welcomed Pompey's army into the city, and rather than attacking during the Sabbaths, they used the time to build siege ramps against the wall that surrounded the temple complex. The experts in siege warfare constructed a large dam and towers that were rolled towards the wall of the temple. Heavy stones and battering rams were used to break the temple wall, and attacks took place every day apart from the Sabbath. Pompey's soldiers eventually entered the temple terrace where they started to kill defenders.

Many good soldiers, including relatives of Eliud and close friends of Anna's brothers, committed suicide as they did not want to see the profanation of the temple.

Pompey ended up siding with Hyrcanus, who had lost many of his troops, and thus, having pacified Crete, he returned to Jerusalem in the spring of 63 BC to restore the priesthood to him and confront his brother, Aristobulus, who continued to take refuge in the temple and refused to move for three months. An officer eventually forced his way in and Pompey entered the Most Holy Place with a sword in his hand. Aristobulus was then taken away as prisoner to Rome.

It was reported that he had been astonished to see no idol-god. He had expected to see a physical deity as he was accustomed to Greek and Roman gods. Aristobulus was captured, and Jerusalem remained in turmoil. The city bled like an open wound. From the year of 63 BC, Jerusalem was made tributary to the Romans. All the cities that Judaea had subdued were also subjugate to Roman governance, and the entire nation became confined and named a Roman province. Hyrcanus took up his office as appointed high priest. Aristobulus was taken away as prisoner to Rome, and Antipater, the Idumaean, was appointed governor.

Throughout Israel, there was not a household untouched by the news, rumours, and announcements that had spread across the land like a forest fire. The Romans had apparently intervened as peacemakers, and many in Jerusalem were in favour of their rule, seeing it as a lesser evil to that of civil war. Opinion was heatedly divided, for tax was considered preferable to bloodshed. The regime established by Pompey was a protectorate. The Jewish state was deprived of its maritime region and continued to exist as a tribute-paying vassal of Rome.

To add to the bloodshed and horror of this fateful year, it became known that a group of magi from the east had made a presentation to the Roman Senate describing celestial portents that indicated a new ruler had been born. Evidently fearful about the implications of this news, the senate had ordered the death of baby boys within the candidate range.

17

SHEMITAH- THE SABBATICAL YEAR

The year of 57 BC was Shemitah, a sabbatical year. The sacred pause of the seventh year in the holy cycle had arrived. The law required that slaves be set free, particularly those who had been obliged to sell themselves in order to pay their debts. Open-handedness towards the poor and even greater charity and fraternity than usual were legal requirements. Some though did not cancel debts entirely, only the interest incurred on debts. Those selling animals in the temple courts were regularly perpetuating this injustice. The earth likewise was to have twelve months of relief. It was neither to be ploughed nor harvested, no pruning or sowing, no labour on the land. Only the strict necessities of life were extracted from it. Even the grapes and olives were left by their owners, though the peasants and farm animals were permitted to eat them. Anna remembered this sacred season well, and as life progressed, the gap between each Shemitah seemed to shorten. Each farmer knew only too well the benefits of revitalising the earth and allowing the soil to replenish its nutrients. The sixth year was always plentiful as God had promised; hence, there was no lack. The storehouses would always be full. Many of those working in agriculture used the free time to visit family members and spend increased time in the synagogues. The Romans, however, did not respect the custom. The raising of taxes during Shemitah was not renounced, and civil burdens were not lifted. Nevertheless, the earth rested and slaves were set free. Trumpets were sounded and charity was shown. However, the restoration of property to the poor by the wealthy citizens to whom they had sold it as a form of debt relief did not take place. Injustice was rife and Roman dominance was ubiquitous. The hoofbeats of Roman soldiers could be heard approaching at seemingly every corner. Women were so often abused and left suffering by the wells as soldiers walked on, their waterskins filled with fresh water. When passing through town, or country, tracks or highways, there was a new sight and scene that constantly imposed itself, awakening indignation and revilement. Low muttered curses attended the steps of the publican whose restless eyes ensured that nothing escaped his menacing net. This was the sight of the foreign tax gatherer, a new and hated symbol of Israel's servitude and subjection to foreign domination. The tax farmers, 'Moches', and the tax collectors, 'Gabbai', were seemingly omnipresent. Ever since their return from Babylon, Jewish ancestors had talked of the foreign taxation, which had led to poignant memories from the time of Zattu. Ground tax had been paid to Persia, and later, there had been taxes imposed by Syria on salt and crops. Yet now it was becoming far more onerous and unbearable as it included income tax, property tax, import and export tax as well as house tax. These exactions and stipulations weighed heavily on a population that was predominantly agricultural and comparatively poor. On top of this burdensome civil taxation, there were, of course, the religious obligations. Every town and community continued to levy its own tax for maintenance of synagogues, elementary schools, public baths; support of widows, orphans, and the poor; repair of public roads, city walls, gates, and other municipal and social requirements. This taxation applied by the Jewish authority was done with ease and kindness in so far as the public welfare system was outstanding. Rabbis ensured that all those who devoted themselves to the study of the law were exempt from such taxes.

The Roman taxation was a different story. It was systematic, relentless, ruthless, and cruel. The two main taxes were ground tax and poll tax. The latter was dual tax as it consisted of head money and income tax. Women were liable from age twelve and men from age fourteen. Landed property was subject to a tax of one-tenth of all grain and a tax of one-fifth on fruit. There was additional tax on imports and exports levied on the highways and at seaports. On top of this, there was bridge money, road money, and a regular duty on all that was bought and sold in the towns.

In order to avoid any possible loss to the treasury, the proconsul of Syria, Quirinus Cyrenius, initiated a regular census to confirm the size of the population and their means. This was a terrible crime in the eyes of the rabbis who knew that in the scriptures such an act had been forbidden and punished. Chaos increased as soldiers arrived with the decree. Tributes that previously had been offered exclusively to Jehovah were now being paid to a heathen emperor. Israel was being shaped according to the whim of a pagan idolater. Roman reality was a knife that cut deeply, leaving open wounds and raising constant questions as men placed the emperor's poll tax beside the half shekel of the sanctuary and saw the tithe of their fields, vineyards, and orchards, claimed by the tax gatherer, a tithe that had hitherto been given to God alone. The questions and revolts that arose were to cost Israel rivers of blood.

The whole cost of tax collection was thrown upon the taxpayer. Roman knights who were great capitalists formed joint-stock companies with revenues of a province at public auction, generally for five years. The board had its chairman and its officers in Rome (known as the publicani) underlet certain taxes. These employed either slaves or some of the lower-class citizens as tax gatherers. Harbour dues were higher than ordinary tolls, and smuggling or false declaration was punished by confiscation of goods. The publicans thus also levied import and export dues, bridge toll, road money, and town dues. Farmers, tradesmen, and all such workers were equally exposed to the exactions of the gatherer. Travellers, caravans, and pedlars encountered their seated presence at every bridge, along the road, and at city gates. Every bale had to be unloaded and all its contents tipped out and searched, letters were opened, accusations were usually unjust, and price fixing was arbitrary. No one appealed against them, for although the law allowed appeals to be made, the judges themselves were direct beneficiaries of the revenue, and accusations had to be made before the knights, who were themselves the very ones being implicated in the farming of the revenue. The joint-stock company of publicani in Rome believed themselves to be entirely worthy of such handsome dividends. Likewise, the gatherers in the provinces all intended to profit from poor people. The more that was collected, the greater the cost of taxation, for the collection costs also had to be covered. Extensive personal revenues were yielded, and this was a lucrative and highly corrupt trade. Fictitious values were more often than not placed on property and income, and the tax of those who were unable to pay was advanced with usurious interest on what had thereby become a private and thus potentially damaging debt. Creditors treated debtors with contempt and often cruelty; rarely did one encounter a creditor with a kind and patient disposition. The publicani were considered by Rome to be the ornament of the state and the strength and valour of the republic. The rabbis deeply hated the publicani and forbade them to exchange money from the temple treasury. They were ranked as harlots or heathens, robbers and murderers.

Shemitah year announced liberty; however grace, mercy, redemption, and freedom were lost values. Israel was in bondage. The shackles were stronger than they had ever been. In fact, quite the opposite to the essence of Shemitah was taking place. Added to the crushing weight of Roman taxation was the ongoing conflict surrounding Aristobulus. Alexander, his escaped son, invaded Judea, deposed Hyrcanus, and began rebuilding the walls of Jerusalem that Pompey had destroyed. In the year of 56 BC Aristobulus and another son, Antigonus, escaped from Rome and came to Judea in order to continue Alexander's fight against Gabinius. Amidst the fighting, Aristobulus was badly wounded, captured, and sent back to Rome—only to escape again. Word spread rapidly that Aristobulus and his sons were back in Palestine raising their own troops. Civil war thus recommenced, and the Romans had to continually intervene, trying to find a suitable regime that would be suitable for Israel.

Fear of the unknown pervaded the atmosphere, and the nation remained in a state of fragility. As the majority of the population worked in agriculture, something had to be done in order to keep them fully occupied during Shemitah year and enable them to make a proper living. As such, during the six years of labour, the government took a share of grain, and when Shemitah arrived, they paid the farmers to work at construction and other types of labour. As the available labour force was so huge, many of the nation's larger projects, new buildings, construction of walls, road building, and irrigation projects were initiated. Due to this diversion of labour, it was normal for men to have had two trades, or at least a secondary trade that they learned and developed during Shemitah.

It was during this time, a few years after the Roman invasion, that several of Anna's brothers left the hill country and went to work on the roads. This year was different to past years as they were no longer working for Israel but for Rome. There were six main highways of commerce that had been developed—the chief objectives being Jerusalem, Caesarea, and the military. The southern road led from Jerusalem by Bethlehem to Hebron and then west to Gaza and into Arabia. The road to Hebron was full of priests and pilgrims. The old highway along the sea known by the Romans as the Via Maris passed from Egypt up to Tyre, a fairly straight route led from it, passing by Caesarea Philippi to Damascus. The seashore road touched Gaza, Ascalon, Jamnia, Lydda, Diospolis, and finally Caesarea and Ptolemais. It was probably the most important military highway in the land as it connected the capital with the seat of the Roman procurator, keeping the sea board and harbours free for communication. This road branched off at Jerusalem at Lydda where it divided, leading either by Beth-Horon or by Emmaus, which was the longer way. A road led from Jerusalem by Beth-Horon and Lydda to Joppa where it continued close by the seashore to Caesarea. A road led from Galilee to Jerusalem straight through Samaria, branching at Sichem eastwards towards Damascus and westwards to Caesarea. It was full of travellers. Many travellers preferred to face the danger of robbers who awaited them on this road than pass through Samaria. This road led from Jerusalem by Bethany to Jericho. Here the Jordan was forded, and the road led to Gilead and then either southwards or north to Peraea, from where the traveller could make his way to Galilee. All of these roads, whether commercial or military, were considered Judean and led to or from Jerusalem. The road that passed through Galilee was not Jewish but connected the east with the west—Damascus with Rome. From Damascus it led across the Jordan to Capernaum, Tzippori, and Nain towards Nazareth and then to Ptolemais. Hence, from its position, Nazareth was on the world's great highway and a springboard from which news rebounded throughout Palestine and could be carried east and west. There were many secondary routes that led in all directions. The roads to the cities of refuge were always kept in good order and provided with bridges and signposts where roads diverged.

It was whilst working on the main road towards Jericho that Anna's brothers and nephews made the acquaintance of a prominent figure by the name of Raphu. Raphu lived in Jericho, the place of his birth. His family was the leading road builders by trade and over recent years had become increasingly established and engaged in various new projects between Jericho, Ramah, and Jerusalem. They had seen the economic climate evolve and strengthen as vast amounts of money poured in from Rome and systems of transport were being developed in order to further enable trade, commerce, and urban development. As this new influx of labourers was constantly on the roads, much time was spent away from families, and many nights were spent in inns and lodgings of friends. When they returned each Shabbat, stories would be told and updates would be given regarding the latest developments, commissioning and tensions arising from the increasing weight of road taxes. Experts in their trade, Raphu and his brothers had been commissioned as overseers to those employed during the sabbatical year and those who were newcomers to the trade. Anna's brothers and nephews were fast learners and at times found themselves as far out as Jericho and beyond. There was much to learn. Military roads were paved and provided with milestones. Primary roads were annually repaired in spring in preparation for the feasts. No subterranean structures were allowed; overhanging branches of trees had to be cut so as to allow a man on a camel to pass with ease. Likewise no balconies or projections were permitted to darken streets, and nothing could be left to accumulate on the road. Regulations in towns and neighbourhoods were strict. Rotten trees or dangerous walls had to be removed within thirty days of ordinances being issued by police. Water or any other material could not be thrown or left on the road as these were seen as a threat to public sanitation. As political and commercial engagements increased, so did the number of travellers and pilgrims. Journeys were on foot, asses or carriages or carts being used for the transportation of goods.

It was during one evening working on the main road towards Jericho that the brothers were invited back to the home of Raphu for the Shabbat meal. The road from Jerusalem upon which they had been working was steep, rocky, and tortuous passing through large stretches of isolated territory before it arrived at Jericho. The home of Raphu was near the centre of the city, and their time there opened their eyes to a whole new world.

Jericho was home to around twelve thousand Levites. The city sat at the base of the primary roads that ascended from the Jordan

Rift Valley up the Judean hills. Seventeen miles to the northeast of Jerusalem, this city of palms stood eight hundred feet below sea level, and it was the lowest city on earth, its position at the top of a deep gorge contributing to its hot tropical climate. The city was bounded by Mount Nebo to the east, the central mountains to the west, and the Dead Sea to the south. Aside from these natural fortifications, Jericho also benefited from natural irrigation afforded by the Jordan River approximately four miles to the west, and from underground tributaries from the central mountains that fed into its famous oasis. This irrigation resulted in teeming plant life and had helped to transform the region into a flowing sea of green in an otherwise barren desert.

Other Shemitah workers too had family and acquaintances in Jericho whose doors were wide open to them on Shabbat, for it was far to journey back to their families in Jerusalem. Working on the roads was a tiring and tedious job radically different to working in the terraces. The generous hospitality offered to the brothers was thus received with gratitude. The wider family of Raphu gathered in a large house. They were God-fearing people who talked much about their faith and their hope that Messiah would come soon. The brothers of Raphu's wife and most of his cousins worked in the balsam trade, whether on the plantations or in exportation. Several of the women and children worked in the sycamore groves incising the figs in order to force ripening and gathering them in season. The fruits were sold and the rejects used as cattle fodder. Trade was thriving in Jericho. The land possessed an exotic charm and a seductive opulence. It was a true oasis in the desert. Its jagged silhouette stood out against the base of the mountains, and to eyes acquainted only with Jerusalem and her environs, it was a place of drama, mystique, enigma, and exoticism. The oasis of Jericho was rich in balm. The vegetation near to the river was dense and looked tropical, lavish with willows, wild bananas, jujube trees, vast quantities of plumed reeds, sweet calamus used to scent the holy oil, and huge beds of papyrus that grew in the water itself. It was a region that in its luxurious growth contrasted dramatically with the shores of the Dead Sea. It was a place of magnificent colour, scented Persimmon groves, with an abundance of flowers of all varieties. The land was bursting forth with life, rich and fertile orchards, flourishing vineyards, and vast spaces for the cultivation of roses. There was a great caravan road that connected Arabia with Damascus. Traders and buyers alike were attracted to the fertility of Jericho's soil and its tropical produce, palm groves, rose gardens, balsam plantations, and sycamore trees.

Rome transformed Jericho into a central station for the collection of tax and custom, and it was here that the chief publicani acquired their wealth. With its trade and traffic in balsam it was the reputed home of the sweetest of perfumes and highly prized medicinal potions. The town was considered a gem within its surroundings, a thriving, dynamic centre for tradesmen, pilgrims, priests, and robbers alike. It was the true home of the soul through which the winding Jordan was reluctant to lose its waters into the slimy mass of the Dead Sea. With the increase of labourers shipped in from the rural areas where the ground was resting, Shemitah year saw a rapid acceleration in the development of new roads and the vast improvement of already established trade routes and other key roads. Jericho's natural resources, beauty, and natural defences caused her to become the ideal locus for trade. These attributes also made her the source of envy and a coveted possession for invaders of ancient Palestine. Access to her neighbouring city-states was a major key to Jericho's importance, the location being ideal for the establishing of trade routes and for communication exchange.

By the end of Shemitah and the year of new labour and new horizons, Raphu and the brothers had become longstanding friends sharing a common passion for the Torah and a resoluteness to walk righteously, honour the law, and await Messiah. Mutual visits to Jericho and the Judean hills continued into the years to come. Indeed there was much to talk about as years passed by.

18

ANNA
MOTHER AND INTERCESSOR

It was Rosh Hashanah, the start of New Year. As the high priest Hyrcanus raised the shofar and announced the feast, he had no knowledge that that this would be his last announcement of another New Year. The day not only announced the New Year but also it was a day for remembrance of covenant, judgement of evil, and exhortation towards repentance. The horns were blown all day long in Jerusalem. The day was observed as a Sabbath and a holy convocation of prayer, sacrifice, and procession, a day in which no servile work was to be carried out. The various prescribed offerings for the day were made and a psalm of David was sung: "Ascribe to the Lord glory and strength. His glory thunders. His voice upon the waters, powerful and majestic, His voice breaks the cedars; it shakes the wilderness and strips the forests bare." Three books were opened inside of the temple—one representing good, another evil, and a third those whose case was to be decided on ten days later on Yom Kippur, the Day of Atonement. During the entire of the day, trumpets and horns were blown throughout the city, and the jubilant blasts resonated over the hills. Even when the feast fell on a Shabbat, this ceremony was carried out, though not outside of the temple walls. Rams' horns were used rather than the horns of calves, oxen, or antelope, for the ram had become a sacred symbol of Abraham's obedience in sacrificing his son. For this holy day the mouthpieces were fitted with gold rather than the silver used on fast days. Those who blew horns were dispersed in between those who blew trumpets, and the sound of the horn was prolonged by that of the trumpets. The people were encouraged to listen and not just hear, to turn their hearts intently towards God. Though Jerusalem was in deep mourning, devastation, and spiritual destitution, inextinguishable flickers of light and hope rested amidst a very small number of the population. Hearts and minds contemplated what this next year would bring. For so many, the future did not look hopeful at all. The melted silver taken from the temple tax and the half shekel continued to create trumpets whose blast heralded nothing more than death and despair.

The summer heat, intensified by siroccos and strong desert winds, had finally lifted. Farmers were starting to dry figs for winter and convert grapes into raisins, syrup, and wine. The pomegranates and bananas had already begun to ripen—the long summer drought finally broken by the early rain. The labourers were busy dealing with the last of the grape harvest, and preparation for ploughing was already starting to take place.

Anna's sons were now ten years of age and working for her brothers, tending the small amount of land around her own house. They were close companions to their cousins and, in stature and mind, robust like they father. The boys had been raised well by their mother and had spent time with their grandfather and uncles frequently. Though they did not remember their father well, they often asked questions about his life and death. Talking of the past had helped Anna to accept the truth and cherish memories. For as long as she had known Joash, he had embodied one thing—hope. Hope in the future, hope in the deliverer. It was in the very centre of this divine hope that she would continue to raise her sons. Now approaching manhood, they were already known in the synagogue as diligent young scholars of the Torah. As soon as Bezalel was of age, they both attended lessons with rabbis who had been influenced by Hillel and the teachings of his son Simeon Ben Hillel, a teacher known for his kindness to the young and for his quiet and gentle wisdom.

It was hard to believe that Ezra was now fourteen years of age. The years had seemed to pass by slowly since the death of Joash, yet at the same time, the two sons had grown up quickly into young men. Ezra and his younger brother Bezalel had grown up with their little parchment rolls made especially for the use of children containing such portions of scripture as the Shema and the Hallel, the history of creation and the first eight chapters of the book of Leviticus. They had attended a synagogue-school, and having reached the legal age, they had been taken up to the temple to observe the festive rites. Local rabbis had taught the boys well, and their uncles had played the role of their absent father. From the age of three years the boy had grown up reciting verses, benedictions, and wise sayings. Ezra still remembered sitting on the ground with other young children repeating sentences, verses, and rhymes, reading aloud and starting to read the Torah at the age of five. At six years of age, they had attended the classroom of the rabbi attached to the local village synagogue and later had been able to sit in discussions of the Sanhedrin with other boys of similar age. At the age of ten they had begun to study the Mishnah, and in one year's time at the age fifteen, Ezra would start to study the Talmud. Also, like all young boys, they had both learnt to swim.

In their mother's eyes, the most important part of their education was about the future, not the past. They had been taught well regarding Israel's expectation of the Messiah and had studied national history, starting with the birth of the expectation during Assyria's conquest of Israel when the prophet Isaiah had introduced the promise concerning the establishment of Messiah's kingdom and the righteous remnant. They had learnt how during Babylonian exile the views had been further developed through Jeremiah and Ezekiel studying various writings from this period. They had learnt of how the Maccabean revolt and the overthrow of Syria and the Hasmonean conquests had dramatically changed the view and expectation of the nation. Maccabee and John Hyrcanus of the Hasmoneans were both from the tribe of Levi, yet the Jews had proclaimed them as priest and king forever. However, when they eventually proved to be corrupt and self-seeking, the people had looked again to the Davidic line from which the deliverer would be sent forth. As God had promised, the royal seed would be preserved through the bloodline of David. Israel's heritage and legacy would not be withheld. A whole new kingdom would arise from this seed, an unending rule of peace. The king of promise would have a dominion beyond measure. The seed had been preserved through Abraham, Isaac, and Jacob, and it would come forth from Judah's tribe. Even when Israel had forsaken her theocracy and cried out for a king, Jehovah in his graciousness had merged the two together in order to preserve and bring forth the seed through the House of David and the royal line. David, in his worship, had gazed into the heavens and seen the seed to come from a king set aside from all others. This king would receive all earthly nations as his inheritance. He would be radiant, glorious, highly anointed one, Messiah. The prophets had listened and taken heed, speaking forth the wonders of the new era that was to come. The serpent's head would finally be crushed. That which lay dormant as seed would bear a mighty forest of strong trees. As the prophet Zechariah had stated, there would be peace for the seed, and as Balaam had prophesied to King Balak, the Moabite, the seed of Jacob would be sustained 'by many waters'. The armies of the king would be valiant and undefeatable, and Judah would retain the sceptre.

It was important to Anna that the boys fully grasped these truths and remained close to those who had conviction and revelation regarding Messiah and prayed in every way possible to hasten the day of His arrival. It was important that these boys received sound teaching and revelation from those who could impart divine wisdom rather than being carried away from truth by winds of false doctrine. The Essenes continued to search for two separate Messiahs, one military and one religious. Others were convinced that Messiah would be primarily a military leader, others viewed him as a prophet, and others looked for a priest-king. Many saw the kingdom as an earthly political one with Jerusalem as capital, and others saw it as being limited to the heavenly realm. The diversity of views made it challenging for young scholars to grow in accurate learning and understanding. They had to judiciously search out the scriptures and the wisdom of the sages before adopting a view of their own. The common point of agreement within all conjecture interpretation and opinion was that Messiah would bring radical change and would deliver the nation from misery, servitude, and peril.

As Anna watched her sons eat the meat and fish stew that she cooked for them each day, the prospect of either of them leaving the home became quite unbearable. By his sixteenth birthday, Ezra was betrothed to the daughter of a local bronze worker. Though he would never be far from his mother, she would miss his hearty laughter and insatiable appetite. Ezra was handsome and robust like his father, and to lose him would be to lose a part of Joash from the house. It seemed only a short time ago that he was playing with clay birds and wooden animals, burying his soft ruddy face in fragrant flowers, jumping off terrace walls with his curls bouncing up and down as he climbed fig trees, hid in watchtowers, and lived the adventures of any young boy growing up in the hill country. His younger brother, Bezalel, had finished his schooling at age thirteen, having celebrated his Bar Mitzvah. He was now a 'Son of the Law'. Leaving childhood behind, he had begun the daily praying of the 'Shema Israel', three times per day, fasting regularly, and studying further the statutes and ordinances of the law. A man in his own right, he was now able to enter the Men's Court when attending the temple. The boys knew that they would always recall that sacred, memorable moment when they had read a passage of the Torah at the ceremony, perceiving the unvoiced pride of their absent father, only wishing that he had lived and not died.

The boys were deeply affected by the death of their great-grandfather Heber who had been like a second father to them along with Grandfather Phanuel. Heber had lost his sight over time, and though lucid in mind, he had become increasingly weak and frail. It was just after Yom HaTeruah, the Feast of Trumpets, and a few days before the Day of Atonement that he died peacefully in his sleep. The mourners had been many, for he had lived a good long life and had been admired by many. Forever they would remember Heber's stories of how his own father, Imnah, had lived as a young man under the heroic leadership of Judas Maccabeus who had drawn an army around him in order to fight for religious freedom. Likewise, his ancestors' involvement in rescuing persecuted Jews who had fled under the terror of Antiochus 1V and who were being restored to Judah were family testimonies that would live on and continue to inspire hope for a stronger redeemer.

Ezra and Bezalel journeyed towards manhood aware of the realities of life and death. Their lives were not unshielded from the harshness of life or the ills of the times. They would continue to grow up in a fragile and war-ridden era rife with crime, compromise, and exploitation. Yet their mother reassured them daily that Jehovah was a refuge and strength, a mighty fortress. For those who abided in His shadow, death itself would not, and simply could not, be their end.

These promises became a lifeline as the tensions grew and dark oppression cast its sinister shadow over the land. It was as if the hills, the trees, the very earth itself was lamenting. Storms and dryness increased in extremity, and a certain disharmony, unrest, disenchantment permeated creation itself. When would Eden return? Would there ever be a full restoration of that which Adam had lost? Would Messiah be like a new Adam who would go forth and multiply faithful rulers of the land? Would toil, labour, fear, and strife ever end? When would Israel rise to her feet and worship in unity free from perversion, greed, malice, rebellion, compromise, and distrust? When would the priesthood be purified? Would her people ever bow the knee in one accord? Where were the tender-hearted and single-minded Davids, the reckless worshippers who would pursue the heart of God? Where were the fearless, unrelenting Josiahs who would abolish idols and foreign gods in the high and low places?

Israel desperately needed a new leader like Moses, Joshua, Joseph, Daniel. Would God raise up intercessory voices in their midst like those of Samuel, Esther, Jeremiah? Where were the prophets and prophetesses? The deliverer had preserved them time after time throughout the ages. At each crisis, their destiny had been redirected by the very finger of God, the divine kinsman redeemer. Where were those anointed with the Spirit of the Lord, those who would stand up with the rod of the Lord and part the waters of oppression, denouncing the rising tide of corruption? When would one come to declare the righteous judgements of Jehovah and administrate the justice and wrath of Heaven? Fear swept across the land like a dark angel, a terrorising spirit that spread its cloak over the city. When hope diminished, those who sought and awaited consolation found it only by holding fast to the divine promises that had echoed throughout the ages. The scarlet thread that spoke of a brighter future found its origins in the sacred covenants, oaths, and promises made to their ancestors. There was no other assurance. When darkness, torment, and despair set in, those who prayed and fasted did so because they trusted in His faithfulness, His mercy, and the steadfast surety of His nature. They prayed that Jehovah would grant to them the faith of Abraham who hoped against hope, the sharp-sightedness of Elisha who saw the chariots and heavenly hosts tearing through the skies. They prayed that Heaven would breathe life and resurrection into the dead bones of Israel. Jehovah—the holy, unchanging one—had provided constantly throughout the lives of their ancestors. He was the great merciful one, eternal in promises, abounding in loving-kindness, El-Berith the great covenant maker, the promise keeper. He was Elohim, the magnificent creator of the galaxies who had stretched out the heavens and set a seal upon the stars, forming with His hands the chambers of south. He was the one who had wrapped up the waters in His clouds and spread out the skies as a cloak, quieting the seas with His holy breath as He walked upon the vault of Heaven.

He was the omniscient, omnipotent, omnipresent, omnificent one, the uncreated creator of all things Immanuel, the King of Glory, righteous judge, El Elyon, seated far above. In Him there was no shadow of turning. He was eternally God, faithful and true. He had sent forth his angels to war against His adversaries, and Joshua himself had met with the captain of the Lord of hosts. Not only were myriads of angels at man's disposal, dispatched to serve the will of God, but the very spirit of Jehovah who had hovered over the void and brought symphony and order into chaos was still breathing. The great Holy Spirit, Ruach HaKodesh, the living breath of the living God, had anointed Gideon and Samson with the Spirit of Might and quickened those who had skilfully built the tabernacle. God was not alone in the heavens, and as the prophet Isaiah had stated, His anointing was sevenfold. Many cried out for knowledge, wisdom, counsel, revelation, understanding, and for increased reverent fear of the Lord. There was too much at stake to stop hoping, believing, interceding. There was too much of Him to find, know, and comprehend. He was the unfathomable one, the sovereign living God, perfect in nature. He was Hashem, the only true and living God, holy and pure, worthy of all worship, devotion, and sacrifice. Uplifting her soul with these thoughts, Anna looked out across the pastures. She knew that if all the unblemished lambs in Israel be slain and sacrificed that night, if all the incense, grain, peace and sin offerings were multiplied to the nation's utmost, this worship would never be enough. It could never be enough. He was a holy God.

Frequently when interceding for Jerusalem and her people, Anna saw golden ladders with angelic beings ascending and descending from Heaven to earth. She saw angels of deliverance stepping down upon local soil. When this happened, she would gaze at the ladders and become light in body and mind. The angels held scrolls and unravelled them as they descended from Heaven. The letters announced local and regional births. Whenever this happened, Anna prayed for her dearest Mezahab who had not yet conceived and still remained barren. Could these visions be a sign that God's favour and mercy were coming to her and Shimei?

49 BC

Memories of solitude returned whenever Anna was invited to weddings and listened to the constant flow of stories of betrothals, banquets, and celebrations from those who gathered to exchange news within the temple courts and inside the city gates. Stories of anticipation and fulfilment inspired both joy and sadness within her soul. With memories, images, conversations, and moments of laughter racing through her mind, she learnt to cherish the past rather than resist it, to behold rather than decry, to embrace the illuminated path of the past without allowing its shadows to haunt her. There was always a joy that came in the morning, a jubilance and gratitude for all that had been given, and a deep tenderness towards those in poverty, sickness, and despair. As the years passed, Anna relearnt to behold the truth of hope. For many, hope was merely the opposite to despair, a sentiment, a sensation, an emotion that countered hopelessness and diminished the clouds of helplessness. Yet she had understood this was not hope. True hope was a person. Hope did not simply disperse and dissolve the dark clouds of oppression. Hope was more than this. Hope wore a robe. Hope was crowned. Hope was enthroned—sovereign, living, breathing. Though Messiah had not yet been born, He was already tangible, touchable, and visible to her soul and spirit. The hope that David had known in his darkest moments, the hope that Gideon and Samson had known as death cast its infernal cloak across the fields of battle—this hope had not just come from the word and assurance of Jehovah but from His very breath. This was Ruah Kodesh, the divine spirit that had breathed His holy presence upon them. There were indeed moments when Anna felt His breath upon her body, inside her soul, energising her being. At times, she felt as if the very blood inside of her was a river of hope. This divine breath brought life, vision, joy. It infused into her mind thoughts and images of Messiah, forcing her to imagine, compelling her to pray and fast, exhorting her to posture herself with arms outstretched. At certain moments, it felt as if the very substance of Heaven, oceans of living water were ebbing and flowing through her physical frame. She felt rivers of revival and renewal passing through her, and at times she awoke in dismay and awe, unsure whether her body was indeed laid out on its pallet and not floating in a stream. In these sublime moments of bliss, ecstasy, divine desire, and union, she knew that Messiah was hope. He was not magnified simply by the darkness of Jerusalem. Even if Jerusalem were free of oppression, idolatry, and corruption, she would still need hope. Israel needed hope. Hope was her portion and her inheritance. Messiah was the hope of Heaven enrobed. He was no less a part of hope than His Creator and His Creator's spirit. The three of them were hope.

She was filled with daily assurance and expectation. Just as Ruach HaKodesh had hovered over the dark chasms of the deep and brought form to formlessness creating the heavens and the earth, He would, at the appointed moment, breathe His presence into the vacuum of blackness, idolatry, and rebellion that had drained the lifeblood from Israel. Jehovah would father Israel, breathing life into the chasms of death. Joy and restoration would once again be their portion. The great advocate in Heaven would lead captivity captive. He would heal the broken and lift the humble. He would set the prisoner free. He was creator, He was breath, and He was Prince of Peace.

Anna was a familiar face of great dignity and diligence, spending many hours in the temple, being given to devout prayer and fasting. This daughter of Asher was a provider, one who yielded fruit and birthed destiny, labouring not in pain but in joy despite extensive times of deep travail. Prophesying into the future, her tribal heritage and legacy became an integral part of her battle cry. The words of truth spoken over Asher by Moses and Jacob permeated her spirit and soul. Asher was to be blessed with children, with a lavish inheritance. Asher would dip his foot in oil. The oil of His presence over her life would leave a trail, a legacy for future generations to follow throughout the ages to come. Her shoes were of iron and brass. She was a widow with the mandate of a queen. She was commissioned to seek divine strength and justice. Her feet would spread truth and hope amongst all those waiting for the consolation of Jerusalem. Jerusalem would not remain without a saviour, for she was Hephzibah, a city desired and not forsaken. Hers were the feet of a prophet to Jerusalem. Her strength and vision were renewed daily. As an eagle, she soared to new heights and nurtured the young. There were several younger women who drew on her wisdom, counsel, and unrelenting faith. Her lips ignited hope and assurance in the hearts of many who otherwise would have believed Messiah's arrival to be an ancient and popular ideal. Her daily presence in the temple, her well-known stories regarding Asherite ancestors who had returned from Assyria, and her declarations of tribal promise led most to distinguish her as Anna of Asher. To others, she was known simply as the daughter of Phanuel, who was increasingly present at the temple during his later years. There were few either in the temple or inside the city who did not know this family, even fewer in the hill country. When Anna spoke, her words carried an unusual resonance and conviction for a woman of the time. Her name meant grace, and it was with the weight of great grace that she spoke.

It was right that Anna had moved to the city. She had left the hill country as soon as Ezra and Bezalel had married. Ezra remained working with his uncles and cousins in the family terraces, and Bezalel moved to the city in order to study train as a scribe. Here, he would be able to learn from distinguished professionals and associate with lawyers, governmental ministers, judges, and financiers. It would be a long learning process and a tedious profession. He was only to use clean animal skins, both to write on and to bind manuscripts. Each column of writing would have no less than forty-eight and no more than sixty lines. The ink would have to be black, and of a special recipe. He would be obliged to say each word aloud whilst writing, wipe his pen, and wash his entire body before writing the most holy name of God each time he wrote it. As with most scribes Bezalel would be copying large parts of the Torah; hence, this would be a regular obligation. There would be a review carried out by senior scribes within thirty days, and if as many as three pages required corrections, the entire manuscript would have to be redone. The letters, words, and paragraphs would have to be counted, and entire documents would be rendered invalid if any two letters touched each other. The middle paragraph, word, and letter would have to correspond to those of the original document, and when completed, the documents could only be stored in sacred places such as synagogues. Despite the tedium and high level of concentration demanded by this process, it was the profession to which the young, agile-minded Bezalel felt called and the reason for which he left the serenity of the hills. Anna lived with him and his wife in a small house not far from the temple.

Heaven was open over Anna's life. She had inherited her husband's fiery heart, and this double flame had never diminished. The inner blaze continued to intensify as a raging furnace. The lion and the sceptre would rise from Judah. Judah would wash his garments in wine, his robes in the blood of grapes. She declared that this glorious day would soon arrive. Her eyes were like dove's eyes and her face set like flint as she prayed with a fiery, unwavering faith. Her life had been set as seal upon the heart of Jehovah. She knew the effervescent blaze of unquenchable love and the jealous longing of the bridegroom to restore His bride.

Life inside the city was vibrant. The smoke-ridden air and constant noise meant that even the roof of the house was not a real place of meditation. It was radically different to life in the hills where even the smallest of houses possessed gardens in which to grow flowers, herbs such as mint, dill, and jasmine and fig trees that shaded the family. The nearest place for retreat was the Mount of Olives across the Kidron Valley and the popular Gat Shmanim, the garden of the olive press. There was a large olive press located in a nearby cave just near the garden, and this was one of the largest presses in the area. The garden itself was situated at the foot of the Mount of Olives, and it was a popular location to which city dwellers withdrew for moments of tranquillity and meditation. The scents of the olive groves and fragrant flowers and the sounds of the birds caused Anna to crave the rural surroundings in which she had been immersed for so many years. Anna missed the pure air, the vast spaces, the terraces, vineyards, trees, and open skies. The air had become so heavily polluted here with the constant billowing of smoke from the temple. The night sky was never quite as clear. Life here was so different and in many ways less rich. The garden at the foot of the mount became an oasis of comfort and serenity. Sometimes for hours, she would stare at the trees and meditate—like all olive trees, the older trees preserving their dynasty through shoots that grew directly out of the roots. The shoots were fertilised after a certain period of growth. The rod grown from the stem would always grow into a flourishing tree, but it was the branches growing from the roots that would fertilise. Some of the older branches, once thicker, started to grow as small trunks. As she stared at the older trees with branches growing from their roots, she contemplated the words of the prophet Isaiah that a new branch would grow out of Jesse's roots. These words, spoken under the reign of Hezekiah, affirmed that Messiah would come from the house of David, anointed and holy. He would stand firm in His kingship until the end of the age. He would reap a harvest of righteous trees.

Other times when walking through the dense array of groves, Anna had familiar visions of the olives being spread out and crushed by the heavy stone, the oil running through the surrounding channel into the rock-cut vat. She saw the baskets being stacked on top of the pressing platform beneath the long timber beam and being pressed down with the heavy stone-weighted beam with the oil flowing into the vat beneath. She knew the process well as she had watched the treaders and workers crushing the olives so many times back in the hills. The juice contained water and oil, and after a few days the oil would float above the water. Visions and sounds of the crushing vibrated through her being as she saw the entire garden flooded with oil.

At times, Anna envied the high priest and those entitled to constant residence in the temple—such as the guards on night watch who remained there from sunset until sunrise. Like David, zeal for the House of the Lord consumed her. She desired to spend whole nights there both alone and together with those to whom she had been yoked in intercession and fasting. She knew that those truly on night watch were those who were praying and interceding whilst others slept. The law was heavy. Its weight was unbearable. How she longed for righteous ones to be raised up and for corruption and deception to end. Men, women, and children failed perpetually to adhere to it. Even spending every day at the temple, she knew that she also had failed. She continued to fall short of the holiness and sanctification that the law demanded. Things had to change. The words of the prophets and the voice of God would not return void. Things would change.

The scarlet thread of redemption that had been set in motion through the sacrifice of the animal in Eden had woven itself through Israel's history through mercy, deliverance, covenant, and blood on doorposts. It was the same scarlet thread in Rahab's window that had woven itself through time in the provision of prophets, priests, judges, and kings; intercessors, deliverers, and restorers. Yet this thread had not frayed either in wilderness or in exile. Moreover she saw a bolder, more glistening thread, the golden thread of kingship. The full and complete kingship that Adam had abdicated in the garden would be restored by Messiah and his ever-increasing reign. The golden thread entwined itself with the scarlet thread. Together, they were the threads of the priest-king. God had provided sovereigns only because Israel had refused to bow down to an invisible king and had requested an earthly monarch to rule them. The golden thread of kingship had not stopped with Solomon, and despite Judah's rebellion, there had always been a king in Jerusalem, including righteous kings who had followed after the heart of David such as Jehoshaphat, Josiah, and Hezekiah. These kings had understood that they were merely subjects of the one king of Heaven and earth, sovereign royal master of all mankind.

As she prayed and meditated upon the scriptures, the prophetic insights increased, and Anna watched the scarlet cord of redemption that forgave the harlotry of the nation, and the golden thread of kingship become intricately entwined and woven together as one eternal cord that continued to weave itself through the era to come. Messiah would be the end point into whom the scarlet and the gold would be absorbed. He would sit on David's throne and establish justice and righteousness across the earth. His kingdom would be one of ultimate sovereignty, redemption, and restoration. He would require no royal counsellors as He himself would be the wonderful counsellor. He would bring a reign of peace that would far surpass Solomon's. His kingdom would spread across the entire earth, and all the nations would know of the richness of his wisdom.

Caesar was in power now as the first Trimumvirate of Rome had been established. It was a time of increased fighting and unrest with Aristobolus, who had escaped again from Rome, returning to fight in Jerusalem. It was during this year of further bloodshed that Eliab, son of Jahath, now just over thirty years of age old, finally entered the priesthood. His childhood desire to hear the audible voice of God had not left him. It seemed as if Heaven had been watching, for it was during Eliab's second year of priesthood that the long silence was broken. Just before Passover he mounted the temple steps and, in his usual manner, turned east and searched the horizon. Crowds of expectant pilgrims were flooding into the courtyard below, their songs resonating through the temple complex: "As the mountains surround Jerusalem, so the Lord surrounds His people." He carefully surveyed the landscape straining to see beyond the slopes of the Mount of Olives and over towards Bethany as sojourners continued to press their way through the western gates. As he looked again towards the east, he saw the tip of the sun finally rising above the horizon illuminating the eastern hills as far as Hebron. As the crowd began to applaud and the priests raised their silver trumpets, Eliab stood motionless, as if paralysed.

It was assumed that the young priest had been stricken by illness, but this was not the case. In the trance, a flamelike being appeared before him and spoke the following words: "When you see the voice that I shall send, rejoice that your prayers have been answered." In awe and wonder, Eliab began to search out the meaning. He often dreamt of revival amongst future generations of priests as truth drew them in. The moment had been blissful and frightening. Words could not describe what had taken place, for it had happened so suddenly and so quickly. He pondered the words 'when you see the voice', for voices were heard, not seen. Eliab wept as he returned home that night and clutched his youngest son, Aaron, in his arms, having gently lifted the sleeping child from his pallet. He wept with awe and holy fear.

19

NEW BIRTHS

It was the year of 49 BC. Shiprah embraced her newly born grandson, Jacob. She had not been blessed with other children since the birth of Matthan and had longed again to hold a newborn child. She uncurled his tiny fingers that gripped her veil, wondering whether in the future these hands would also become rough and cut like those of his father and grandfather who were constantly cutting stone and wood. She gazed into his sapphire blue eyes, his dark soft wisps of hair blowing as a light breeze passed through the open door of the house. Never since the late birth of her beloved Matthan had she seen anything so exquisite. Shiprah did not care that she was not wealthy. To behold a grandson was more valuable than all the wealth of Jerusalem. This joy was priceless. As she handed the child back to his mother, she smiled contentedly with tearful eyes. Jehovah had been merciful. He deserved all of her worship.

The latest news was that Roman tension had reached a high point. Caesar had defied Pompey by refusing to relinquish control of his army before returning to Rome to involve himself in politics, and hence there was civil war in Rome. Aristobulus had been freed by Caesar to take over the position of the Roman general Crassus who had died in battle and had been given Roman legions in order to subdue Syria and Judea. However, rumour had it that agents of Pompey had poisoned and beheaded Aristobulus before they reached Judea. As always, tales, gossip, and updates were somewhat vague. What was clear though was that peace was far from Jerusalem and peace was far from Rome.

Shavuot, the Feast of Pentecost, had just ended. The apricots, plums, green almonds, and vines were in blossom, and the spring fruits had ripened. The heat began to increase, and rain would not be seen for several months. Work went on as normal—though in the small village of Ein Karem, one family was rejoicing. Eliab's oldest son, Zech, after marrying the daughter of a priest from Hebron, had just become a father. They had chosen the Greek form of his name and called the child Zacharias, for Yahweh had remembered them and would continue to remember Israel. Jahath, still a trembling man who had carried the word of the Lord deep within his heart and lived in the fear of the Lord, arrived at the home just after his grandson's birth and blessed the child. It seemed that Jahath was always weeping, his tender heart always lost in some state of elation, yet on this day his gaze was fixed in a different way. No one knew how difficult Jahath was finding it to stand upright. No one saw what he saw, as he stared at Eliab and blessed the child. No one felt the intense presence that he felt. No one knew what he was thinking.

Back in the towns, political and societal change was rapid. News spread that Roman generals had looted the temple, confiscating its gold as punishment to the people for failing to pay the required tributes. New orders, procedures, and regulations were introduced with each passing day. Some were highly restrictive and unnecessary, others constructive. Aulus Gabinius, proconsul of Syria, had divided Palestine for juridical reasons into five districts, each presided over by a Jewish council. Jericho, Jerusalem, Sepphoris, Amathus, and Gadara were the centres of these districts. Rome believed strongly in the principle divide and rule. Division facilitated subjugation and dominance. Each town had its own Sanhedrin consisting of various numbers, depending on the number of inhabitants.

In each town and village, new sanitary regulations had been implemented and were to be strictly adhered to. The police had prohibited open wells and pits, faulty ladders, fragile staircases, and dangerous dogs. Cemeteries and tanneries had been removed to at least fifty cubits outside of a town. Bakers and dyers shops or stables were not permitted to exist beneath family dwellings. Jerusalem was repaved with white stone. In order to minimise arguments and strife, neighbours were not permitted to have windows that overlooked the courtyards or rooms of others. Shop owners were not permitted to have their entrances lead through a court common to two or three dwellings. In each town, the houses differed in size and in elegance, ranging from small cottages to the mansions of the affluent, embellished by rows of pillars and adornments. Flat roofs were made to slope downwards slightly in order for rainwater to pass easily through pipe networks and drain into the cisterns below.

Despite the changes, the family roof still remained a common location for banter and gossip that regularly passed from roof to roof. When not around fountains or in shaded courts below, family members gathered above their homes for conversation and song. As the most elevated part of the home, it was the coolest, airiest, and stillest location. Neighbours leapt from roof to roof whether to make an escape or to quicken their route. Unlike the rural roofs, the urban roof was more of a place for hospitality and discussion than for quiet prayer, meditation, and contemplation. A place for pilgrims to stay and for victims to hide from enemies and a stage from which one could survey the skies and foresee the gathering storms or witness the red and golden light of dawn slowly illuminating the edge of the horizon as the priests prepared for the morning sacrifice.

Though much had changed, some things had not. When each head of the house returned home on the Sabbath eve from the synagogue, he found it festively adorned with the lamp brightly burning and the table spread with the richest that each household could afford after tax. Before eating he would bless each child and as always prepare to rest from work until the Sabbath light faded out and the soft glows of clay lamps danced over the windows as the moonlight streamed in.

It was after the last Sabbath in the month of Adar just after the blossom had started to bud that Shimei sent word to Anna in Jerusalem that Mezahab was finally with child. A few weeks later, the couple travelled over from Galilee, and Mezahab remained with Anna for a month. Though the wait for a child had been long, the praying and believing had been constant. Hope had been deferred but not denied. It soon appeared that a double portion had been indeed given. God had been gracious to Mezahab and Shimei, and their portion was bountiful. There was much rejoicing in Galilee amidst families and relatives who later gathered there to reunite and celebrate the births. The son was named Jair, and his sister, younger by just a few moments, was named Jemimah. Mezahab had consistently prayed the prayer of Hannah, and her supplications and lamentations had been responded to in double. The almighty had shown regard for her and lifted the shame of barrenness. It was true that for those who delighted in Him, their desires would be granted. He would exalt the horns of His godly ones.

20

CONFLICTS INTENSIFY

The next eight years were marked by increasing tension, oppression, and darkness. News broke out that the General Pompey had been assassinated in Egypt and that Egypt itself had now broken out in civil war. Meanwhile, the high priest Hyrcanus and his friend Antipater, the Idumean, had assisted Julius Caesar (who was now dictator of the Roman Republic) by sending Jewish armies to Egypt. As a reward, Hyrcanus was permitted to rebuild the temple complex walls that Pompey had torn down. Many builders and stonecutters were called to work on this rebuilding project including Eliud, Eleazar, and Matthan. Whilst working on the temple walls, they found themselves within a whirlpool of news and speculation regarding the Roman control of Jerusalem and more distant conflicts and movements abroad. It was during this time that Anna's acquaintance Rizpah, the wife of Rabban Simeon, a former priest and prominent teacher in the temple, gave birth to her third son. There had been much talk amongst the women regarding the event since the midwife had delivered a dead child. For three hours they had prayed that God would send the Angel of the Lord to restore the child and that divine breath would enter his body as it had for the widow's son who had been revived through the prophet Elijah. The tiny body remained cold and blue, and the heart did not beat, yet in the third hour as they continued to pray in desperation, a miracle took place. Life entered the tiny body. The heart began to beat, the lungs filled with air, and the babe began to cry. The news surrounding this birth spread rapidly throughout the region. It was the source of amazement and the subject of discussion for many days to follow. The God of miracles was still living amidst the darkness.

As a further reward for Jewish and Egyptian assistance, Caesar declared Jerusalem exempt from taxation, Joppa was restored to Jewish jurisdiction, and Hyrcanus was recognised as the Jewish Ethnarch. Hyrcanus had charge of Roman power on behalf of the Jews, whilst Antipater helped him in the role of procurator of the kingdom. Despite the relief, the weight of taxation had already taken its toll, and people were only too conscious that this period of respite would be short-lived. Furthermore, though the people were grateful for the status granted to Hyrcanus, it was understood that his autonomy was restricted and that in reality he was under the full control of Antipater.

As injustice and suppression intensified, the corruption and exploitation of the Roman regime remained unconcealed. It was a tangible everyday reality. Knowledge that Antipater's family had been appointed Roman citizens yet remained exempt from taxes aroused further unrest, as did the latest news that this dislikeable Idumaean had been designated chief steward of Judea, official to Hyrcanus, the high priest and ethnarch of the Jews. Appointing his own sons to positions of great honour and authority, he assured that if Jews sought cooperation with him, Hyrcanus, and Caesar, peace and prosperity would be reestablished. This promise was met with widespread mistrust and contempt, and when word spread a while later that Antipater had been poisoned, few were surprised. By 44 BC Caesar himself had been assassinated by republican conspirators. There was war and bloodshed both in Jerusalem and in Rome. Antipater was succeeded by his sons Phasael and Herod. Phasael ruled over Jerusalem and its environs whilst Herod, just twenty-five years of age, was assigned Galilee. Though many were suspicious and reluctant to accept any foreign ruler, Herod became a popular hero by eradicating Jewish gangs who had been terrorising the region. Songs were composed in his honour, and he was later commended by Rome. It seemed that the young ruler had inherited the ambition and ability of his father, Antipater.

In 40 BC Antigonus, the nephew of Hyrcanus, offered financial support to the Parthian army to enable him to recapture Jerusalem. He was supported by many patriotic Jews, and those incensed by Roman levies marched on to Jerusalem promising the invaders a thousand talents and five hundred women in exchange for their departure. Antigonus was successful in his bribe and assigned himself the double title of high priest and king of Judea. However, the horror amongst the people lay in the crimes that he committed against the high priest, Hyrcanus. Not only was Hyrcanus stripped of his title of high priest and king but also he was left mutilated. The evil wretch Antigonus had lacerated his ears, thereby leaving him unfit for priesthood. For fear of the same destiny, Herod escaped to his fortress of Masada south of his castle on the western shore of the Dead Sea, and learning of the news he left for Rome in midwinter. Rumours were divided regarding Herod's brother, Phasael. Some said that Antigonus had dashed out his brains against a stone; others claimed that he had committed suicide. Such abominations left the people sick with horror, many full of hatred and fear, lamenting the unbearable weight of violation and oppression that was relentlessly crushing Jerusalem and draining hope from her veins.

21

A Heretic Takes the Throne

It was in the year of 38 BC and by decree of the Roman senate that Herod was assigned the royal status of king of the Jews and provided an extensive army. Following Herod and the Roman general's defeat of the Parthians in northern Syria, Herod had regained Judea, culminating in the siege of the city. By this time he had become engaged to Mariamne, a Hasmonean princess. Furious wars and massacres followed Herod's conquest, and the Sanhedrin was decimated due to its refusal to recognise his kingly status.

Many asked where this man had come from, how these matters had come to be, and since when had this family of Idumeans been of any significance whatsoever. It had been in the year of 126 BC during the time of Grandpa Heber that John Hyrcanus, the first Hasmonean king, had ruled Palestine, conquering Idumea, the land of ancient Edom south of Judea, and decreed that all of its inhabitants convert to Judaism. This had brought multitudes of Jews, Arabs, and Greeks into the fold. The grandfather of Herod, Antipater I, had profited connections with John Hyrcanus I and had been appointed governor.

This manipulative, self-exalting figure who called himself king remained the object of bitter hatred. Though he was valued by the Romans, he was now deeply despised by the Jews. Not only was he a non-Jew occupying the very throne of David, he employed networks of spies, relying on threats and murders in order to maintain the throne. Furthermore, he was turning Jerusalem into a Greek city with his endless Greco-Roman styled buildings, flamboyant and costly building projects that were filling the sacred land of their ancestors with castles, temples, parks, gymnasiums, fortresses, and libraries. His reputation as a murderer and an evil man erased any positive perception that the people may have had, particularly regarding his civic improvement plans. It was said that he was a brutal, heartless murderer, an evil man who murdered relatives and enemies alike.

Though Herod did not take the position of high priest himself, he alone had the power to appoint a man to this office. Hyrcanus was reinstated, but as he was defected due to his torn ears, there was little that he could do. With regard to defects, the law was clear. Herod always chose priests from priestly families of modest social standing so that he would not fear their influence. By the year 36 BC, the seventeen-year-old Aristobulus III was named as high priest, and this caused a great uproar amongst the Jews. For a start, how could one so callow and inexperienced be appointed to such a sacred office? The following year the sudden news that the poor boy had been 'conveniently' drowned in a swimming pool at a party in Jericho Palace was received with both horror and relief.

All of Herod's conduct was contrary to the statutes and ordinances of the Mosaic Law. He was overtly amoral and intentionally inhumane. The hostility of the people towards him led to more fear on his part and thus greater restraints. He heavily relied on spies as well as initiating his own investigations. He would walk through the streets in disguise, asking any random passerby what the people of his village or quarter thought of the new king. He was constantly devising plans to prevent plots and conspiracies from being initiated. It was not difficult for conspirators to find willing accomplices within Herod's own family. His inner circle was divided, and he was surrounded by division, potential civil revolt, and palace revolution. He eliminated all the descendants of the Hasmoneans and governed

Jerusalem as a police state. Fear and suspicion permeated the land whilst news and updates continued to strike horror in the hearts of the people.

The people knew that the visual splendour, constant festivities, magnificent architecture, and lavish expansion projects were all methods of diverting their attention and encouraging them to forget their loss of freedom. The empty facades meant nothing in the minds of the people. In fact, for many citizens, it was the cause of deeper hatred. Ruined cities like Samaria were rebuilt, yet such restoration was not enabling Israel to restore her identity when the new cities bore all the hallmarks of her oppressor. The hatred increased when it was heard a few years later that 31 BC Hyrcanus had been charged with treason and executed by Herod. With the loss of a man who had been faithful in his priestly role and who during his office had been considered by many as a source of security to the people, the level of fear and despair reached a new height.

22

THE EARTH GROANS (31 BC)

They had seen it coming. Several had seen it. In fact, they hadn't just seen it; they had heard it, felt its ominous, turbulent presence invading the night hours. Some had talked of it, and others had kept silent, not wishing to add more dread to the atmosphere of trauma and unrest. Some had discussed it in the temple and others like the fragile, aged Elisheva had spoken of it only to her family, who had stood at her bedside as she breathed her final breath. It was not long after that Anna realised she was not alone in the knowledge that a mighty earthquake was about to ravage Jerusalem. Whilst holding her dying mother's hand, relief came in the midst of mourning. At least Elisheva's days would not see the horror and destruction that was about to occur. Some had not been sure whether their visions spoke of the spiritual state of the city or whether physical tragedy was going to befall it. Others had seen the Jordan Valley quake and crumble as the ground groaned and trembled, crashing open, folding up, and breaking beneath Jerusalem, engulfing animals and crops, swallowed up young and old, rich and poor. The land itself was groaning and repelling the iniquitous climate of the hour as it regurgitated the hideous idols and abominations draped across its scape.

This tragic year was marked by the death of over thirty thousand people, as well as thousands of animals. There was serious damage in Jericho and in the Galilee region. Extensive damage was done to the temple, and large portions of its walls instantly collapsed. The city walls had also crumbled in places, leaving Jerusalem open to attack. Beneath the surface of glamour, change, and progress was the chasm of the deep. It seemed that Israel had reached her darkest hour. The entire nation was in deep turmoil and inconsolable mourning. Many saw this as the darkest hour yet and just the start of greater judgement to come. Every man and woman had some relative or acquaintance who had been either killed or injured during the disaster. The nation waited in anguish for several weeks before the death toll was complete.

Pride and fear caused Herod to respond with haste. No time was wasted. Rebuilding started immediately, and hundreds of men were recruited, including many who were unskilled and had no knowledge of the trade. Faithful to Pax Romana, he knew exactly how to adapt to circumstances and use the occasion to unite diverse communities, presenting himself as a heroic sympathiser.

It was months after the earthquake and the death of Elisheva that Anna saw the birth of her first grandson. Ezra had named the child Joash-Omri. He was born a month earlier than expected, a tiny lamb, the supreme joy of his grandmother. Amidst the darkness and turbulence of the times, the faithfulness and steadfastness of Jehovah was somehow still evident to all who raised their eyes and reached to hope. Anna knew that this birth was one of the several written announcements upon the scrolls that she had seen the angel announce as it descended the golden ladder. A generation of zealous ones would be raised up. Along with others who prayed and fasted, posturing themselves to see more, she hoped, prayed, sensed, and somehow knew that this child's generation would see the dawning of the new age. This generation would see the great transition. It would cross into a new era marked by the superior covenant of which the prophet Jeremiah had spoken. The more she mediated and prayed over Joash-Omri, the more she believed and declared into the heavens that before the birth of this grandson's last child, Messiah would be in Jerusalem and a new era would commence. She prayed that this child, named after her beloved, would walk in the fiery faith and single-minded conviction that Joash had done during his short life upon the earth. She prayed with all of her strength that the eyes of this child would see the land of promise.

It was around 30 BC, and Phanuel continued to mourn the death of Elisheva, who had not been old at the time of her death. Though she had lived her three score and ten, he had expected and hoped that she would live much longer. He could only imagine the pain that his daughter had been through, losing her husband so young. At least he had years of history to cherish. He was still a strong and sturdy man even now, approaching the age of one hundred years. He was loved dearly by his children, grandchildren, and great-grandchildren, who kept him youthful. He had never moved from the hill country, and the boys and their sons continued to work and expand the land. Only Anna and Bezalel lived in Jerusalem. In his older years, Phanuel continued to ponder and to believe that the deliverer would come soon. He still attended the synagogue and travelled to the temple for feasts. His friendship with Eliud had never faded, and he remained as close as ever to so many of his aged friends in the hill country and in the temple. For his generation, it was an era of passing from this life, an era of agedness. Loss and mourning were known by so many who had been shaped and seasoned by the dramas of the times. He pondered on how the years had changed since the birth of his seventh child, beloved Anna. Who had ever thought at that time that a queen would be on the throne? At least Salome had eased the tension and reduced the bloodshed. The years had seen such increase in physical and emotional torture. The hill country had always been a haven and a sanctuary away from strife, gossip, and commotion of the city, yet now it seemed that in every vineyard, at every well, up every watchtower, in every synagogue, and in every village, anger and fear were enveloping the people. Peace had diminished and the chasm between rich and poor had become larger. The burden of tax, from which no man could hide, was a fierce and heavy yoke to bear. Conversations were not what they used to be, and many of those who taught in the synagogues were fragile, precarious, and ridden with doubt, fear, and disillusionment. Tensions and arguments were rife, and the only thing that men agreed upon was that something had to change. The temple had become a haven for iniquity, the sanctity of the priesthood devoured by avarice and corruption. The city lay morally derelict, besieged by perversion and oppression as the ever-flowing blood of empty, ritualistic sacrifice streamed out like an endless river. The proud and arrogant were yet to be abased. The cords of falsehood strangled young men and oppressors continued to grind the faces of the poor.

It was during the long season of rebuilding after the earthquake that Eliab took his grandson, Zacharias, on an important journey to Jericho to visit a priest whose young son had been injured in the earthquake. Despite holding on to life for several months, it had been affirmed by the physician that the child had only a few days to live. They had prayed fervently for mercy; however, Avi had steadily declined, and it seemed that all hope had been lost. Eliab joined the family in fasting and prayer and took his son Zacharias to pray also for the child. As the young, faith-filled boy zealously prayed, hope gradually returned. Within three hours, the child sat up, asked for food, and began to recite psalms. Throughout their remaining days in Jericho, Eliab and his grandson visited the child. Like many, they were alarmed at the physical progress his young body was making. Twisted bones were straightening, wounds were healing, his crushed arms were regaining strength, his weak lungs had been revived, and his shallow breathing had regained depth. As young Avi reported a steady decrease in pain, the physician could offer no explanation, confirming to the child's family that their prayers and lamentations had been heard. A divine presence had been felt by all who surrounded the child, and even the young Zacharias had spoken of an unusual heat in his own bones as he had prayed for the boy.

It was Zacharias's first visit to Jericho. Towards the end of the previous year, shortly after the suicide of Cleopatra, Octavian had given the city to Herod, who had previously been leasing an area of it from Cleopatra. This was a great asset as the land was a coveted jewel, rich in minerals and a fountain of wealth and productivity. Zacharias was inspired by every moment of his visit and had been given money by his father to acquire balsam salves, oils, fragrances, and fruit. The soothing aromas of balsam, persimmon, and citrus blossom that fragranced the region were a refreshing contrast to the smoke-filled air of Jerusalem.

When Herod had claimed the throne of Judea, he built a new hippodrome theatre and a network of aqueducts to irrigate the cliffs and reach his winter palace at Tulul Al-Alaiq, surrounded by splendid gardens. Jericho remained an agricultural centre, a major crossroad of trade and commerce, and a winter resort for Jerusalem's aristocracy. The palace had lavish royal gardens, a grand opulent reception hall with mosaics and frescos, gold and marble columns, and it straddled the ancient road that led up to Jerusalem. There were also several new synagogues that had been built there a few years before Rome invaded.

Jericho remained a region of deep beauty, flourishing vegetation, and lucrative trade. No part of the balsam tree was wasted. The costly sap was added to olive oil to formulate fragrances. Likewise resin taken from the trunks was a prized commodity converted into solid balm. Juices were released from the bark by making incisions with sharp stones, and these were used for ointments and salves, a major source in botanical medicine as it was known to cure headaches, cataracts, and dimness of sight. The wood was used as construction timber, and the leaves were used to weave baskets, mats, brooms, beds, ropes, and furniture. The balsam trees grew easily within the date plantations, and trees were often intermingled, growing side by side. This mixed cultivation led to an intense melange of rich aromas that saturated the region. As his grandfather continued making visits, Zacharias spent time with his young cousins, helping in the plantations owned by relatives of his mother. He never saw trees quite so lavish and dense back in the hill country. The date palms had a straight soft trunk capped with a canopy of deep, vibrant green leaves that unfolded like a botanical starburst. The honey-sweet dates had nourished the nomads throughout the ages, and the leaves continued to shade the bright desert sands. The palm tree was a great national symbol of fertility, peace, victory, and grace—its dates being a major product in commercial fruit export. The palms created a microclimate by providing protection to under-crops from heat and wind as well as reducing damage caused by sandstorm and wind erosion. Sycamore trees grew all over the land, producing thick clusters of figs ranging from yellow to orange. It was a common tree bearing fruit similar to the fig tree, though a little sweeter and more aromatic. Its leaves were very similar to the leaves of the mulberry. The tamarisks were evergreen shrublike trees forming dense thickets of green-grey foliage. The bark of the young branches was a smooth reddish-brown turning to bluish-purple with age. Its flowers ranging from pink to white could be seen in dense masses from March to September. The tamarisk's leaves offered constant shade, and the wood was a common supply to the carpenter. It was a graceful tree with long, slender feathery branches, particularly visible in the Jordan Valley and the maritime plain. The excitement of the landscape and lavish vegetation captured the heart and mind of this young, inquisitive visitor. He eagerly asked his grandfather why they could not all live there as so many other priests did. His grandfather explained that whilst this was not God's will, he would be able to accompany him on future visits and return to Jericho whenever his father granted him permission to leave Jerusalem.

23

ZACHARIAS MEETS ELIZABETH

It was during one of these later visits that Zacharias made the acquaintance of a young woman from the priestly line. She was radiant in countenance and beautiful in speech. The youngest granddaughter of Phineas, her name was Elizabeth. Phineas, alongside his brother Aaron, was a long-serving, sincere, and God-fearing priest and, not least, a beloved friend of Zacharias's grandfather and father. Though the two were considered too young to marry, there was an attraction on both sides. This, of course, could be sensed by the older and wiser who had observed the mutual gazes.

Back in Jersualem, Rosh Chodesh had just been heralded with the sounding of the shofar. As always on the day of new moon, the women refrained from spinning, weaving, and sewing, and people made their way to the temple.

As was the custom, the day of the new moon had been sighted the previous day by at least two observers who had noted the day and hour that the moon was visible as a waxing crescent. The reader holding the Torah scroll had already announced previously the exact day of the forthcoming week when the new month would begin so that the people could prepare. The law regarding this day of sanctification and prayer for the new month had been given to their ancestors after they had been delivered from Egypt and had marked a departure from the solar tradition of the Egyptians. The emergence of the moon from darkness to light was symbolic of divine mercy and redemption. As the various sacrifices and convocations were made, prayers for the restoration of the temple, the words of psalms resounded through the courts. The earth and the heavens would continue to declare his praise, gladly receiving Him as the majestic provider who covered Himself with light. What other idol or god had stretched out the heavens as a tent curtain, made the clouds his chariots, sent forth springs in the valleys, provided faithfully for every living creature, watering the mountains from His upper chambers? Who else could cause the grass and vegetation to grow and bring joy to man that his face glistened with oil. The moon and the sun were the works of His wisdom. The glory of the Lord would endure forever. The people must rise and sing to Him for as long as they live. The earth had no doubt regarding the identity of her owner and creator, and she gladly received from His hand. She trembled with reverence and joy as He turned His face towards her. Those who prayed fervently cried out for total restoration and for the glory of Eden to return. Each new month as Anna left the temple ceremony and prayed in solitude, she entered that month hoping that it would be the month of change, the month of consolation.

It was just a few weeks after Rosh Chodesh that an announcement was made regarding the engagement of Eliab's grandson Zacharias to Elizabeth, the daughter of Phineas. Zacharias had already begun the arrangements to have a house built near to that of his parents at Ein Karem in the hill country. He had not intended to marry so young, but since his first glimpse of Elizabeth's face, it had seemed that he was surely destined to do so.

24

EXPANDING JERUSALEM (29 BC)

Following the death of his first wife Mariamne, whom Herod killed along with his closest friend, it was said that the so-called king was turning insane, his treacherous acts being constantly fuelled by fear of being usurped. Nevertheless, Rome continued to admire and support him. He was considered to be a man of courage and skill, a successful diplomat able to reverse any unfavourable state of affairs, an excellent administrator with immense ideas and far-reaching views, a tireless builder and known by many abroad as Herod the Great. To those with minimal insight, it was clear that his entire policy rested on serving, protecting, and honouring Rome.

His expanded kingdom was almost as extensive as King Solomon's territory had been. His army was great and his territory vast. He raised tribute money for Rome but also had the right to levy his own taxes, a right that he thoroughly abused. Political and socioeconomic tension were reflected in the rise of social rebellion and banditry, even though it had lessened under him originally in Galilee.

The year of 28 BC following the death of Herod's wife was marked by an enormous festival in Jerusalem to celebrate the completion of the theatre and amphitheatre. Gladiators from abroad came to compete, and the spectacles within the hippodrome drew great crowds despite the people's disrespect for heathen festivals. Though many Jews attended the festival, news of further executions due to suspected conspiracy, including that of Herod's brother-in-law, ensured that the dark cloud of fear enshrouding the city did not lift. On the contrary, it grew darker and heavier with each passing festival.

By 27 BC Herod's next completed project was the construction of the northern city of Samaria. In honour of Emperor Augustus, he renamed the city Sebaste, and it soon became known that during this time he had married a Samaritan woman. As prestigious developments and extensive building work expanded, Herod drew nearer to being the new 'Master of the Orient', and clearly this was his intent. Cities rebuilt by him received names in honour of the Roman emperor. For example, there was Caesarea on the coast and Jerusalem with her palaces and the Antonia Fortress, which was being built to overlook the temple, being built.

Herod intended to participate fully in Pax Romana and to show himself as a completely loyal subject to Rome. In the same year that Sebaste was completed, the republic of Rome officially transformed into an empire. Many older men and women had foreseen that this would happen. They had been alive when the great bloody battle of Corinth had taken place and the Romans had defeated Greece. This had been a sign to their parents and ancestors, some of whom had lived in Corinth at the time, that Rome would eventually take over the world. As it was, this great city, resting upon seven hills, situated where the Tiber River met the Mediterranean Sea, had become the largest and most magnificent city of its day, and under the reign of Augustus, it reached the heights of his splendour. It was the city of theatres, baths, aqueducts, arches, pagan temples, theatres, and roads—the centre of progress and invention.

Under the leadership of its senators, Rome made huge territorial and political advances, and Octavian laid the groundwork for extended tax laws, vast networks of roads that would succeed in linking the empire, reinforcing of social order; facilitate military organisation; and strengthen Pax Romana. Any disruption of this military-enforced 'peace' was considered by Rome to be a cardinal violation.

People knew though that this order to which the Romans aspired was not peace. Peace in Jerusalem could only happen when she was in possession of her divine identity and destiny. As her very name confirmed, this city had been created and ordained to behold peace and to embody peace. Peace was not the absence of friction. It was a presence and a force that could come only through godly government and righteous rule. Those who eagerly awaited Messiah prayed that He would come soon to return the city to her rightful name as a place of peace. Herod and his enforcement of Pax Romana was merely the counterfeit for the presence of the everlasting Prince of Peace of which the prophet Isaiah had spoken. Messiah would not just claim the throne. He would be perfect in counsel and judgement. He would be Ben Elohim, the Son of God Himself, and His rule of peace and unity would be far greater than that of any known earthly regime. He would reconcile the nation to her Creator and reveal the policy of Pax Romana to be nothing less than usurpation and bondage.

25

FAMINE AND TORMENT

As with the earthquake, certain prophets of the day had spoken of it, seers had seen it, intercessors had sensed it. In the year of 25 BC, great famine struck Israel. Countless times before Israel had seen drought, yet not for several hundreds of years had such deadly arrows fallen upon them. In the minds of many, this was undoubtedly divine judgement and rebuke. Israel was cursed. Right across the land, her streams were consumed by drought as deep darkness consumed hills, valleys, and plains. All life was languishing. The trees ceased to yield fruit. Flocks and herds were dying as the sky withheld its due and the earth, its produce. As weeks passed, storehouses were gradually emptied, and homes, plundered. Workers of the land longed to see the early and latter rains, yet the sky withheld all water. Desolation and death ravaged the people. Thousands died as the soil lay barren, scorched and parched like arid desert land. Other than those who lived by the coast, no part of the land was untouched. Each family looked after their own. Orphans, widows, beggars, and the frail suffered first. As weak bodies became wasted by lack, many feared that earthquakes, plague, and pestilence would follow. The burning heat intensified until no man could bear it. As the deaths continued, the nation stooped in grief and disgrace, besieged by foreign hands, rejected by the hand of God.

It seemed that the only good thing Herod ever did was sell his golden plate in order to buy corn in Egypt. He had vast quantities of Egyptian grain imports and, in response to the famine, attempted to launch a major aid programme whilst lowering taxes by one-third. His assistance though was too little, too late, and the devastation, disease, and death continued. Meanwhile his lavish palaces, houses, hippodromes, amphitheatres, and colonnaded courts towered in silence over the carnage. The palaces were glamorous, but their gardens were graveyards, and their fountains were dry.

The following year, as the rains returned and ploughing resumed, the nation struggled immensely to regenerate its economy. Herod's expenditure continued to far exceed his capital. The taxes imposed became increasingly heavier. Any real recovery relied on revenue. He continued to attack anyone who he considered a threat, and his elimination of all political rivals did not bring him closer to the Jewish people. He had slaughtered the representatives of the Hasmonean house and transformed the Sanhedrin into a puppet institution. He brought pagans into his court as council members and administrative deputies. He established a military contingent at Batanea in the Golan region to watch over the northeast portion of his empire, and as his military support increased, so also did his extreme self-importance and related paranoia. He would soon marry another wife whose father he named as high priest.

In order to create a facade of community, society, and well-being, Herod arranged for houses of public entertainment to be built in various locations selling pickled locusts fried in flour or honey, Babylonian beer, Egyptian drinks, and homemade cider or wine. Animated banter and games of chance were indulged in by those who frequented such places. As time passed, many wasted their income on riotous living. Herod employed secret police who acted as spies and assessed the opinions of the populace as they drank and talked. Likewise it was not unusual for spies to circulate the rural regions and the hill country in order to overhear conversations. People often reported on having seen Herod himself undisguised, lurking in the streets at nighttime in order to eavesdrop on conversation and banter. At one point demonstrations, public meetings, and banquets were all suddenly banned in the city within a day's notice. Any of the monarch's suspicions—random or otherwise—led to acts of vengeance and torture even if no evidence could be furnished. Such was the authority and prerogative of his office.

26

TUVYA

Tuvya was a poor man born from a family of peasants. He had grown up in poverty and from a young age had been forced to make a living, be it through robbery or through honest means. His brother had died at birth, and the young Tuvya had lived a somewhat isolated life. As an unskilled and uneducated worker, he accepted any jobs that he could find, ranging from loading and unloading the camels of tradesmen, well digging, and fruit picking. At times, his unusually short and robust stature had proved an asset as he was hired by various farmers to repair awkward machinery, mainly ploughs and carts. Though untrained and unrefined, Tuvya was physically versatile and known for his stamina and perseverance as well as his eagerness to be productive. Tuvya was also known in the town for his dishonest tendencies; hence, all who dealt with him kept a close eye on affairs and transactions, as they did with all ignoble characters of ill repute. Not long after the age of twelve, Tuvya was orphaned, losing both parents to a contagious infection. After this crisis, his reputation worsened, and his liaison with the various groups of robbers who attacked tradesmen passing on the road from Jerusalem to Jericho became known in various circles. Tuvya became greatly disliked, and though his guilt could rarely be proven, the majority of locals refused to deal with him. Nevertheless, compassion was extended by certain gracious families who tried to care for him and provide him with food and gifts during feasts. None of Tuvya's attempts to restore his reputation in the town were successful, especially those that involved alleged thefts and shameless raids of widows' properties, taking their garments as pledges. At times he was seen amongst the more familiar faces, begging outside the city gates hoping that passers-by would not recognise him.

Tuvya's life changed dramatically when a distant relative discovered him whilst visiting the temple during Purim. The relative had not known of the recent death of both parents, and upon learning of the tragedy, he offered to take Tuvya back to work for him in Jericho in return for a place to stay. From this moment, Tuvya's life took a radical and eventful turn, leading to a dramatic transformation, seemingly erasing his first painful fifteen years of life. The relative was resolute that he would make a respected and honest man out of Tuvya and relieve him of the hardship and poverty of his past.

Tuvya had never visited Jericho though he shared in the common knowledge regarding its status as a desirable place of great opulence, productivity, and commercial venture. He had never travelled beyond Jerusalem and its environs. Jericho, a figment of his imagination, was a mysterious, exotic paradise to which rich tradesmen travelled, departing after sunset in time for the next day's trade. He had heard the stories of those who loitered with other villains in the dark shadows and rocks lining the long, winding roads that the merchants and rich Levites knew so well. He had only ever imagined the affluence and palatial majesty of this treasured oasis in the Jordan Valley. It was thus in his sixteenth year, at the end of Purim, that the imaginations of this young man began to become his future reality.

After one year of attending synagogue with his distant uncle who had legally adopted him, Tuvah stood as a renewed and transformed man. His eyes shone with contentment and gratitude as he began to readily embrace all forms of charity, compassion, and benevolence. Thanks to both his uncle and his robust frame, Tuvya had a stable job as a hired worker. His labour was mainly in the sycamore groves collecting figs and in the date palm orchards gathering dates, preparing them for wholesale trade and maintaining the plantations. After a few years of working in the plantations, Tuvya became betrothed to Peninnah, the daughter of Raphu's cousin, a balsam plantation owner. He had considered himself unworthy of Peninnah, yet he had gained her father's respect through association at fruit markets and trade circles as well as gradually making his acquaintance at synagogue. Tuvya had often been called upon to help as he became quickly known for his unusual physical strength. His short, stocky stature had continued to prove an advantage when needing to repair machinery. Though he was uneducated, Tuvah was considered a stable, solid, and worthy match for Peninnah, and his genuine kindness and zeal for life had been recognised by many. Jericho had given him a clean start, and the shameful garments of the past had been forgiven and stripped away. Moreover, Tuvya loved Peninnah with a tenderness that was reciprocated. Jericho had breathed life into him. The deprivation, poverty, and rejection he had known as a young boy had been exchanged for comfort, love, and purpose. His dishonest ways had been replaced with a zeal for righteousness; his lack of knowledge had been replaced with an understanding of the Torah; his worn-out rags, replaced with fresh white linen garments. Everything that had been tainted and filthy had been made pure and white. Tuvya had enough to provide for a family and here. He would always have his new reputation. Though he would never be a wealthy man, he would always be a forgiven man.

Jericho too had been a victim of the great famine that had engulfed the nation, leaving her parched and languishing. At least for a few years, she was not the oasis of plenty that he had envisaged. At every level, life had been affected whether in the plantations or on the plains. As Tuvya continued to build life and develop trade, he found that there was little in Jerusalem that he missed. Furthermore, the city had changed and was now in the hands of a foreigner representing the lifestyle of corruption and blindness to which, be it on a smaller scale, he himself had once been victim.

The following year was Yovel, the year of Jubilee. With land and economy still recovering from drought that had devastated it two years before, it did not feel like a year of freedom. Yovel did not just mean 'Ram's horn' but it meant 'to be carried'. However, such declarations of ease rung void, and the still waters that restored the soul could not be found. Every fifty years, the law of Yovel was for all slaves without exception to be liberated. The rules were more emphatic in their requirements than those of Shemitah, the Sabbath year. All property that the poor had sold to the rich was to be restored to them without delay at a legally regulated price. Had the law been carried out fully, this would have set Israel far in advance of surrounding nations regarding the question of slavery and the monopolisation of land by the wealthy. Social justice, aside from Roman exploitation, would have most certainly increased. However, greed, fear, and economic complications meant that little more was done aside from the vacuous blowing of the Shofar on the tenth day of the seventh month of the forty-ninth year. As always, those who did follow the law responded only partially in order to protect their reputation rather than for the sake of freedom and justice.

As the prophet Isaiah had declared, Messiah would bring good news to the afflicted and bind up the brokenhearted, He would fulfil this discarded law completely and proclaim liberty to every slave and captive. He would sound the ram's horn and declare Jubilee. Messiah would restore Yovel. Those who mourned and wept would be reestablished as strong oaks of righteousness. There were several in the temple who prayed and believed wholeheartedly that this would be the last Jubilee before the fulfilling of prophecy and the arrival of Messiah. Numerous sages and rabbis were of the opinion that fifty years from now, on the next Jubilee, Messiah would take his throne. Others saw things differently and believed that the words of the prophets pointed to a new era of constant Jubilee—a regime of constant justice, constant conversion of slave into brother, prisoner into freeman, orphan into son.

By the end of the year word had spread that building had started on Caesarea Maritima, a huge city and harbour that would be developed into the biggest port on the eastern seacoast. Herod's building empire was proving to be a highly strategic and geographically tactical project. Furthermore, Rome would continue to reward him by adding new regions to his rule.

27

EXPLORING THE TEMPLE

Lying between the east and the west and placed between the great military monarchies of Egypt, Assyria, and later, Rome and the east, the temple naturally became the battlefield of the nations and the highway of the world from the top of the Mount of Olives through the plains and over to Jericho, the tortuous windings of the Jordan and the Dead Sea, the mountains of Moab and Ammon. To the south were the king's gardens as far as the hill country. Westwards the view was the mountains of Bether whilst the haze in the distant horizon marked the line of the great sea. To the north were Mizpeh, Gibeon, Ajalon, Michmash, Ramah, and Anathoth. As bands of pilgrims came up from all parts of the country to the great feasts, they were enthralled at its beauty. Jerusalem had turned into a city of palaces and royally enthroned as no other city. Placed on an eminence higher than the immediate neighbourhood, she was cut off and isolated by deep valleys on all sides but one, giving her the appearance of an immense natural fortress. All around it on three sides, like a natural fosse, ran the deep ravines of the Himmon Valley and of the Kidron Valley, which merged to the south of the city. The deep natural cleft of the Tyropoeon ran right through the centre of the city then turned sharply westward, separating Mount Zion and Acra. Mount Acra was divided by Mount Moriah, and Moriah was divided by an artificial valley from Bezetha or the new town. From these encircling ravines rose the city of marble- and cedar-covered palaces. Up the middle cleft down in the valley and along the slopes of the hills crept the busy town, with its streets, markets, and bazaars, but alone and isolated in its grandeur stood the temple mount. Terrace upon terrace, its courts rose until high above the city, within the enclosure of marble cloisters, cedar-roofed and richly ornamented buildings, the temple itself stood out as a mass of snowy marble shimmering in the sun against the half-encircling green background of the Mount of Olives. Pilgrims entered from Jericho or Galilee on the well-known road that led over the Mount of Olives, from the south beyond Bethlehem, from the west, over the heights of Beth-horon, or from the north, journeying across the mountains of Ephraim. All pilgrims coming from these directions could see the city looming in the distance; however, for those approaching from Bethany and the east, the Negev Desert was the final stage for caravans on the spice and incense route from India and southern Arabia to the Mediterranean. The city was hidden from view until the final moments of the journey. The Mount of Olives was always fresh and green, even in the earliest spring or parched summer, and many enjoyed the sheltered walk. The valley of Jehoshaphat lay at the base of the Mount of Olives, as did Gat Shmanim, the garden of the olive press. Many wished to be buried there as it was widely believed that this mount would be the place from which mankind would be resurrected on the Day of Judgment. At the southern end of the valley were the tombs of Absalom, Jehoshaphat, and Zechariah.

Across the road the temple and the mountains flung their broad shadows, and luxuriant foliage spread a leaf canopy overhead. Gardens burst into orchards, and orchards extended into fields whilst higher up, olives, figs, cypress, and pine freely intermingled. The stony road over the mountain wound along terraces covered with olives whose silver and dark green leaves rustled in the breeze. Gigantic fig trees twisted themselves out of the rocky soil; clusters of palms with rich coloured fruit, myrtle groves, pines, tall fragrant juniper trees, cedars, cypresses scented the landscape. To these shady retreats, the inhabitants still came to stroll and meditate.

A sudden turn in the road where the descent of the mountain began allowed travelling pilgrims a first glimpse of the city. The temple still hidden but across Ophel, the busy suburb of the priests, the eye would range to Mount Zion and rapidly climb its height to where Herod's palace covered the site once occupied by King David. Further, the pilgrim would hurry onto the ledge of rock from where the entire panorama was in full view. With one glance, they would see the whole city, its valleys and hills, walls, towers, palaces, and streets and its magnificent temple—almost like a vision from another world. Smoke from the sacrifices billowed upwards against the blue eastern sky and music of the services drifted across the busy city as the bright sunlight shimmered across the gilt roofs and the marble streets of this transformed city. The temple, made of marble of three different shades and ornately gilded, was an eye-catching masterpiece that looked like a snowcapped mountain sparkling in the sunlight.

The first feature to attract attention was the city walls. The first wall defended Zion, Ophel, and along with the temple walls, Moriah. The second wall enclosed Acra and terminated at the Antonia Tower. This meant that all the city and temple were protected. Stairs descended from Antonia Tower into the northern and western porches of the Gentiles' Court. Antonia was occupied by a Roman garrison that kept watch over Israel. The tower overlooked and commanded the temple so that a detachment of soldiers could rush to the scene of a riot at any time. The city walls were further defended by sixty towers in the first wall and forty in the second. The most prominent being the three new ones—Phasael, Mariamne, and Hippicus. All the towers were compactly built of immense marble blocks, square strongly fortified and defended by battlements and turrets. The city stood on four hills—Zion, Acra, Moriah, and Bezetha. The new town rose north of the temple mount and of Acra and was separated from them by an artificial valley. All of the streets were narrow and paved with white marble. An elevated footway was used by those who had been recently purified in the temple, and the streets derived their names from the gates and bazaars. Hence, there was Water Street, Fish Street, East Street, and other such titles. The timber market and the tailors were in the new city, and the grand upper market was on Zion. The wool and the braziers' stalls were on streets such as Baker Street and Butcher Street. Herod's palace at the northwestern angle of Zion stood higher within the shelter of the new towers, a marvel of splendour with its majestic roofs, gardens, courts, and porticoes. On the southeastern corner behind the temple was the great sheep market, and to the south of it, the Hippodrome. Originally the royal stables built by Solomon had occupied this area south of the temple mount, but now it had become Herod's royal porch. Other magnificent monuments and pillars had been erected all over the city, and new synagogues had been built. The towers and castle of Antonia with its colonnades looked almost like a small town on its rocky height. Beyond the city, numerous large gates opened everywhere into the country upon the slopes and crests of the hills covered by gardens and dotted with grandiose villas.

The Shushan Gate opened from the eastern wall onto the Mount of Olives. From this gate an arched roadway by which the priests brought out the red heifer and on Yom Kippur, the scapegoat, led to the Mount of Olives. Near the spot where the heifer was burned, there were extensive lavatories and booths for the sale of articles required for purifications.

Five gates opened into the outer enclosure, the Gentiles' Court, one from the south and four from the west. The southern Huldah Gate was a double gate that served many worshippers including the priests coming from Ophel. They passed through its gigantic archway and vestibule and then by a double tunnel, which ended at a flight of steps leading straight up from the Gentiles' Court into that of the priests', close to the place where they officiated.

The boundary line between Judah and Benjamin ran right through the middle of the city and the temple. It was said that the porch and sanctuary were in Benjamin and that the temple courts and altar were in Judah.

A huge bridge on arches spanned the valley of Tyropoeon, connecting the ancient city of David with the royal porch of the temple. From the royal bridge one could see suburbs and orchards, the royal gardens to the south, the garden of roses, so celebrated by the rabbis, and the hazy outline of mountains in the distance. The porches ran all around the inside of the temple wall and through the outer enclosure of the Gentiles' Court. They consisted of Corinthian pillars of pure solid marble. The royal porch was the most splendid, consisting of a treble colonnade, and along with other porches formed the southern enclosure of the first and outermost court of the temple—that of the Gentiles. These porches that were in fact the size of small halls around the Gentiles' Court were convenient meeting places for socialising, meetings, and discussion. Solomon's porch ran along the eastern wall of the temple and faced its great entrance. This was the only remnant of Solomon's Temple.

It was the rule when entering the temple to enter by the right and exit by the left. The great Gentiles' Court, which formed the lowest enclosure of the sanctuary, was paved with the finest variegated marble. It was open to both Jew and Gentile provided they observed the prescribed rules. Here there were eating and sleeping apartments for the Levites and a synagogue. It was also in this court that oxen, sheep, and doves selected for sacrifice were sold. The place was thus in part a market near which tables were stationed for money changers to do business. Within a short distance in the court, there was an ornamented marble screen that bore Greek and Latin inscriptions warning Gentiles not to proceed. Failure to observe this rule could result in death.

The sanctuary consisted of three courts, each higher than the former, and beyond these courts were the Inner Court and the

Most Holy Place. Entering by the principal gate on the east, one passed first into the Women's Court, then into the Israelites' Court, and from here into the Priests' Court. The eight side gates that led from the terrace into these were thickly plated with gold and silver. Far more magnificent than these eight gates was the Eastern Gate known as the Beautiful Gate. It was richly engraved and made of fine Corinthian brass. Its doors were so huge that the strength of twenty men was required to open and close them. Beggars were often placed near this gate as it formed the principal entrance into the sanctuary.

The Women's Court was not for the exclusive use of women. Men were free to worship there, but women could proceed no further except for sacrificial purposes. The Women's Court was in fact the most common place for worship. The women occupied a raised gallery along three sides of the court.

It had been in an attempt to appease the people that Herod had initiated this elaborate reconstruction and renovation programme.

Through his ambitious plans to rebuild the temple, Herod sought to establish a residence with Jewish history, for the temple became one of the architectural marvels of the ancient world. The religious prestige of Judaism was increased, and a positive balance of trade throughout Judea was facilitated. Herod was a skilful strategist who knew how to create and maximise a space that could accommodate an enormous number of pilgrims and tourists. His ability to bring local resources as well as foreign resources to bear on his civic and entrepreneurial ambitions was unparalleled. Those who acknowledged his talents only wished that he was a righteous man, not least divinely appointed.

The largest of Herod's towers was Phasael Tower named after his brother. There was also Hippicus Tower named after his friend and Mariamne Tower named after his beloved wife, whom he murdered. The towers were located in the citadel. They contained water reservoirs and dwelling rooms and were decorated with turrets. Mariamne Tower was smaller but the most beautiful and luxurious. In front of the towers were the monumental tombs of John Hyrcanus. Within the area encircled by the second city wall there was the timber market and other markets and storehouses. South of the towers were the barracks and Herod's palace, which was protected on the western side by the first wall and on the other sides by a wall that separated it from the rest of the town. The palace consisted of two main buildings, each with banquet halls, baths, and accommodation for the king's family and hundreds of guests. The buildings were surrounded by gardens, groves of trees, ponds, and fountains. At night, its lit windows cast an ominous glare over the town.

East of the palace were the rich quarters of the upper city and its new lavish buildings. Here the aristocracy and the priests lived. The streets were parallel and perpendicular to each other according to the principles of Hellenistic town planning. Near Herod's palace stood the Upper Agora surrounded by porticoes. This was the forum, the civic centre of the city where people assembled for business and social needs. Inside the upper city was a magnificent palace with residential quarters and open courts adorned by two conical-shaped towers. East of this palace lay another open public square, and in front of it was the house of the high priest. Behind this was a monument marking the tomb of David, which was similar to that of Zechariah in the Kidron Valley and equally visited by pilgrims. There were many other luxurious buildings furnished with large rooms, frescoes and mosaics, bathrooms, water cisterns, and ritual baths. Many people drew consolation from the total absence of statues. These were forbidden by the law, and there had been fear that those which were spread across the Roman Empire would soon appear in Jerusalem. Inside the corner of the first city wall was the dyer's quarter where woolen garments were washed, bleached, and prepared for sale. In the courts there were wells, vats for dyeing, and stands for drying the cloth. The city was built on two hills separated by the deep Tyropoeon Valley. On the slopes of the upper city were smaller buildings marking the residential quarters of the poor population. Above the slope was a new magnificent theatre. Standing in the lower part of the valley was the Pool of Siloam, and this was the only permanent water source within the city. The waters of the Gihon spring were diverted here through King Hezekiah's tunnel. In the face of Assyrian invasion, this wise and righteous king had had a new tunnel designed in order to channel water directly to the city, thereby concealing the source of supply and protecting the city from her adversaries. The tunnel ran from a spring to the Pool of Siloam, which was surrounded by gardens and workshops. There was a bridge that connected temple mount with the upper city. In the lower city there was a synagogue and the new Hippodrome in which horse and chariot races took place. A little farther, near, the two southern gates of the temple mount, which is known as the Huldah Gates, there were shops and ritual baths for the use of pilgrims. The basilica that stood on the temple mount was one of the largest buildings in the Roman Empire, used for huge gatherings, money changing, and large administrative tasks. In the eastern wall of the temple mount was the Susa Gate, and the esplanade above it was surrounded by porticoes on the south by the basilica. These porticoes sheltered worshippers from sun and rain, opening onto the esplanade. The temple itself was surrounded by a balustrade with inscriptions that warned Gentiles from entering. Inside there was a narrow raised platform that surrounded the temple on three sides. The Beautiful Gate led to the Women's Court, beyond which women were not permitted. There were small court chambers in each corner of the Women's Court, each with its own function. To the right of the gate was the wood store, and to the left was the Chamber of the Nazirites. People with defects were admitted to menial offices here in the Wood Chamber and entitled to temple support.

The oil store lay to the far left, and the court on the far right was for the purification of lepers and had its own ritual bath.

The Women's Court was surrounded by galleries and porticoes. The Gate of Nicanor, distinguished by its copper colour, led from the Women's Court to the innermost court. The gate was named after a rich Jew from Alexandria who had donated the doors. The story that circulated was that these doors had been miraculously saved from sinking whilst transported from Alexandria by sea and that therefore the original copper had not been gilded like all the other gates. The gate was approached by fifteen curved steps upon which the Levites stood singing and playing music. The innermost court was divided into two sections. The eastern strip was named the Israelites' Court, belonging to priestly and Levite families, and they were not permitted to pass beyond this point.

The area west of the Israelites' Court was accessible only to priests. Behind the porticoes of this court, there were various chambers including the Chamber of Salt, the Chamber of Hewn Stone, where the Sanhedrin sat, and the Chamber of the Hearth where priests on duty spent the night. In the middle of the courtyard stood the great altar, made of stones that had not been touched by iron. The whitewashed altar was ascended by a ramp attached to it by the south. North of the altar was the Place of Slaughtering with marble tables, posts, and hooks. The altar stood slightly south of the centre in order to enable the priest sacrificing the red heifer on the Mount of Olives to see the temple portal, a huge gate. The reconstructed facade of the temple was very high and wider than the rest of the temple. The main hall and the Most Holy Place preserved the dimensions of Solomon's Temple.

Attached to the temple in the northwest was the recently built Antonia Fortress named after Mark Antony. Prisoners were guarded here. This was a stronghold of Herod, connected to the temple by staircases. North of the temple was the double pool of Bethesda known as the Sheeps' Pool, and north of this was the monument of Alexander Janneus. It was crowned with a conical roof similar to that of Absalom's tomb in the Kidron Valley. This part of the city was Bezetha, the new city. It was less densely occupied and contained many gardens and agricultural fields. To the north were the Women's Gate and Tower.

Amongst the crowds that attended the temple there were several who believed that in their quietness and contemplation there was a place for constant intercession, prophetic declaration, solitude, and fasting. These calm frequenters of the temple courts were known as the Quiet in the Land. These were the ones who held firm to the words of the prophets and interceded for Israel with passion and humility, not with empty words. As Jacob had declared, the sceptre would not depart from Judah. Zechariah had seen the righteous branch, the stone with seven eyes, the corner stone, the tent peg, the battle bow, the cleansing fountain. They cherished these images and prayed for faithful leaders, restorers, and rebuilders like Zerubbabel, Nehemiah, and Ezra to be raised up in their midst. They cried for one who would be a sign and preach a message of repentance and reconciliation as did the prophet Jonah. They clung to the words of Haggai that this new temple would be one day full of glory as Messiah himself entered it. As Malachi had prophesied, Messiah would come suddenly to the temple once the messenger had prepared the way. They prayed that the messenger would arrive soon and present the scrolls of good news so that Israel would have time to prepare herself for the great coronation and the new era of kingship. Many within this small group had visions, dreams, and trances, meeting regularly inside the courts to discuss what they had heard and seen. Several visions lined up with the words of the prophets, others yet to be affirmed by a new scroll, a new testament. Such was the flow of visions amongst these righteous few. They required a faithful servant who would record each vision, each word, each scene, each portrait. Joahaz, the nephew of Mezahab, was a scribe and acted as keeper of records.

28

THE RECORDS OF JOAHAZ

The Throne

Anna saw a golden throne in Heaven. Oil was flowing from the throne, forming a river of oil whose stream became a steady flow cascading out of the heavens. Rising above the throne was a swirling steamlike vapour. The vapour looked like ripples of man's breath on a cold day. As the vapour thickened it billowed into torrents of air, released like mighty winds across the heavens and into the skies beneath.

A Sign of the Forerunner

It was during the final night of Passover that Hephzibah, the wife of Hiddai, saw the Passover cup of Hallel, Elijah's cup, overflowing with new wine. The flow continued for what seemed to be hours, until eventually the garments of each person were covered in crimson stains. As Hephzibah surveyed the family gathering, she noticed that the empty seat traditionally reserved for Elijah had been removed from the table.

The Book of Blood

Over several nights, Theophilus saw a vision of a large unsealed book made of linen cloth, animal skins, and papyrus leaves. The book was ancient yet new with a golden-green tinge and strengthened with the inner bark of trees. The pages appeared to

be living, breathing. As he fixed his gaze and reached to survey
the pages, he gasped and shut them immediately, for the writing
had been penned in lamb's blood.

The Holy City

Shelesh saw a majestic city framed by jasper light walls with their
twelve foundations of precious stones. Within the jewelled walls,
a crystal river flowed from the throne and thick fresh oil flowed
from its rocky ravines. The plains of the celestial city were rich,
fragrant, and verdant expanses of floral grandeur, emanating a
holy glory far surpassing the loftiest conceptions of mortals. There
was no sun and no moon, yet the entire city was illuminated with
the whitest of light.

Observing his surroundings, Shelesh surveyed the resplendent
beauty of velvet lawns, lavish verdant foliage, and superlative
glory. He felt the life flow of the anointed one energising every
created thing. The city was pulsating with life, a million voices
blending into one. Wave after wave of holy adoration swept over
the plains, infinite palm branches waving to the rhythm of a great
celestial symphony. Divine perfection breathed from every corner,
and everything was being made constantly new and infused with
bright white light. There was an eternal exuberance, a perfect and
unbreakable harmony, a limitless realm of vision. Love flowed as
a river. The cadent rhythms of adoration flooded this paradise.
Pure love was itself the constant inflow of life.

The End of the Law

Joahaz saw the administration of the hidden mystery, a living
Jerusalem, birthed in peoples' hearts. He saw a new priesthood
arising from Judah yet wondered how this could be when Levi
alone was the priestly line. The new priest wielded a sceptre to the
sound of a thousand trumpet blasts announcing an anointing and
a coronation. He was a priest-king, sitting, not standing. As he

raised his sceptre, the clay tablets that he held in his other hand began to disintegrate into a heap of dust. As he gazed at the heap, it turned into the small hill of Golgotha Then in amazement, he watched this small skull-shaped hill transform into a majestic purple mountain rising towards Heaven.

Brit Chadashah: The New Covenant

Eliab saw Mount Zion blazing and towering into Heaven as clouds of glory billowed and formed majestic peaks that pierced through the skies. He saw Sinai erupt into flames and crimson ink being penned on the hearts of men all over the earth. It was the inscription of a new ordinance given not by angels but by God Himself. In a second dream, he saw Aaron's rod blossoming in the Gentiles' Court, illuminated with a shaft of white light.

A Light unto the Gentiles

As was often the case, Simeon stood in a whirlwind with the universe rotating around him. This night, as the oceans and lands rotated before his eyes, he saw a thick golden signet ring encircle the equator. A new covenant encircled the entire world. As Simeon watched, he fell to his knees, revelation consuming his body. He then travelled back inside the sphere and saw a long banquet table that ran the expanse of the entire sphere from east to west. Seated at the royal banquet were men, women, and children of every tribe and land. Jews were interspersed with Greeks, Romans, Ethiopians, Persians, and multitudes of other nations. He saw above the table a golden banner. Written upon the banner in scarlet were the words 'Many sons to Glory'. He was then taken back outside the sphere and again saw the golden ring around the equator. Trembling with amazement, his eyes became transfixed at the awesomeness of the vision. He reached out to touch the ring as it seemed so real, so tangible. As he touched the ring, he found himself embracing the entire sphere. He placed his arms around the sphere and held it close to his body. His heart beat faster, and he felt vastness flood his being. It was the vastness of passion, the vastness of promise, the magnitude of a new dispensation, and the greatness of Olam Haba, the Age to Come. Not simply Israel, but the entire earth itself was to become wedded. Why else would this ring of royal love be placed around her?

The Measuring Line

Ishvi saw a costly cornerstone and the measuring line of righteousness and justice. Every building that did not align with the level instantly crumbled and dissolved. This line marked the fall and rise of many. As he looked further, he saw a carpenter extending a measuring line and marking an outline on cedarwood with red chalk. He worked and planed it, outlining it with a compass, turning it into the form of a cross.

Patmos

As Zacharias fell into a deep sleep, he saw two voices appearing, one from a desert and one from a rock. Both voices came from two men, one young and one old. Both looked poor and deprived, having been banished to desolate places. He strived within the vision to see their faces. Their voices could be seen and heard resounding through the lands, swift, unrelenting, pounding like hammers. These were voices that men had tried to silence, yet they echoed across the four corners of the earth, penetrating everything they touched. These human sound waves resonated through his entire body, and the visions recurred for numerous days until one night the strangest thing happened.

As his eyes followed the coastline northwest of Jerusalem and round to the west, he saw within the expanse of water a large crescent-shaped piece of volcanic rock, illuminated by rays of white light. Inscribed upon the rock was the phrase 'rock of revelation'. His eyes fell upon an old, frail-looking man. As the man spoke, he realised that this was one of the voices he had encountered in previous visions. The man's eyes were deep and penetrating, and he had the air of a seer. He was not resting but labouring with other men inside the chasms of the rock. Though the man's countenance was radiant, he looked physically weak and was clothed in prison garments. As Zacharias surveyed this scene, he saw that this rock was actually a sizeable piece of land of rugged formation, surrounded by water. As he climbed onto the rock to pursue the man, he saw a ladder reaching up to Heaven and wondered whether this elderly man was not his ancestor, Jacob.

The following night, Zacharias found himself standing once again upon the rock; however, he could not find the old man. He called but heard no reply. Anguished and alone he searched the island only to encounter crowds of downtrodden criminals and prisoners fighting, some dying. He walked anxiously through the crowds of bruised, beaten, and oppressed men, searching their faces yet unable to find the old man. As he raised his eyes, he saw the same ladder standing in the centre of the rock reaching up to Heaven. At the sound of a trumpet blast, the ladder vanished. He lifted his head once again towards Heaven and traced the vertical line where moments earlier the ladder had stood. Yet all he could see was a magnificent rainbow of jewels, sapphires, rubies, diamonds, and onyx. As the rainbow glistened, it cast its majestic arc over the entire rock. Encircled by colour, the crowd of exiles rested their tools raising their eyes towards the sky. As each tired, vacant pair of eyes traced the arc of the rainbow, the small population fell silent. As Zacharias awoke, his body still trembling, he felt fresh moisture in his eyes, as if eye salve had been applied. From that day on, his natural and spiritual vision gained fresh clarity.

Flames in the City

During the Feast of Shavuot, as the procession of farmers from the hill country arrived at the temple to present bikkurim, the first fruits, Japhlet saw tongues of flames and thick orange vapour consuming one of the narrow streets that led up from the lower market.

New Oracles, New Testaments

Phineas, friend of Simeon, saw in his dreams the outlines of illuminated nations. After each new dream, he searched the images out on maps that his cousin had acquired. He saw Greece, Rome, Persia, and Spain and a blazing forest fire spreading rapidly through the Roman province of Galatia igniting the cities of Antioch, Iconium, Lystra, and Derbe. A second blaze flooded through Macedonia and into a series of other major Greek cities. The scrolls he had seen falling from Heaven in earlier visions multiplied in number and young, zealous men of revolution voyaged across the oceans in Phoenician boats. They ran through nations wielding swords that consisted of enflamed parchments. These flaming parchments were threefold in function: they were oracles, torches, and weapons. Phineas was led by an angel to a trophy room and a court in Heaven, where he saw the commissioning of divine alignments, apostolic mandates, and heavenly coronations. He saw celestial hosts assigned to co-labour with an army of young men and women who had emerged out of darkness. As he looked further, he saw ecclesia, chosen ones, drawn out and assembled together under the full administration of the new covenant, mantled with the spirit of Elijah and marked with the mandate of the establishment of an eternal kingdom. These torch-bearing warriors established kingdom outposts across the named lands. As he surveyed the scene, he heard angelic voices, trumpets, earthquakes, prison gates crashing open, stones being hurled, shipwrecks, human desperation, acts of human kindness, the songs of peaceful communes, and the violent winds of revolution.

The Lion of Judah

Eliab saw the head of a majestic lion with emblazoned eyes, golden mane, and royal gaze. Yet the lion had no body. As golden rain fell upon the earth, a perfect body began to form beneath the head of the lion. As Eliab watched the body gradually merge with the head, he gazed into mysteries hitherto disclosed.

A Veil Torn

Hiddai of Arimathea watched in horror as the seventy-two twisted plaits of the temple veil rapidly unravelled, the twenty-four threads of white, scarlet, blue, and gold violently ripped apart with no priest officiating. The scene was quite terrifying. All of Israel knew that two teams of oxen, pulling in separate directions, could not cause this veil to tear apart.

As the thick woven fabric split, Hiddai's bones vibrated. After a few such moments, the drama merged into an image more horrifying still. He saw a beaten man nailed to a tree wearing a crown of thistles, his flesh torn, and blood streaming from his veins. The man was alone, isolated, just near the small hill, Golgotha, yet encircled by wailing, screaming, and shrieks of savage laughter. For a few short seconds, Hiddai fought for breath as his heart sank into spiritual agony. As he cried out in torment, his baby son Joseph awoke and ran to his father's pallet. As Hiddai stared in horror, the vision became more real than reality. Why was the veil torn, and who was the man? Oh, that the torment would end.

Signs in the Skies

On the eve of Passover, Issachar entered a deep sleep and watched the moon rise. Its colour was a spectacular blood-red. He heard the sound of the earth quaking and a cataclysmic vibration as if the very fabric of the cosmos was being shredded. As he reentered the vision a few hours later, he saw the moon returned to the foot of Bethulah, the virgin planet. Now it was a full moon, so complete, so radiant, and so glorious.

Glory Covering the Earth

As Simeon prayed in the temple, other worshippers found him sitting in a trancelike state. In his visions he was carried across oceans of vast blue water and surveyed formations of land that he knew nothing of. He saw the demarcation line of two hemispheres, and passing from one half of the sphere to the other, he conversed with foreign tribes in an unknown language. On one occasion a divine constellation of other spheres and celestial balls of blazing fire exploded around him with divine glory. On other occasions, he saw the two hemispheres covered with Shekinah glory. He saw the kingdoms beneath the oceans, every plant, animal, and created thing saturated with glory as the very face of God himself reflected over the waters of the sphere.

New Scrolls

As Joahaz faithfully listened to reports and recorded the visions, he saw multitudes of scrolls descending from Heaven and multiplying on the earth. As the walls of Jerusalem collapsed under the weight of golden hailstones the size of rocks, young men ran from the city towards the coast carrying letters penned in golden ink.

Like others, he saw the temple veil torn down the middle, from top to bottom, and saw Jews and Gentiles dancing within the Most Holy Place as a river of crystal water flowed out of it and flooded the courts. As he gazed at the spectacle, he saw the Torah turn into a human figure and pass through the temple walls, ignoring every gate.

Gethsemane

During spring Bezalel awoke early and spent the early hours at Gat Shmanim, the garden on the western slope of the Mount of Olives. It was a place where the oil of revelation saturated his eyes. The garden was a place where all of his carnal thoughts were crushed and where thoughts of Messiah sustained him. When his eyes were not closed, he stared at the aged stumps of olive trees cut down to encourage future growth. His stares were not vacant; they were lengthened and sustained by hope. The shoots growing from them were strong and full of promise. With eyes closed, he heard the intense crushing of olives with huge stones and saw thick streams of oil flooding through the garden.

A New Mandate

Anna prophesied that there would emerge armies of overcomers armed with flaming scrolls containing reports and testimonies. These reports would boast not simply in the birth of Messiah and the physical beholding of Jehovah in human form, but they would somehow speak of moments fuller, a reality more complete, more consequential, more final. She saw crowds of witnesses, both within Jerusalem and beyond, armed with parchments that mapped out a new and living way for people to be redeemed by an eternal sacrifice. In night visions, she saw herself running through the streets of the city with a lamp.

Messiah

Meditating on the words of the prophets, Anna became consumed by the spirit of prophecy, knowing that this infilling was the testimony of Messiah. Though she knew not the hour, she prophesied that the new covenant spoken of by Jeremiah would be initiated just over thirty years after His birth and that thereafter there would be a new priestly order in which animal sacrifice would no longer be required for the remission of sin.

A New Order

Commotion and rupture dominated many of Elizabeth's nights. As the city gates crashed wide open, breaking up the earth beneath them, she saw Herod's palace fall to the ground. Marble remnants dissolved into powder—every tower, castle, fortress, theatre, and hippodrome crashed to ground. In another dream she saw a timeline descending from Heaven showing key people with crimson stamps on their foreheads.

Olive Trees

When ascending the Mount of Olives, Ezra saw wild olives being grafted into cultivated ones and entire groves merging together into a gigantic tree of life, unguarded by cherubim.

Seven Furnaces

Crispus and Jair regularly saw seven great fires lit across the land of the Greeks.

Rain from Heaven

As heavy rains lashed against the columns and porticoes of the temple, Mezahab and Zibia saw rain turn to hail and hail turn to majestic jewels, jasper, sardius, turquoise that poured from the skies above.

The Rise and Fall of Many

Jashobeam saw the sky splitting apart as a rolled-up scroll, mountains melting as wax, stars falling, islands becoming submerged, kings being exiled from palaces, and rulers hiding in caves with vultures feeding on their flesh.

Phanuel's Last Sukkot

Phanuel saw a great sea of Gentiles waving palm branches. The scene was far more immense than the crowds of foreign pilgrims who normally arrived to celebrate major feasts. Amidst the rejoicing, the words of the prophet Hosea resounded throughout the courts: 'I will call those who are not my people, my people, and those who were not beloved, beloved; sons of the living God.' As Phanuel surveyed the multitudes, he saw the temple transform into an immense sukkah, a vast tabernacle that spanned the expanse of the skies, its poles reaching down into every nation.

New Songs

Many visions of Grandma Hadassah included fountains, rainbows, harps, songs unheard, sickles, vast fields of fine golden wheat, stretches of sea becoming sheets of glass, white horses riding the skies, captives and exiles exchanging prisoners garments for white linen, sealed books of names, blood turning into wine, and gigantic olive presses.

The New Jerusalem

Shimei saw a gigantic jasper stone crash to the ground and turn into a city. It was a glorious city, a city of shalom. Later in the dream, he rode through the city on horseback as flames of white illuminated every corner. Shimei rode on in search of the temple but was unable to locate it. Approaching the centre of the city, he saw infinite lines of righteous kings and queens enrobed in scarlet, purple, and gold assembling as if for a royal ceremony.

Bride of Many Nations

Simeon saw an ancient treasure box made from ebony wood. The box was enchained with thick gold. An angel holding many keys unlocked the box. Inside the box was a collection of thick golden rings of the same size and dimension as the rings of the chain that locked the box. The angel informed him that these were covenant rings for the nations of the earth. A day would come when every nation would be called beloved and invited into a great covenant with Jehovah. The rings themselves would form a linkable chain across the earth, as strong as the one that locked the ancient treasure box. People from every nation would be joined together in covenant. The angel then closed the box and locked it securely with the golden chain, affirming that these covenantal treasures could not be given until the appointed time.

The Eye of God

Ezra saw his grandfather's name 'Phanuel', 'Face of God', written with human blood across the sky. As he examined the writing, he saw the stars forming the shape of an eye that was scanning the universe whilst the planets were swirling as if in a celestial dance. As Ezra opened his eyes at sunrise the following day, he saw a shaft of bright violet light illuminating the ancient watchtower of Bethlehem.

Agony

In his sleep, Simeon encountered a young shepherdess holding a newborn lamb and a ferocious wolf lying in wait to snatch the lamb from her arms. Suddenly, the sword of an angel descended from Heaven and pierced the head of the beast, casting it to the ground. In other visions Simeon saw the same shepherdess lying in a field with a Roman spear cast upright through her heart and a blood moon over her head. The agony he felt was unbearable.

The King-Priest

Shiprah saw scarlet rain watering the nations and gigantic jars of frankincense being tipped into the oceans as the substance of global salvation was being prepared. Trumpets blasted as vast armies of priests in royal attire were gathered from the four corners of the earth.

Another Massacre

Anna heard bitter lamentation throughout Jerusalem. Families were lost in inconsolable torment as the angel of death came as a thief in the night. The piercing shrieks of young children and anguished screams of agonised mothers awakened her for several nights. She saw a river of blood in Ramah and heard the violent clashes of silver swords.

Trees Falling

When walking through Jericho through the sycamore groves, Raphu had open visions of strong, flourishing trees falling to the ground as small dry trees regained moisture and began to flourish.

Resource from Above

In a dream, Jerioth, mother of Issachar, was called up to a high place on a mountain far above the earth. On the summit was a man with raven-black hair and piercing eyes, dressed in a crimson robe. The man smiled and reached out, his hand pulling her up to join him on the summit. As the high winds gained speed, he spread his robe over her. His hair blowing and swept back in the rapid winds, his eyes transfixed, roaming to and fro across the infinite realm below, he raised his right arm whilst holding her inside his robe with his left. He then began to release from Heaven infinite hosts of angels armed with sharp-bladed sickles, axes, silver trumpets, and glistening armoury to be transported to the earth below. These gifts, he said, were for the new kingdom fighters. These kingdom fighters would act in the spirit of David, Jehoshaphat, Josiah, and Hezekiah. They would tear down principalities, gather the harvest, and declare the restoration of all things.

In the Order of Melchizadek

In the night hours, Zacharias encountered a holy celestial figure who served him bread and wine. The man introduced himself as the King of Righteousness. His eyes were like flames of love, and his robes were made of light. As he departed, the awestruck priest saw an immense infinite pile of priests' garments and accessories being quickly thrown into a red-hot furnace that blazed within the centre of the temple.

29

TEMPLE LIFE

It was in the Women's Court that Anna spent most of her hours.
A colonnade ran around the edge of the Women's Court, and
inside it were thirteen chests placed for charitable contributions.
Narrow at the mouth and wide at the bottom, these chests were
known as trumpets. Nine were for legal dues, and four were
for voluntary gifts. The first two were for the temple tribute
that had been introduced by the Pharisees under the reign of
Queen Salome. The third was money redeemed for turtledoves
that were bought for sin or burnt offerings, the fourth was for
money received for the value of young pigeons, the fifth was for
contributions towards the wood used in the temple, the sixth was
for contributions towards the cost of incense, and the seventh
was for the cost of golden vessels. If a man had put aside a certain
sum for a sin offering and there was money left over, this was
placed into the eighth trumpet. The remaining five trumpets were
for leftover money from trespass offerings, the Nazirite offering,
the offering of the cleansed leper, and other voluntary offerings.
The contents of the thirteen chests were taken into a special
treasury chamber. As well as the thirteen trumpets, there was
the Chamber of the Silent where people could secretly deposit
money that was used for educating the children of the poor.

In each of the four corners of the Women's Court were
chambers that looked like unroofed courts. One was for priests
who were unfit for services other than menial tasks on account of
bodily blemishes. The job of these priests was to pick the worm-

eaten wood from the wood that was destined for the altar. A second court was for the lepers to be washed before presenting themselves to the priests at the Gate of Nicanor. The third court was where the Nazirites polled their hair and cooked their peace offerings whilst the fourth court was used for storing the oil and the wine for the drink offerings. The musical instruments used by the Levites were deposited in two rooms under the Israelites' Court to which the access was from the Women's Court.

The western colonnade of this court was open, and forty steps led from it to the Gate of Nicanor into the Court of Israel. It was on these steps that, during the Feast of Tabernacles, the Levites stood to sing the fifteen psalms of ascent. Two steps led up from the Court of Israel to the Priests' Court. Three semicircular steps led up from these to a platform upon which Levites also sung. The priests pronouncing the blessing occupied the steps at the other end of the court, which led up to the temple porch. As with the Women's Court, there were receptacles for the priestly vestments.

There was also the chamber of the high priest's meat offering where each morning, before attending duties, the officiating priesthood gathered from the Beth-ha Moked, the house of stoves, which was built on arches and contained a large dining hall that communicated with four other chambers. One of these was a large apartment where fires were continually burning for the use of the priests who ministered barefoot. The heads of the ministering courses slept there in a receptacle under the paving, near to where the keys of the temple were hung at night. There were also chambers for the lambs that were kept for regular sacrifice. It was a place designed for preparing the showbread, storing of salt for the altar, salting the skins of sacrifice, washing the flesh of the animals, and storing wood and machinery that supplied the laver with water. Finally there was the Chamber of Gazith, square polished stones where the Sanhedrin assembled for meetings. Above some of these chambers were other apartments such as those in which the high priest spent the week in study and meditation prior to the Day of Atonement.

A nearby passage led to an illuminated subterranean bath for the use of priests. Along the southern side of the court, one could see the Water Gate through which the pitcher with water was brought from the Pool of Siloam during Sukkot. Above the gate was a chamber where the priests kept guard at night. Then the Gate of the Firstlings through which the firstlings to be offered were brought, and the Wood Gate through which the altar wood was carried to the Wood Chamber. Above and beyond these gates were the apartments of the high priest and the chamber of the priestly council that engaged in affairs that were strictly connected to the temple.

Along the colonnades, both around the Gentiles' Court and the Women's Court, there were seats and benches for the accommodation of the worshippers. The most prominent object in the Priests' Court was the immense altar of unhewn stones that were whitened twice a year. Nearby was the great heap of salt from which every sacrifice was to be salted. On the altar, three fires burned: one (east) for the offerings, the second (south) for the incense, and the third (north) for supplying the means for kindling the other two. The four horns of the altar were straight, square, and hollow. The one at the southwest had silver funnels into which the drink offerings and (during Sukkot) the water of Siloam were poured. The system of drainage into the chambers and canals below had been carefully designed, allowing the blood and refuse to be swept down into the valley of Kidron and towards the royal gardens. North of the altar there were vessels, marble tables, and hooks for fastening the sacrifices.

Between the altar and the porch of the temple and positioned towards the south was the immense laver of brass, supported by twelve huge lions. This was drained each evening and filled every morning by machinery, and there was room here for twelve priests to wash at the same time. Unlike the high-level aqueduct, which collected water in a rock-hewn tunnel on the road to Hebron and wound along delivering water to the upper part of the city, the low-level aqueduct that supplied the temple derived its waters from three sources: the hills of Hebron, Etham, and the three pools of Solomon. As well as this there were various rock-hewn cisterns in which the water transported by aqueduct from Solomon's pools near Bethlehem was stored. These were connected by a system of channels cut out of a rock so that when one was full, the surplus water ran into the next, and so on until the final overflow was carried off by a channel into Kidron.

The entrance to the porch was covered by a splendid veil. Right and left were depositories for the sacrificial knives, and inside, there were dedicated gifts such as the golden crowns presented by the Maccabees. There was a marble table for the new showbread and a golden table on which the old bread was placed as it was removed from the Holy Place. Two large doors plated with gold and covered in a rich Babylonian curtain of the four temple colours—scarlet, blue, fine linen, and purple—formed the entrance into the Holy Place. Above it hung the symbol of Israel, a huge vine of pure gold, each cluster the height of a man. To the south of the Holy Place was the golden candlestick, and to the north, the showbread. Beyond them was the altar of incense, just near to the entrance to the Most Holy Place. The Most Holy Place was the home of the Ark of the Covenant with the cherubim and the Mercy-seat, the Tablets of the Law, and the Book of the Covenant. Aaron's rod that budded and the pot of manna were no longer there, their absence indicating to some that the Aaronic priesthood was soon to be rendered obsolete and to be replaced by a superior priesthood. Moreover, the fire that had descended from Heaven upon the altar was extinct, and the Shekinah, the visible presence of God, was absent. The will of God could no longer be ascertained through the Urim and Thummin, nor could the high priest, on his annual entrance into the Most Holy Place, be anointed with holy oil, for the very composition of the oil of the day was unknown. Everything in Israel was defiled and contaminated, even the oil. Despite this the rabbis fought rigorously to preserve their own illusion of purity and sanctity. A wooden partition separated the Most Holy Place from the Holy Place, and over the door hung a veil. The veil of the Most Holy Place was a handbreadth thick and woven of seventy-two twisted plaits, each consisting of twenty-four threads. There were six threads of each of the temple colours: white, scarlet, blue, and gold. Two of these veils were made every year, and it was said that around three hundred priests were required to accomplish this.

As with the ministering priests, the worshippers were to walk backwards when leaving the immediate area where the service was performed, and at the Gate of Nicanor, each one was to stand with his head bowed. Once a week the sanctuary was thoroughly cleaned. Priests and Levites carried out repairs, and if they were unable to, other Israelites were called in. No man was able to go on to the temple mount with his staff in his hand as if for business or pleasure or with shoes on his feet. Sandals alone were permitted, neither with dust on his feet nor with scrip or with money tied to him in purse. Any offerings or contributions had to be carried by hand. Just before Purim, the money changers opened stalls throughout the nation to change the various foreign coins that Jewish residents at home or settlers abroad might bring into Israel. Only the regular half shekel of the sanctuary could be received at the treasury. During this time the temple tribute had to be paid, but it was not accepted from heathens or Samaritans. The rate of discount of the money changers was also regulated by law.

30

Offerings and Worship

For pilgrims and those dispersed in nations abroad, the temple was a physical bond of national and religious life. Patriotism and religious ritual caused them to give generous gifts. The richest contributions came from crowded Jewish settlements in Mesopotamia and Babylon to which those in exile had originally been deported. Armed escorts carried the gifts from the collecting treasuries placed within their own cities. In the temple this money was emptied into three large chests that were opened at certain points during the three great feasts. The revenue went towards the cost of sacrifices, temple repairs, the salaries of staff and officials, such as those who prepared the showbread and incense, ensured the exactitude of copies of the law used in synagogues, examined the Levitical fitness of the sacrifices, instructed the priest in their list of duties. The fees of curtain makers and rabbis were also paid from this source. After all the expenditure, there still remained enough to pay for the repairs of the city walls, road and public buildings in Jerusalem, and to accumulate a wealthy reserve in the treasury.

The real service of praise was in the voice of the people. Instrumental music was merely to sustain the song. Levites alone were choristers though other distinguished Israelites could take part in instrumental music. The trumpet blasts were performed by priests only. On ordinary days, they blew seven times, and this was a symbolic proclamation of the kingdom of God, divine providence, and the final judgement. The first blast were blown when the gate of Nicanor was opened; then when the drink offering was poured out, the Levites sung the psalm of the day in three sections. After each section there was a pause when the priests blew a second blast and the people worshipped. This was repeated in the evening service. On the Sabbath eve, a threefold blast summoned the people to prepare for holy day. As the sound was carried over the city, another threefold blast announced the commencement of the day and again at intervals during the singing of the psalm of Moses: "Thou hast been our dwelling place in all generations. Teach us to number our days that we may present to thee a heart of wisdom. Satisfy us with thy loving-kindness that we may sing for joy and be glad all our days. Let thy majesty appear to our children. Let thy favour be upon us and confirm the work of our hands." There was one pair of brass cymbals, harps, and lutes of different types that were all used in the temple orchestra.

As well as the silver trumpets, the priests played the ram's horn, the shophar mainly at New Moon, New Year, and to proclaim Shemitah, the Year of Jubilee, which was always announced in advance at Yom Kippur. It had loud far-sounding tones and was used also in the synagogues. The flutes and reed pipes were played during the main feasts and by festive pilgrim band on their journey into Jerusalem whilst others sang psalms of Ascent. A good voice was a valuable gift for a Levite. The female choristers were not counted within the temple services though their voices were often heard in dirges in honour of the dead.

31

The Life of a Priest

Ophel was a densely inhabited quarter. Half of the twenty-four courses into which the priesthood was divided were permanent residents of Jerusalem. Many others lived in Hebron, Jericho, and Ramah. When a course was on duty, all of its members were bound to be near Jerusalem. Those who were unable to do so had to meet in their local synagogues in order to fast and pray for each day of their week of service apart from each day around Shabbat, as this was considered a detraction of the joy attached to the sacred day.

Everything connected with the priesthood was intended to be symbolic. The fundamental design of Israel itself was to be a kingdom of priests and a holy nation. Israel was sinful and could only approach Jehovah in the manner in which He Himself had appointed. Direct choice and appointment by God were the conditions alike of the priesthood, sacrifices, feasts, and every detail of service. Reconciliation through atonement and mediation through the priesthood were at the heart of everything. The high priest was the exceptional provision made. The gold plate worn on his forehead bore the words 'Holiness unto Jehovah'. The qualifications required for entry, the mode of ordination, and every aspect of their dress was to express holiness.

Those Levites who were not priests were priests' assistants, singers, and musicians, gatekeepers, and guards. The duty of the assistants was to take care of the sacred vessels, storehouses and their contents, and the preparation of the showbread, the meat offerings, and the spices. They also assisted the priests generally in their work and attended to the cleaning of the sanctuary and taking charge of the treasuries. At night, the priests kept watch of the innermost places of the temple, and the Levites took charge of the outer gates and the Courts of Gentiles and Women. If a leper or anyone who was defiled (including a priest in a state of uncleanliness) ventured into the sanctuary, he was dragged out and beaten to death.

Each course came on duty for one week, and the service of the week was shared amongst the various families that formed the course. On feast days, priests from any course could officiate, and during Sukkot all twenty-four courses were present. Whilst engaged in services, they were not permitted to drink wine. Other families of the course on duty who were not actually on duty were also unable to drink wine in case they were asked to stand in for another. Priests had to arrive in Jerusalem properly washed, trimmed, and attired. Their income was moderate as there was no law by which to enforce the payment of tithes and offerings.

In the days of Herod, the political influence of the high priest continued to decay. High priests were often unlearned and unreliable. There was a huge turnover of occupants of this office, and bribery, corruption, and manipulation were rife. The high priest could officiate in any part of the temple services, and he had exceptional rights including the right to take whatever percentage of the offerings he chose. He had a house inside the temple where he lived by day, retiring only at night to his own home, which had to be in Jerusalem. On the Day of Atonement the people would reverently escort him from the temple to his home. The permanence, holiness, and hereditary nature of the office was, however, being replaced by crime, bribery, greed, rivalry, jealousy, and at times mutual destruction through witchcraft.

As well as the various officials that formed the temple council and the priestly assistants, there were overseers who summoned people to their respective duties. There were overseers for the guards, the captain of the temple, the singers, the trumpeters, the cymbals, the lots that were drawn each morning, the turtledoves and pigeons, the meat and drink offerings, the sick and the infirm, the water and drainage, the showbread, the incense and the garments. All of these overseers chose and employed helpers either for the day or permanently. As well as this, there were important roles such as those held by the temple physician, instructors, examiners of sacrifices, and others who supported the daily life of the temple.

It was, thus, a highly elaborate and intricately orchestrated system, a complex living organism that had tragically become infiltrated and diseased with invasive sin and iniquity. All sacrifices had to be brought before sunset although unconsumed flesh was allowed to smoulder on the altar until the following dawn. Temple guards who fell asleep at their posts were beaten and often had their clothes set on fire by the captain of the temple.

Each evening when the last notes of the temple music died out, worshippers slowly retired, some after lingering for private prayer, or else tarrying in one of the marble porches. Already the short eastern day was fading out in the west. Far over the mountains of Gibeon, the sun was sinking. The new company of priests and Levites who were to conduct the service were coming up from Ophel under the leadership of their heads of houses. Those who had officiated during the day were preparing to leave by another gate. They had removed their priestly dress, depositing it in the appointed chambers, and resumed their normal clothing and sandals. Though sandals could be worn in the temple, priests were to minister with bare feet. As those arriving at the end of their week of service left the temple through the enormous gates, there were at times twenty men holding them open. Then the temple keys were hung up in a hollow square under a marble slab in the fire room that also served as the chief guard room of the priests. Now as the stars were shining out on the deep blue eastern sky, the priests leaving the temple gathered for discussion, often sharing the evening meal together. This consisted of pieces of sacrifices and the oil and flour from the first fruit, Therumoth offerings. Those Levites in charge of collecting the tithes and other business details needed to buy the meat and drink offerings for the following day in order to sell it to the worshippers. This was the source of great temple profit. On payment of a monthly fixed tariff, the sacrifices were purchased. The accounts for all transactions had to be reconciled and checked each evening though one could only imagine the levels of dishonesty to which the priesthood had stooped.

The temple was to be guarded throughout the night as throughout the day. With the proximity of the Romans to deal with as well as the overwhelming crowds during feasts, the captain of the temple had a great responsibility. During the night, the guards were placed in twenty-four stations around the gates and courts. Each guard consisted of ten men. They were responsible for all three watches. Older priests were permitted to lie on the floor having wrapped their priestly garments beside them whilst the younger men kept watch. The chiefs of the courses could recline on couches. However, those reclining had to be ready to prepare the morning sacrifices. The priest whose duty it was to supervise would appear suddenly, and no one knew exactly when. They had to have all taken a bath before his arrival. A subterranean passage lit on both sides led to the bathrooms where each priest was to immerse himself. Their hands and feet had to be washed again throughout the day each time they came for service. After this the preparations commenced, the lots were drawn for the various services of the day, and the high priest's meat offering was prepared. Meanwhile the earliest glow of morning light streaked the eastern sky. Much had to be done before the gates could be opened, the lamb could not be slain, and the sacrifice could not be made anyway until the sun had lit up the whole sky as far as Hebron—without having fully risen upon the horizon.

32

A JOURNEY TO BETHLEHEM

It was the year of 20 BC just towards the end of the wheat harvest when Shimei and Mezahab took Jair to see his newly born cousin in Bethlehem. The younger sister of Mezahab had moved to the town after marrying a well-known landowner in the region who rented out his pastures to local shepherds who paid him for grazing rights. They had already been blessed with four girls and had finally borne a son. It was custom for them to pass through Bethlehem after stopping first in Jerusalem.

Bethlehem was a small town surrounded by fertile hills and valleys with a huge grain-producing capacity. Farmers and shepherds were drawn to its vast pastures and valleys. Not only was the soil there rich but also it was a place of great historical significance. The fields of Boaz, Ruth's kinsman redeemer, continued to produce an abundant harvest of wheat, and of course, it was the ancestral home of King David, son of Jesse, the Bethlehemite. The grafting of foreign lineages into the royal lineage that Ruth, the Moabite, had represented ensured that blood in Bethlehem was already crying out for the salvation of the Gentiles. This humble place named Ephrathah for its fertility and known as Bethlehem, the 'House of Bread', remained a site of great significance both within Israel and beyond her borders.

From Galilee to Bethlehem, their most simple route was along the plains of the Mediterranean, coastal road, or through Jordan Valley, but as always he desired the quickest route and thus joined the long string of Mesopotamian caravans on the trade route through the rocky highlands. At least with this company they were under guard and thus protected from bandits, robbers, and mountain lions. They gradually descended through the Galilean hills with Mount Tabor rising in the east through the plain of Jezreel, passing by Mount Gilboa. Lines of heavy-laden animals advanced slowly through the mountains and through Dothan near various walled wealthy Samaritan cities that served as thriving commercial centres where caravans stopped to trade. They journeyed on towards Shomrom-Sebastea and south to Shechem, passing around Shiloh where merchants continued to sell their wares, and stopped to pray at Bethel. Eventually they reached Ramah where they could see Jerusalem and the pinnacles of the temple glistening as jewels in the setting sun. Near to Bethlehem on the road from Jerusalem was Migdal-Eder, 'The Watchtower of the Flock', a principal station from where local shepherds kept watch of their flocks—most of whom were destined for sacrifices in the temple. The quality of the soil here was so well known that animals pasturing as distant from Jerusalem as Migdal Eder and within that radius on every side were deemed fit for sacrifice. The males were offered as burnt offerings and the females as peace offerings. After bringing gifts to the newborn cousin, Shimei and Mezahab planned to journey on through the hills so that Jair could spend time with younger relatives before visiting Anna in Jerusalem.

It was during a visit to Bethlehem that Jair made the acquaintance of Zibia, an attractive beauty whose father, Barzi, owned land and flocks in the area. Her mother had died the previous year after a tragic fall, and Zibia had been left to look after her father and older brother. Barzi was a tall and humble man well acquainted with labour and resistant to political conversation. As well as renting out land to local shepherds, he had his own flocks to take care of, and this occupied his full attention. Barzi had been deeply grieved after his wife's death but drew solace from his daughter's presence. It was at the well in the centre of Bethlehem that Jair encountered Zibia. The two had been introduced by a friend of his mother's sister who was passing through the town. From this day on, Zibia became the cause of many more journeys to Bethlehem.

It was just after Purim of the year 18 BC that a large crowd of guests were invited to the home of Eleazar, son of Eliud, to say farewell to his grandson Jacob. Jacob had married in Bethlehem and his wife had borne him a son, Joseph, who was now two years of age. They were leaving their home, close to the house of his parents Matthan and Jehosheba, and planned to relocate for a year or two in order to acquire new building and carpentry work in the city of Tzippori. This was the largest city in Galilee, and the Romans had recently taken it over, renaming it Sepphoris. It was an old city that had been subjected throughout history to the dominance of diverse nations and fortified by the Assyrians. The city was a vibrant centre of political action, and now under Roman influence, its identity as a thriving commercial town had continued to grow.

Jacob and his wife Miri had saved enough money to buy a home not far from Sepphoris in the small valley from which Mount Tabor rose in the east. It was a fairly isolated village by the name of Nazareth, with its own synagogue and a population of roughly five hundred people—fairly dense compared to the scattering of homes across the hill country. The settlement lay between the Jordan valleys and was one hour's walk from Sepphoris, which was just to the northwest. The streets of Nazareth lay in a very irregular chequered pattern with wide areas between, each containing mazes of houses and courtyards. Jacob and Miri had bought one of the regular modest homes. These looked like whitewashed cubes with a few openings and a single room inside. Rooms were divided into two sections so that animals could also be kept there. Some of the other houses around the area were partly cave dwellings built up against limestone rock face that was hollowed out. Though there would not be a lot of space in their new home, the flat roof would house the tools and provide extra sleeping space if necessary as well as sufficient space for young Joseph to be active. There were many relatives and friends who gathered in Bethlehem to bid farewell to the couple. Many who had grown up with Matthan and Jacob, including the several generations of Phanuel's family, had wept when receiving news of the latter's departure. The couple promised to return home with the child as frequently as possible. Bethlehem would always be home—the hills, the land of their youth.

Jacob and Miri were not alone in their plans, for there were several in the building and carpentry trade who were relocating to be in closer proximity to the new Roman Sepphoris. Rumour had it that building plans were already in place for the reconstruction of roads within the region as well as eventually the renovation of the city itself.

33

FAMILY SORROWS AND JOYS

It had been a painful few years for Jair and Zibia. God alone knew their pain. A year after marriage they had been blessed with a daughter, Jedidah, and several years after her birth, a son was born to whom they gave the name Jairus, the Greek version of his father's name. Both children had been healthy and had lived close to their grandparents Shimei and Mezahab in Galilee, paying regular visits to Barzi, father of Zibia, who continued to shepherd flocks in Bethlehem. However, at twelve years of age, Jedidah had collapsed on the ground in the middle of the day and fallen into a deep sleep. She had been alone in the courtyard when this had happened, and Zibia had been out working in the flax fields. The housemaid had found Jedidah lying prostrate on the ground, and young Jairus had run to get help, but it was too late. Her head was bruised and heavy, her eyes vacant, and her final breaths had been taken. Helpless and desperate, they had attempted to breathe life into the young girl, crying to Heaven for help. Yet it was all in vain, for the body lay stiff and cold inside the house. The family was distraught, and for years to follow the young Jairus lived haunted day and night by the harrowing memory of finding his sister lifeless and running for help until his young fatigued legs could run no more. His beloved Jedidah had been his guardian angel, his second mother, and oh, how he had adored her. Though another child, Jemuel, was later born, nothing would ever replace his beloved Jedidah. His parents too had lived painful days. For some, life seemed to be such a mixture of mercy and silence.

It was a few years later that Hephzibah, the wife of Hiddai, son of Jashobeam, finally gave birth to a son. This was a surprise and a relief after ten years of marriage and a large family of young girls. Hiddai had followed in his father's footsteps, excelling in the oil trade. He had also overseen the construction of a large wine press in the family garden, that lay just outside of the city, near to the hill, Golgotha. The brothers of his wife Hephzibah were successful merchants with various links to Greek, Syrian, and Phoenician ship owners. It was during business transactions in Arimathea and new connections that the brothers had introduced their sister Hephzibar to Hiddai. Though the brothers had maritime trade links, they were not involved in shipping themselves, for the Palestinian coast was not good for shipping. The wind from Africa blew upon it with great force, moving great masses of sand, which made the sea shallow so that vessels of a considerable draught had to anchor far out in order to avoid the shoals. Even the curved coastline that lay in the shelter of Mount Carmel was dangerously exposed to the north wind. Palestine lacked the small creeks and islands that had rendered the Greeks a maritime nation. The ports that Simon Maccabaeus and later John Hyrcanus had taken such pains to hold such as Dor and Joppa had only been very modest roadsteads used by small fishing vessels to gather the shellfish that were used in the production of purple dye. Even now, Herod's newly built port of Caesarea was controlled by Rome and managed by Greeks and Syrians. Nevertheless, the port served its purpose well as it was protected from the waves by enormous blocks of stone, and its entrance on the northwest was positioned so that the wind could not affect the harbour. The place was thoroughly equipped with docks and warehouses. The fine harbour that King Solomon had built for trade with India had long been replaced with a small, inferior port. As such, Jewish merchants—many who lived in Hebron, Arimathea, and the surrounding regions—hired the services of foreign shippers for their own voyages and movement of merchandise. The brothers of Hephzibar had an increasing number of commercial links, and their wealth continued to expand.

Hephzibar was a faithful mother to her daughters, and along with their father, she taught them to pray earnestly and to read and memorise scriptures. She was known for her generosity to the poor, and God alone knew how much of the money passed to her by wealthy relatives had been poured out to meet the needs of orphans and widows. Jashobeam and Ishvi still remained close, though now both too frail to journey far. Nevertheless, now in their old age, their gazes remained fixed upon the words of the prophets concerning Messiah. Jashobeam prayed that Joseph, the newborn son, would be one who increased in divine understanding and one who would truly bless Jerusalem.

34

THE OLYMPIC GAMES (13–12 BC)

News circulated that Herod had made his firstborn son Antipater his primary heir. The king had ensured that great festivals and celebrations were in place. There was to be a spectacular celebration for all to see, and at no cost. As always, lavish and exorbitant amounts of money were poured out freely on any occasion that was seen to magnify his power, influence, and splendour. The stories of how he had rescued Greece and ensured the future of the Olympic Games seemed far from heroic in the eyes of so many who remained crushed and choked by the onerous weight of his ever-stretching tax regime. The citizens of Olympia lacked money to continue funding the games as the task of holding this great prestigious event every four years had drained the city's financial resources. The financial burden had simply become too heavy to carry.

This was because the city of Olympia did not just feed and house all the competitors and spectators, but was obliged to pay for the hundreds of sacrifices offered to the Greek god Zeus in whose name these international games were held. As well as honouring and sacrificing to Zeus, the people sacrificed to his consort, the goddess, Hera. The first and last days of this festival were devoted purely to sacrifice. As word spread regarding Herod's sudden offer of substantial financial support (including a huge down payment of money for the future) as well as his recent departure to Olympia to preside over the game, anger and frustration burned in Jerusalem, for not only was the revenue created by levied taxes being spent on endless vacuous building projects, but also evidently on futile entertainment and worship of foreign gods. It became known that he had paid for renovation and reconstruction at the ancient athletic site, as well as financing the opening ceremony, official sacrifices, and banquets, and the cost of functionaries, and even the victors' statues. In return for his generosity, Herod had been proclaimed president of the Olympic Games for life—a position that many concluded must have been created especially for him. After his return from Rome, he reintroduced Greco-Roman athletic culture to Judaea on an unprecedented scale, appointing solemn games to be celebrated every fifth year, in honour of Caesar. Those in Jerusalem who had not seen the spectacular chariot races, horse races, wild beast chasing, gladiatorial competitions, and gymnastics taking place in the hippodromes and stadia in Jerusalem had certainly heard about them. Many continued to ask how this could be a serious priority of any king in any nation.

It was known by those who worked at the palace that Herod also possessed a considerable private fortune obtained through the ruthless execution of numerous important individuals in his kingdom. Furthermore, the great copper mines of Soli in Cyprus had recently been given to him as a gift from the emperor Augustus, and his personal wealth was rapidly multiplying.

Herod's temple was publicly dedicated and the great festivities, spectacles, rituals, and ceremonies surrounding the event attracted infinite crowds of pilgrims, governors, and royal dignitaries from many nations. Whether for religious, political, or social reasons, thousands of people passed through its gates. Yet amidst prestige and pomp, the land and the people were crying out for a lawful king to be upon the throne. The current throne was founded upon gross injustice and unrighteousness, and lurking beneath the magnificent beauty of this extraordinary glistening jewel-like edifice was grotesque ugliness. The temple stood as an aberration, a disfigured monument. Jerusalem had

become a distortion, violated by foreigners and violating herself.
No earthly flamboyance could disguise this reality.

The year of 9 BC saw the spectacular inauguration of the now
completed Caesarea Maritima. The port became the finest in the
nation with Caesarea itself as the administrative capital for Jewish
territories and the seat of the Roman prefect. The grandiose
inauguration included musical contests, athletic exercises,
horse racing, and fights by gladiators with wild beasts. It would
be here in the Judaean port that Greek-style Olympic Games
were henceforth held. As with all these innovative architectural
accomplishments, the ever-strengthening power of the oppressor
was embodied within the stones.

35

THE EXPECTANT ONES

Amongst some of Anna's close acquaintances was Rizpah, the wife of Simeon Ben Hillel. Rizpah and Simeon were the parents of the miracle child Gamaliel of whom thirty years later the story lived on. The child had died at birth, having been choked by the cord around his neck. The story, however, did not end here, for after several hours of prayer, the child miraculously came back to life. Rizpah did not fail to live out the meaning of her name. She was a 'burning coal'. She had fiery faith, tenacity, and passion for the prophetic promises of God. It was as if she was permanently with child, always expectant, forever declaring the truth in order that divine promises would be birthed. Phoebe, the wife of Theophilus, was another close friend, their young son Nicodemus aspiring to follow in his father's footsteps as a respected, erudite guardian of the law, associating with the intellectual elite of the temple, teaching and expounding the scriptures in synagogues. Theophilus was a member of the Sanhedrin, the ruling authority of Israel. He was known amongst others on the council for his thirst for knowledge and his hatred of all forms of corruption, particularly that of the money changers. The boy Nicodemus had a long way to progress, but even at the age of ten years, he had a mind as sharp as a blade, and an extraordinary capacity to memorise overwhelming portions of scripture in a single night. He was a great defender of the scriptures and uneasily challenged or disarmed, holding firm to his humble position within the religious hierarchy. Many teachers had expressed awe at the child and had fought to be his teacher.

Shelomith, the wife of the priest Azarel, cousin of Zacharias, who was now serving as a priest, was another devout, zealous woman of prayer, and another close friend was Jerioth, the mother of Issachar. Issachar was a Persian Jew well known amongst the younger men of the temple. His mother, Jerioth, a very close friend of Anna's, had ancestors of Jewish descent who had been deported from Jerusalem to Babylon centuries back, during the exile, and had resided there during the seventy years that the prophet Daniel had worked in the king's courts. Indeed her own ancestral line was traced back directly through the lineage of Daniel. Her husband, Aquila, was a Jew of Persian origin, and it was in Persia the two had met before marrying and returning to Jerusalem. Jerioth had been amongst one of the first families of many to return, and despite the turbulence of the times, she did not regret it. She had grown up knowing that one day she would not just visit the temple for pilgrimages but that in the great city of Jerusalem she would be replanted in home soil. She was a devout and sincere woman who spent a great amount of time praying and serving in the temple.

Aquila had been a close acquaintance of Jerioth's father and brothers with a shared interest in astronomy as well as being a highly gifted physician and a pioneer in botanical knowledge with much insight into remedies. He was known to be a man of reverence, intelligence, and scientific insight. Their son, Issachar, was a tall, handsome, erudite young man who had also acquired great insight. His father Aquila's ancestors had been of noble origin, attending one of the highly prestigious Babylonian schools that had been founded by the Chaldean astronomer and mathematician Kidinnu in southern Babylonia. These ancestors had associated with magian priests who worked assiduously for kings and princes of the Medes, Persians, and Babylonians relaying detailed divine information about daily matters involving governmental affairs as well as interpretation and evaluation of dreams, visions, and astronomical signs. They also contributed to the performance of ceremonies and coronations, offering secret teachings and insights and closely studying a wide array of literature including the prophetic writings of Daniel. They understood how celestial occurrences were motivated by symbolic principles. Zoroaster, an early religious leader and teacher in the region, had taught that, sometime in the future, a great king would arise who would raise the dead and transform the entire world into a kingdom of peace and security. Zoroaster had taught and reiterated that this king would come forth from the lineage of Abraham. The school was linked to the Chaldeans, a highly educated seminomadic tribe renowned for their study and knowledge of astrology and astronomy.

Aquila's ancestors had not returned to Jerusalem at the time of Zerrubabel or Ezra but had returned much later after the defeat of Persia by Alexander the Great and his conquest of Jerusalem around two hundred years after the majority of exiles returned. Greek influence on Jerusalem during this time had included the infiltration of tradition and learning from major Greek and Jewish astrologers. In adjoining countries, the skies became the object of a united gaze and intense scrutiny. With more conjecture, assumption, knowledge, and understanding in circulation, several men whose ancestors had associated with the Babylonian schools maintained their interest in surveying the skies.

Like his father, Issachar had been raised with this curiosity and passion for the deeper meaning of the skies. Of course in Israel, it was normal practice to lie at night on the flat roof, gazing into the patterns, formations, and constellations that beautified the heavens. However, there were certain self-made scholars of the sky who studied out matters in great depth, acquiring an intricate understanding of stars, planets, and galaxies. Issachar was one such scholar, and he often met with rabbis, sages, and chief priests to report his findings. For Issachar, the decor of the sky was an eternal celestial poem. As his eyes surveyed the night sky, he gazed with awe at the starry dance of the heavens. Certain bodies and constellations he was able to decipher quickly, and night after night he recorded patterns, calculations, movements, and measurements of all description. He was convinced that the sky was part of a clockwork universe and that Elohim, the Divine Creator, had scripted every event in the stars before time began. Like Job, Issachar stood in awe of the living God who stretched out the heavens, trampling down the waves of the sea. He alone was the great artist of the skies, the designer of the constellations, the painter of the Bear, Orion, and Pleiades, and the chambers of the south. The omniscient one enshrouded in mystery—His secrets, the spreading of the clouds, and the thundering of His pavilion. He laid the foundations and cornerstone of the earth, setting its measurements as the morning stars sang together and the heavens declared His majesty. He enclosed the sea, setting the recesses of the deep and causing the dawn to know its place. He was the magnificent sustainer holding the entire expanse of the heavens and the earth in His palm. The intricate ordinances of the heavens were but a figure in His mind, the clouds as vapour in His hands.

Issachar regularly attracted crowds at the city gates. People of all ages gathered to hear his findings—his charisma irresistible, his knowledge indisputable. Moreover, he had recently taken up a position as a lawyer and was becoming increasingly known for generosity and great passion for the administration of civil and social justice.

There were other known individuals in the temple to whom Anna only occasionally talked but whom she greatly respected as teachers, intercessors, and pioneers who understood the seasons and the times. Her brothers still came regularly to the temple, and now approaching eighty years of age, Ishvi and Jashobeam remained as close as they had been when running through the maze of narrow streets, thirsty for adventure. A small group of older men were having dreams, and younger men were having all sorts of visions, trances, and encounters with angels. They were few in number, but they could see that Heaven was soon to open wide. Several times a week, these men and women assembled in houses, on roofs, and in temple courts to discuss dreams that they had either recorded mentally or written with split reeds on parchment using lamp-black and gum, which was kept dry and only wetted for the purpose of writing. Many of the recordings indicated that several had dreamt the exact same dream and received identical visions, often at the same moment.

36

JACAN'S STORY

Jerusalem was in a desperate position. The façades of wealth and glamour gave an image of opulence that did not reflect the situation of its inhabitants. Palace dramas were escalating, and by 8 BC charges had been made by Herod against his other sons. They had been accused by him of high treason and, as a result, had been speedily executed.

The temple for many was merely a place for trade, gossip, and self-promotion. It felt at times as if the temple complex was more greatly cherished and revered by the many beggars and orphans around it than so many of those who entered its courts and administered its sacrifices. It was not always for money that the poor gathered, but for a chance to be healed of the disease and infirmity that plagued their bodies. Amongst these familiar faces was Jacan, now ten years of age. Jacan's story was tragic. At seven years old, his bones had been severely crushed after being trampled on by an unruly ox in the marketplace. Jacan had been told by the tradesmen to keep away, but the animals were often more awkward than their owners. Both intrigue and passion for adventure had blinded Jacan to the dangers that awaited him. The ear-piercing screams could be heard across the marketplace, and by the time the young boy was rescued, his legs had been so broken and his bones so crushed, he was left crippled. Within a month he was completely lame. The trauma had been compounded by the loss of both parents to a vicious fever before the end of the same year. Orphaned and crippled before beginning adulthood, Jacan had little chance of survival.

There were other young victims of life and circumstance. Jacan was just one of several in this position. His parents had been of humble origin, and his father had found his main work by helping to unload goods on trade routes. This had meant that he returned home only for Shabbat. The Shepelah road along the coast was the best for work, but it ran against the mountains of Carmel, and the road through the Jordan Valley was unbearable due to the heat as well as being dangerous and exposed to wild beasts at nighttime. The main trade route was thus that which ran along the other side of the Jordan—the great caravan route that led to Damascus. Jacan's father had been exposed to harsh temperatures during labour and had suffered from a chronic lung condition resulting in his death. Whether through savage beastly attacks, exhaustion, or dehydration, many died on these routes.

Since the sudden untimely death of both parents, Jacan had been taken in by a cousin who resided outside of the city and spent much time drinking excessively and engaging in raids, assaults on peasants, widows, and pedlars. As Jacan's physical state worsened, he had found his place amongst other beggars near the city gates. Now at ten years of age, the local townsmen, who looked upon this poor and neglected child with pity, often carried him along to the Pool of Bethesda on the path of the Beth Zeta Valley as the waters there relaxed his muscles. Bethesda was a collecting pool of spring water whereas the Pool of Siloam was the end point of the Gihon spring. Pilgrims used both pools for washing and bathing, but this pool was the most spacious. It was located near the Sheep Gate, and rainwater poured down into it. A dam had been built across the valley, turning it into a reservoir for rainwater. A sluice gate in the dam allowed the height to be controlled, and a rock-cut channel brought a steady stream of water from the reservoir into the city. A second pool had been added at the side of the dam. Natural caves to the east of the two pools were about to be turned into small baths. Rumours were starting to spread amongst foreign pilgrims regarding Greek and Egyptian gods who would one day take over the waters and release supernatural cures that would heal those who bathed in them. The rumours and expectations became increasingly mixed and far-fetched, but nevertheless, it seemed a good place for a crippled man to spend his day. Furthermore, it was a good place to receive an income, particularly during feasts when people were more generous and pilgrims liberal and compassionate. Jacan could not but hope that, maybe one day in the future, there would be a miraculous cure released at the pool and that crowds would be fighting to enter the waters. For now, though, whilst the pool was refreshing, there was certainly no healing power hidden in its waters. Nor was there any reputable healer in Jerusalem. Many of Jacan's days were spent there, and fortunately he required little help lowering himself into the water, for though he could barely walk, his young bones had regained some strength, and his arms were strong. He did, however, always need help in exiting the pool. Despite the constant noise and clamour of crowds passing, Jacan often fell asleep at the side of the pool, dreaming that his dead parents had been resurrected. Children who gathered would watch him talking and gesturing to no visible person. People began to consider the child insane and did not expect him to last more than a few more years. It was sad, but Jacan was just one of many beggars and cripples, young and old, whose presence was part of Jerusalem life and whose reliance on charity and kindness was the only shield against trouble and misery. Lonely and rejected he was usually collected and returned to the home of his drunken uncle.

With various murders, massacres, and natural catastrophes taking place, the city was home to more widows, orphans, and cripples than ever. Jacan spent his days wishing that any angel from any god would come and rescue him from a lifetime of infirmity. Did any god truly exist? Nothing was certain, and for Jacan, there were no promises. Where promises were absent, so also was hope.

37

ASAPH'S STORY

As he tossed and turned in the depths of the night, Asaph was eventually drawn out of his sleep by the rowdy voices of his uncles that resonated across the darkened shore, their small lamps illuminating the port. They were not usually this loud, and the chanting could be heard from all the houses that lined this small shore in Bethsaida. The lake of Galilee was vast, and to the children who played at the water's edge, it was an ocean. Asaph's young cousins were not yet old enough to join their fathers on the lake, but there was no doubt that as soon as they were of age, they would do so. The fishermen laboured mainly at night as it was in the dark hours that the fish rose to the surfaces of the waters before sunrise drove them back down. The men heaved the nets, unfurling into the sea, straining at the ropes as watchful herons and cranes readied themselves to dart in and steal the catch. The clapping and cheering that resonated across the shores indicated that it must have been a good catch. The residents would see the evidence soon after sunrise.

Asaph loved to be back with his relatives near the water and wished that his parents had never relocated to Jerusalem. The sounds and textures were so different here, the people spoke differently, and the breeze was clean. The air was fragrant and fresh and the pace of life so much calmer. Life was abundant, and the sounds of water splashing against boats were so much more melodic than the relentless trumpet blasts that vibrated throughout Jerusalem. Furthermore, in Asaph's mind, fishing was the trade of all trades.

The lake was fed and drained by the Jordan. It was known for its abundance of fish, and the fishing trade and export was thriving. Tiberias was the largest town on the western shore and home to seventeen natural hot springs. It was founded by Herod Antipas who dedicated it to the emperor Tiberius and eventually moved the regional capital here from Tsipori, which he named Sepphoris. Capernaum was on the northern shore, and to the southwest of Capernaum was Tabgha where the popular spring Ein Sheva was situated. Although the population consisted of mainly Galilean Jews, there was a small number of foreigners dwelling in towns and settlements near the shores and throughout the upper Jordan Valley.

It did not cost to fish on the lake. Fishing was free for all. The work was constant and intense, only ceasing on Sabbaths and feast days. The lake was surrounded by extremely high mountains, and powerful winds swept down from the peaks along its shores, clashing with heat waves rising from the water's surface often resulting in sudden turbulent storms. The fresh waters were known for the sheer abundance and rich diversity of fish, and the fishermen were a popular team of workers. Fishing was the majority trade for those who lived close to the shores of the lake, and many also owned pastures nearby, envied due to the rich fertility of their soil. The small ports were Bethsaida where most of Asaph's relatives resided, and there was also the Fishery, Magdala, the Fish Tower, and the Dried Fishes where there was an important centre for preserved fish.

The fishing hooks were made of copper, brass, or iron, and there were two types of net. One large, round throwing net with leads surrounding the edge of it—this was designed to catch the fish by dropping over them. The second was a net of Greek origin called a 'seine'. It was extremely broad and deep with light wooden floaters above and sinkers below.

Asaph's older cousins had grown up observing and acquiring the relevant skills from their fathers. When they reached the place where they intended to fish, some of the crew went ashore holding the end of one of the two long ropes attached to either end of the net. The boat then departed from the bank advancing slowly until the rope had been fully unravelled. Then one of the men afloat gently lowered the net into the water whilst the boat travelled in a great semicircle. As soon as this course brought them back to shore again, the men on board got into the water carrying with them the second rope attached to the other end of the net. Once they were back on land, they hauled on the two ropes with equal strength on each side until the net was near to the shore. The nets were expensive and needed a great deal of maintenance and constant repair. The boats were wide and solid, able to resist most winds, but not very fast. Nevertheless they well adapted to the conditions of the region.

When the fish were caught, the nets were emptied into the hulls, and after sunrise, they were sorted out into different kinds as they varied in value. Also some could not be sold as they were considered unclean fish and the Jews had been forbidden to eat them. Those without scales or fins were either thrown back into the waters or hidden and sold privately to pagans who were notably fond of them. Whether related or not, fishermen clubbed together to buy the necessary equipment, and they formed crews usually of six or eight with one man nominated as the captain. Proceeds were shared equally, and some of them formed cooperative unions in order to sell their fish to the salters and wholesalers of Jerusalem on profitable terms. Courage, brave-spirited patience, and determination were the necessary qualities of these fishermen.

Asaph lay imagining the size of the catch and the heaps of silver fish that would be shimmering in the sun as the night skies turned to day. These images were one of many distant recollections that would remain in his mind's eye forever. Asaph had not been blind from birth. He had been born in Bethsaida, and whilst most of the wider family remained there, his parents had moved to Jerusalem four years after his birth in order to seek help from a physician. Asaph had been the first and only son born later after the birth of several daughters. He had made new friends in Jerusalem, all of them musicians: Jehiel, a harpist; Eliphelehu, the son of a lyrist; and Chenaniah, a singer. As an unborn child, Asaph had leapt in the womb whenever music was heard and whenever his mother sang. This was why they had named him Asaph. Yet after a few years in their family home in Bethsaida, the child had become extremely ill. As the fever strengthened, Asaph's vision gradually deteriorated and blurred, causing him to perceived people as trees, objects as mere clouds, and the vast lake, a patch of light. For weeks, the trees and clouds remained; however, by the time the fever left his body, he was completely blind. Over the space of weeks, his world descended into blackness. Local physicians had tried to restore his eyesight, but no suggested cure had been successful.

His parents continued to search out a remedy for Asaph in Jerusalem, but so far, to no avail. His sisters had all married the sons of fishermen apart from the youngest who had married a Jerusalem goldsmith who spent his days smelting ore until dross floated from the top, removing impurities from molten ore and faithfully repeating the process until, finally, he could see his own face reflected in the gold. How Asaph dreamt of the day that he too would look into the gold and see through it. He prayed daily that Jehovah would send a miracle worker like Elijah or to breathe light into his eyes. This would be far superior to the touch of any physician. Recently in a dream, he had seen an angel clothed in glistening garments walking upon the waters towards the edge of the shore. Terrified, he hid in the bulrushes at the water's edge and watched the radiant figure move towards him, gently signalling for him to rise from the bulrushes. As he slowly rose to his feet, the angel lifted him into his arms and kissed his eyes until they were moist. He then whispered in his ear that the healer was on his way to the lake. Soothed by the angel's whispers, Asaph opened his eyes and saw everything as bright as day. Streams of colour and life returned, and blindness left him. Then awakening from his sleep, Asaph arose from his pallet to the familiar sounds of water and breeze but visions of unchanged blackness.

His grandfather was a keen fisherman, and the firm, reassuring grip of his rough hands was a cherished part of his grandson's world. Grandfather told him that Jehovah would recompense him with the brightest eyes of all the young boys in Israel. He would place eyes in his heart as well as restore his physical sight. In Bethsaida it was his grandfather who took him out alone on the boat and introduced him to local fishermen. He swam with a rope, fresh water splashing over his head, whilst in his mind's eye, everything was crystal clear. As the days passed, new dreams came, as did flashes of white light. Whenever Asaph sang, he saw more, and his family continued to listen in awe, for his voice was strong and unique. Back in the temple courts, he drew crowds, and when singing psalms alone in the house, he felt surrounded by a breeze of living beings. It was a strange sensation that caused him to feel that he had left the world as he knew it. Now laid outstretched on his pallet back in Bethsaida, listening to the joyous clapping of fishermen and the energy of the winds that swirled across the waters, he recalled the early images that his young eyes had once cherished: bright orange sunlight glistening over the waters; pale lilies and blossoms that graced the valleys, herds of mountain stags and gazelles that dotted the hills, dense orchards of flourishing nut trees, rich green pastures, towering bulrushes children hid in, lines of huge wooden fishing boats, gigantic nets that hauled in abundant heaps of shining fish, radiant sunsets of pink, violet, and indigo…and he prayed once again that he would be there when the healer came to the lake.

38

HARD TIMES IN TEKOA

Eri was a shepherd in Tekoa and just begun his journey to Jericho in search for a new life. A relative had recently settled there to work in the plantations and sent news that it was a good place to live. His ancestors had been nomads who, since returning from exile, had lived in immense caves and settled in Tekoa to work as shepherds. Eri had left his flocks in Tekoa with his cousin Ebez, who was also a shepherd there. The land in Jericho was richly resourced, and he would have more chance there of finding a wife.

Back in Tekoa, the life of his cousin Ebez remained overshadowed by sorrow. He had lost his wife during the birth of Timaeus, their first child. Ebez had named the child Timaeus, for he was a son, highly prized. Like all shepherds, the flocks of Ebez were his life. The grazing rights in Tekoa were cheap as the soil was not the best and the ground was rocky. He shepherded a special breed of small sheep known for the quality of their wool. The land here in Tekoa—its gullies, rocks, caves, and ravines—had been his only home. He had no house but had made his home in tents with a very elderly relative for whom he provided. Though she was old and frail, Persis ensured that Ebez and Timaeus were well fed, and she treated the tent as if it were a palace. She was a quiet soul, almost speechless, rarely expressing emotion. She had never married, and had it not been for Ebez and Eri she would have no relatives on whom she could depend.

As Timaeus grew stronger and more alert, he helped to take care of the flocks, learning quickly from his father. The two were well acquainted with other shepherds who assisted each other when one was in need. Shepherding was a lonely life, yet in a sense, not so lonely for the flocks were always present, and they became family. They were the object of the shepherds' affection and grew quickly to recognise the voice of their leader. They were totally dependent on good shepherding and vigilant protection from the wild beasts and vultures that awaited their prey. During the winter season, the shepherds kept their flocks in the valleys, and in the summer they moved to the mountain pastures. They used the stones to make sheepfolds and at times depended on natural caves and enclosures. The flocks were fed through winter on a mixture of chaff and barley, and small flocks of twelve or less were often entrusted to a child. Many flocks and herds consisted of thousands and demanded skill and attention. Shepherds were acquainted with solitude, standing alone in vast open spaces under the sky, leaning on their crooks. Though many Jews saw this as a dubious trade never to be taught to one's son, it was not an easy calling. Certain flocks spent the greater part of the year in the open air. They were led out the week before Pesach and did not come back again until after the arrival of the early rains. Wool shorn at the end of summer was better than that of spring because the keeping of the sheep indoors matted and soiled their fleeces. In winter, they spent several months under cover. Watching over these immense flocks demanded a high level of care and attention. Many sheep tried to wander astray, and wild beasts such as hyenas, jackals, wolves, and bears were common. Shepherds were always armed with a solid iron-bound cudgel and a large knife. Burning midday heat and biting night frost meant a rough living. They wore thick woollen cloaks to cover them during the bitterly cold nights. Many grouped together and brought their flocks to the same place in the evening so that each shepherd could watch in turn and allow the others to sleep in the tent. To make the watching easier, it was usual to make huge sheepfolds with dry-stone walls high enough to prevent escape.

Various pasture grounds had watchtowers in them similar to those that were built in the vineyards. Robbers and bandits were also a threat. As the shepherds led the sheep to drink in the morning, they uttered piercing cries that the sheep would recognise and played a reed pipe or flute as they walked with the flocks. They also had to take good care of any sick and injured sheep, gravid ewes and newborn lambs, castrate the male lambs that were not to be kept for rams, and tithe the flock according to the law. This was done by making the flocks and herds pass through a narrow gate, every tenth beast being set aside for the priests. Shepherding was thus a life of duty and affection. Tamed sheep would even come to the call of their own names whilst the loss of any animal caused anxiety. It would be relentlessly searched for and carried back to the flock on the shepherd's shoulders.

It was not many years after Eri had moved away from Tekoa that Timaeus, son of Ebez, married the daughter of a goatherd in Tekoa. The coming of a grandchild was, for Ebez, God's recompense for the sudden loss of his wife. When the baby girl was born, Ebez felt the years of shame and regret lift from his shoulders. The heavy burden of shock and grief began to lighten his soul, though its menacing shadow lingered. His son, Timaeus, had named the child Oholibama, 'Tent of the High Place', after her grandmother. Ebez had always held himself responsible for his wife's death. Though he had helped Persis deliver the baby well, his wife had not been strong, and she had suffered greatly during the birth. He had blamed himself, weeping in anguish for many months to follow. He had loved Oholibama, yet his love had not been strong enough to resurrect her corpse. The cords of guilt and sorrow that had bound his heart started to loosen their grip at the birth of his granddaughter. The seasons were changing, and there was reason to smile again.

Holding the child in his arms, he raised the bundle of cloths against the warm glow of the pink sun as it set over Hebron. The child had her mother's wide green eyes and bronze hair. Ebez had never imagined that he would hold anything of such supreme beauty. The soft fleece of a tender newborn lamb did not compare to the satin glow and silk complexion of the child's cheeks. The delicacy of her fingers, the perfection of this magnificent creation caused him to weep with joy. He had been expecting the child to be a boy, but somehow, everything seemed so right.

When the second child, a boy, was born the following year, Ebez and Timaeus danced in the fields and raised their heads once more to the heavens. After a short time, however, it became evident that the babe was not responding to eye contact. His eyes were vacant and rolled upward. There was no sign of vision, and though he responded to sound, the child's eyes remained expressionless. Sadness and anguish began to haunt Timaeus. How would a child with no sight ever amount to anything? How would he ever be able to pay a physician to cure his son? From where had this second curse come? Timaeus planned to save money to take to the temple. He would travel to Jerusalem with his father Ebez, beg for mercy from the priests, and find a reputable physician. This would not be easy, though, for even here in Tekoa, the price of grazing rights was ever increasing, and they had no money to spare. It would be worth it, though, for every shepherd needed his sight. As the months passed, the plans of Timaeus to go to Jerusalem and gain assistance did not materialise. Instead, he took to theft and strong drink, leaving his young wife in a state of deep despair. As the months passed, Ebez became weak with a broken heart and Persis breathed her last. There was barely enough money for her and Oholibama, let alone another child. Her own relatives were poor, and though Eri, now in Jericho, had been a good uncle to Timaeus, where was he now? It would have been better had this poor child not been born. God alone knew whatever would become of tiny Bartimaeus?

39

FAMILY EXPANSIONS

It was during this same year of 6 BC, at the end of the barley harvest, that Anna's youngest grandson, Jorah, son of Bezalel, became acquainted with Orpah, the daughter of leather workers from Bethany. They had been introduced by mutual friends during the festival, and by the end of the year they had become betrothed. Orpah was a determined soul, full of hope and highly active. She and her sister Apphia were both respected midwives, strong but tender women, extending their hands to the poor on every occasion. Although Apphia was already married with two daughters of her own, the sisters were close, and Orpah did not desire to depart from her family in Bethany. By the end of their betrothal, Jorah was working in Bethany in the leather trade for his father-in-law. The family house had been extended, and there was great feasting and dancing at Bethany. It was a large wedding with an unusual amount of guests. It was a day of rejoicing, and Anna cherished the prospect of great-grandchildren being born whilst she was alive and well. It was not long after the wedding that Orpah had the joy of delivering her sister Apphia's third child, a strong and healthy son, named after his father, Lazarus.

Anna's brothers had stayed in regular contact with Raphu with whom they had worked on the roads during Shemitah years. They journeyed to Jericho from the hill country to visit him, having received news that he was struggling to work due to an injury caused by lifting heavy weights. It was during this visit that the brothers became acquainted with Raphu's niece

Penninah and her husband Tuvya. Penninah's brothers worked in the balsam trade, and Raphu, her father's cousin, had always been like an uncle to her. Tuvya recounted story after story to the brothers about his former life and the merciful relative who had rescued him from a life of crime, anger, and poverty in Jerusalem. Since moving to Jericho he had still not once looked back. His faith was strong, and his knowledge and understanding of the scriptures increased each day. Moreover, after a very long wait, God had finally granted them a son.

Tuvya had vowed to Heaven that he would raise his son well with the care and guidance that he himself had never known. He would take him to Jerusalem for feasts and ensure that he was well schooled. This child would be a peace offering to God for the mercy and deliverance granted to him through the uncle who had redeemed him from a life of destitution and hopelessness. This blessed son would grow strong in stature and purity. He would stand in the reformed ways of his father, opening his home to the poor and providing for those in lack. Until Messiah came to set up his kingdom and crush the powers of Rome, Israel would require more and more bold, pure-hearted young men who would live righteously and remain faithful with clean hands and pure hearts. Purity was thus the name that he gave to his long-awaited son. Zaccheus would live out his name and resist the malice of the day, refusing to bow his knee to the corruption of Rome. This boy would dissociate himself from greed, stretch out his arms to the poor, and faithfully await Messiah. As Tuvya—this short, stocky character, tender-hearted and full of emotion—told his endless stories, he caused laughter and weeping. The man himself was a story, a story of great mercy and redemption. As Tuvya recounted the details of his life, his eyes were flames of passion.

It was during the latter part of this year that waves of anger and lamentation once again spread across the land. Hundreds of Pharisees, many of them young fathers, were being hung publicly in fields for daring to criticise Herod. As usual, there was no discussion, no verification of evidence, no trial. There was no place for justice in this tyrannical regime. Hundreds of employed officers, some Roman and others Jewish, were also hung for having been suspected of plotting in Samaria. The curse upon the nation was thickening. As bloodshed increased, so did the number of orphans and widows, many living in utter destitution. There was no safe place to speak one's mind, all discussions had to be held in secret, the king himself continued to circulate in disguise, and the multitude of officers that were indeed not colluding to plot his downfall operated as spies throughout the city. Those Pharisees who were not hung continued to fear for their lives and were treated harshly by Herod, who feared their unshakeable hope in the birth of a new divinely appointed Jewish king. He was unaware that the bloodshed he caused was not simply arousing militant revolt but reaping a small harvest of fierce and devout young men who pledged to be separate and joined the Pharisees.

Hiddai of Arimathea, Theophilus, and the circle of audacious young scholars with whom they had been raised were amongst the many young men who were now well trained in the law hoping to eventually be part of the Sanhedrin. They followed boldly in the footsteps of those who had been brutally tortured for voicing their convictions. They refused to respond militantly with violence and bloodshed or to walk in the vicious hatred of the zealots who were torturing and slaughtering fellow men who worked for Rome and stirring up the people to fight for vengeance in the name of justice. Rather, they were warriors of the heavens who had learned to pray and fast, declaring the promises set before them. Hope, alertness, and tenacious faith were their weapons, and armed with these, they would become experts in war, wielders of a greater sword. They were destined to be alert and judicious watchmen, stationed on the walls, guarding against the terrors of the night. The turbulence of the time caused them to rise up like eagles and soar to new heights. Their wingspan was ever increasing, and their vision, more acute by the day. Moreover, these were true eagles, for they nurtured their young with the revelation that they had received and they relied daily on fresh manna, the hidden bread of revelation. Isaiah, the prophet, had been sawn in two pieces during the time of Manasseh, and the prophets had paid the price of death. Martyrdom, bloodshed, and torture surrounded them, yet the divine promises that their lives embodied were stronger than the grave.

The economy was flourishing, but the people were poor. Pure sap was now worth twice its weight in silver, and it was to the continued distress of Jews in Jericho that trees themselves were forced to pay tribute to Rome. Young men were still being burnt alive, and several had been stoned for trying to wrench off the golden eagle placed by Herod on the temple gate. It was clear that, in Herod's eyes, massacre and bloodshed were seen as pragmatic and acceptable solutions for any query, any issue. Before the age of forty years typhoid fever drew him close to death, and during this time of great personal fear, the evidence of his brutality and the frequency of family murders radically increased. New types of torture were constantly being invented. The silence of the graves that encircled him was broken only by the revolutionary chants of builders and the wailing of the bereaved. Suspicion, not evidence, was the criteria for brutal action. Antipater, the heir to the throne, was certainly proof of this, for he was also executed as suspect of conspiracy to murder his bloodthirsty father.

40

THE YEARNINGS OF A PRIEST

The priests continued to faithfully perform the daily sacrificial duties and to intercede for the people, but this was to no avail. Who would move Heaven and awaken the hand of God? Who would mediate for this ravaged city and hasten the day of Messiah? Those who prayed united their cries and became a corporate intercessor, a covenantal family. They stood resolute side by side with faces set like flint, doves' eyes with no peripheral vision. They were few in number, part of the Anawim, the Quiet in the Land who were more interested in Israel's redemption and consolation that her reelevation to a former self-governed state of prominence. They postured themselves in prayer and fasting like Daniel whose face was ever set before the temple. In moments of deep adoration, their eyes were opened to visions of the age to come. They waited like Elijah in anticipation of the abundant rains that matched the sounds of their dreams. Like Abraham, they entered the counsel room of the Lord. Like Esther, they called for unified prayer, convinced that their calling was at such a time as this. Like Hannah, they pushed hard through clouds of despair with prayer and supplication. Like Moses, they prayed for great mercy and forgiveness to be poured out upon the nation. Like David, they were extravagant, uncompromising worshippers with hearts tenderised by divine majesty.

In his prayers and meditations Zacharias dreamt of the Most Holy Place. He felt the intensity of Shekinah glory in dreams and visions, and in moments of deep in prayer, his spirit passed beyond the veil. Both he and his wife were ones of prayer and song, their lives a constant incense offering. Zacharias knew no other way of living or being. As he became more acquainted with the divine presence, he meditated on what his ancestors Moses and Joshua had seen. He repeated the prayer of David: 'Let my prayer be set before thee as incense', and lived a life overwhelmed by waves of divine passion. As he read more of the prophet Ezekiel by the river Chebar and the dreams of the prophet Daniel, he became radiant with a heavenly glow, mystified and captivated glory. At times, he saw rivers of fire, rainbows, jewelled mountains, golden rain, and expanses of water set as crystal. The more he prayed, the more frequented this realm. In one vision, he saw a majestic lion, his mane soaked in frankincense myrrh, his eyes blazing with love. In other visions the lion was seated next to the Ark of the Covenant, oil dripping from his mane. He then watched himself kneel next to the lion, his hands cupped in order to catch the flow of oil.

Following such experiences Zacharias often wept for hours. He spoke of it only to Phineas, a likeminded priest within his course. Zacharias had only two desires outside of living to see Messiah. The first desire was that God would grant him a son; the second desire was that one day the lot would fall to him to burn the incense upon the golden altar. He knew, however, that the first was impossible as his wife was no longer of child-bearing age, and the second was improbable as there were one thousand priests to whom the lot could fall. Even though each priest could only be chosen once, there were multitudes who had still not yet been selected and who were awaiting the honour. Furthermore, he would soon be retiring from the priesthood

David had divided the priests into twenty-four courses, and the order of Abijah was eighth in line. Each course ministered twice a year, and each occasion lasted one week. Almost one thousand priests were in each course. Throughout the years the number of priests had multiplied considerably. There were always two assistants: one removed the ashes from the previous day's evening service, and the second entered and carried in new red-hot coals from the altar of burnt offering, placing them on the burning golden altar of incense. This continued for one week.

41

THE LOT FALLS TO ZACHARIAS
(JUNE 3 BC)

It was not long after the end of Shavuot, the Feast of Pentecost, and the course of Abijah was due to minister in the temple. Those in priestly ministry were to minister for the week, and the ministry for each specific day was determined by three lots. The first lot was cast before the break of day, and its purpose was to designate the various priests commissioned to cleanse the altar and prepare its fires. The first man of this group of priests upon whom the first lot had fallen went out immediately, and the other priests reminded him of where the silver chafing dish was deposited and not to touch any of the sacred vessels before washing his hands and feet. He took no light with him, for the fire of the altar was sufficient for his office. The brass laver filled with water as the other priests stood in readiness. As these assistant priests waited, the first priest took the silver chafing dish and removed the burnt coals from the altar. As he descended, the other priests washed their hands and feet and took their shovels and prongs with which they moved aside any unburned sacrifice left from the previous evening. They then cleaned out the ashes, which were later removed from the temple, replacing them with fresh fig tree wood, which provided sufficient charcoal for the incense offering.

The priests then reconvened for the casting of the second lot. The priest upon whom it fell was assigned, along with the twelve who stood nearest to him, for offering the sacrifice and cleansing the candlestick and altar of incense. If the sun was shining and the sky was lit up as far as Hebron, it was acceptable to kill the daily sacrifice. The lamb was then brought from the chamber where it had been kept for the four preceding days. Other priests, amongst the twelve, set in place the gold and silver vessels of service. The lamb, whose Levitical suitability had already been confirmed, was watered out of a golden bowl. The sacrifice was always offered against the sun so the lamb was placed on the stone altar with its face turned to the west. The elders who carried the keys now gave the order for opening the temple gates, and as the last gate opened, the priests blew three blasts on their silver trumpets, summoning the Levites and elders to their duties whilst announcing to Jerusalem that the morning sacrifice was about to be offered. The gates to the Holy Place were then opened to admit the priests who were to cleanse and dress the golden candlestick and the golden altar of incense. As the gates opened, the lamb was slain.

The incense was made of frankincense, cassia, stacte, onycha, and galbanum as well as a small quantity of a certain herb that generated a dense smoke. Whilst one set of priests remained busy offering the sacrifice in the Priests' Court, the two who had been commissioned to trim the lamps of the candlestick and to prepare the altar of incense entered the Holy Place. The lamps that were still burning were trimmed and refilled. The wicks and the old oil were removed from those that had become extinguished. They were supplied with fresh oil and relit from one of the other lamps. The large central lamp was known as the Western Lamp as it inclined westwards towards the Most Holy Place. It was the lamp towards which all the others were directed and could only be relit by fire from the altar itself. As the lamps were being prepared, the daily meat offering, the drink offering, and the offering of the high priest was carried up to the rise of the altar.

It was only then that the most solemn part of the morning service was initiated as the third lot was cast in order to choose the one single priest who would burn incense and bless the multitude who had come to worship. The priestly course of Abijah was on ministerial duty during the month of Sivan (June). For Zacharias, it was a sacred Sabbath. His burning desire was about to be fulfilled as the lot fell to him to burn the incense. His grandfather, Eliab, and his father, Zech, had but dreamt of this moment all their lives. Though no longer serving as priests, they were both still alive and at the temple that day. It was whilst he was in the Holy Place between the altar and the showbread that the angel, Gabriel appeared to him. He had entered alone to burn the incense, and the multitudes were praying outside of the Holy Place.

No one who had officiated in this way before was allowed to do it a second time, so for those chosen it was for once in their lifetime, after which they too were to be called rich, leaving to their fellow priests the lifelong hope that one day they would be chosen. Zacharias was to choose two assistants from amongst his friends whilst the fourth lot designated those who were to lay the meat offerings on the altar and pour out the drink offering. It was only the third lot that could not be repeated in the evening by the same priest, and this was recast for the evening incense offering.

The incensing priest, Zacharias, accompanied by his assistants, approached the altar of burnt offering. A golden censer held in a silver vessel was filled with incense by one assistant whilst the other placed in a golden bowl burning coals from the altar. As they passed from the court into the Holy Place, they struck the resounding instrument known as the Magrephah, which signalled to the priests to gather for worship and ensured that the Levites occupied their places in the service of song. Another priest assembled the people at the Gate of Nicanor. Slowly Zacharias and his assistants ascended the steps into the Holy Place preceded by the two priests who had formerly dressed the altar and the candlestick and now removed the vessels they had left behind. Worshipping, they withdrew from the Holy Place. Next, one of his assistants spread the coals on the altar whilst the other arranged the incense, and Zacharias was then left alone within the Holy Place. It was thus during this time alone that the forty-nine-year-old Zacharias, in his final year of priesthood, had a divine encounter far beyond anything he had hitherto experienced. There, in the Holy Place, he was not alone, for Gabriel was with him. The orbs of bright white light that illumined his night visions reappeared that morning, right beside the altar.

42

TO THE RIGHT OF THE ALTAR

Having heard the word of command signalling that it was time for the incense offering, the multitudes withdrew from the inner court and fell to their knees, spreading their hands in silent prayer. Zacharias remained alone in the Holy Place illuminated by the seven-branched menorah. In front of him at some distance, towards the heavy veil that separated him from the sacred place, there was the golden altar of incense, on which red coals glowed. To his right was the Table of Showbread, and to his left was the golden candlestick

Deep silence rested upon the worshippers as Zacharias, hidden inside the Holy Place, laid the incense on the golden altar. As he carefully performed his duty, the angel, surrounded by intense white light, appeared to the right of the altar and spoke with him as the cloud of aromas ascended. Prayers of thanksgiving, deliverance, and restoration were then offered by the priests and the worshippers. After this, the priest upon whom the fourth lot had fallen placed the meat offering upon the altar. Then Zacharias, followed by the other priests, came to speak the blessing of Aaron over the people. However, as this moment arrived, it became evident to both the crowd of worshippers and the surrounding priests that Zacharias was unable to speak. Trembling and shaking, he gestured and beckoned to them as they stood in wonder, patiently awaiting his benediction. As the delay became increasingly long, the blessing had to be made by one of the other priests. The high priest's daily offering was then presented, and the drink offering was poured out upon the foundation of the altar.

The temple music began with the blasts of the silver trumpets, the priests faced the people, and the Levites crowded the steps that led from the Israelites' Court to the Priests' Court, and all faced westwards towards the sanctuary. Cymbals were struck, and the choir of Levites, accompanied by instrumental music, began to sing out the psalm of the day. Several young, skilled sons of Levi joined their fathers and stood to sing. The psalm of the day was sung in three sections, and at the close of each section the priests drew three blasts from their silver trumpets, and the people bowed down and worshipped. As the morning service officially closed, there was much discussion and enquiry amongst the crowds regarding the health of the incensing priest.

Priests were called up for duty twice a year for one week. Jericho had a large priestly settlement, and those who lived there arranged certain temple supplies. The fertile Jericho valley was, of course, crown property. Others lived in the quarters of Ophel in Jerusalem, but Zacharias did not live here with the elite. Not only was Ein Karem in the hill country the land of his ancestors and the land that he loved, but also it was a calm place to shield his barren wife from idle tongues of judgement.

Zacharias taught and advised several young, devout men who were rising up out of oppression, earthquake, bloodshed, and famine. Even ones as young as nine and ten years old such as Nicodemus, the son of Theophilus, and Joseph, the son of Hiddai from Arimathea, were intently drawing on his wisdom as well as that of their own fathers. There was a visible acceleration of learning and study as anticipation intensified and Israel grew more desperate for the words of the prophets to be fulfilled.

There seemed to be so many logical reasons for why the current climate was conducive to Messiah's arrival. Many were convinced that the fullness of time and the dawning of a new era would soon be upon them. The impossibility of the law continued to torment souls, particularly those who were truly God fearing. The nation had descended into indescribable darkness though knowledge of the scriptures had spread rapidly across Europe and Asia. As Isaiah had foretold, the Gentiles were awakening to the truth. Greek was now a common world language, and the pages of the Septuagint were being read in many nations. The elaborate and economically expedient road system had facilitated and accelerated travel, communication, and territorial gain. Pax Romana had ridden the land of a significant degree of social disorder. Social crimes such as pirates raiding sea vessels and bandits invading highways had been rife during the last years of the republic and had now been minimised by the new infrastructure. The reorganisation of the land into provinces by Augustus and the establishment of common laws and regulations had established a level of social order in the nation. Was this era of social restructuring the sign of a reordering to come? There had certainly been enough bloodshed in the land due to torture, famine, and earthquake. As the prophet Jeremiah had warned, the voice of Rachel in Ramah was already being heard. Were there more massacres to come before Messiah's arrival? At least they would stop after his arrival—surely this was a certainty. The prophet Micah had declared that an eternal ruler would go forth from Bethlehem, the city of David? Had the new king already been born? The prophet Balaam had stated in his oracle that a star was to come forth from Jacob. Was a sign to be sought in the skies? Many who studied these prophecies recalled their parents discussing the horrific events of 63 BC when many young boys were slaughtered following a presentation to the senate by magi who, having surveyed the skies, inferred that a new important ruler had just been born.

Though many rabbis and sages did not agree, to a very small minority of controversial scholars, the recent introduction of the cross into Roman society was a sign of the nearness of the times. Formerly such executions had taken place in Israel by hanging on a tree, and this was infrequent. The cross as a form of execution had been introduced by the Syrian king Antiochus IV, and the Romans were now starting to use it. Several wondered whether this rise in brutality was a sign that Heaven's light was about to shine forth. Was this now the window of time in which Messianic prophecies were to be fulfilled? Certainly some perceived a sense of acceleration and held an expectation that God would act suddenly. Would it be that a new priestly would bud, blossom, and bring forth ripe almonds overnight?

43

Speculation? (3–2 BC)

"Speculation!" they muttered. "Pure nonsense," whispered others. The month of Elul had begun, and it was now the hottest season and two months since the month of Sivan when Zacharias had been on duty in the temple. Neither he nor his wife had been seen since, and rumours had spread in the temple that Elizabeth, wife of Zacharias, was with child. Argument and conjecture ensued for days. As gossip was not always accurate, many assumed that the expectant mother was in fact Elizabeth, the youngest daughter of Amzi, one of the chief Levite choristers. Amzi was a kind and renowned man of tremendous musical skill. His only daughter, Elizabeth, had miscarried a few years earlier and struggled to conceive since. However, when several women approached the wife of Amzi in the Women's Court, a stir was created. Amidst the commotion and confusion, it soon became evident that Elizabeth Ben Amzi was not in fact with child, though she continued to live in hope. The confusion, however, did not die down as tales and reports of all types (many contradictory) continued to circulate about Elizabeth, wife of the priest, Zacharias. As endless gossip and opinion echoed through the temple courts, only those inside the hill country home at Ein Karem knew the truth.

Zacharias had been absent from the temple for several months, and this was most unusual. The multitudes had assumed and concluded that he must have had a vision that day when the performing of the incense offering had left him voiceless. Those priests who had visited him since the drama gave no reports that suggested otherwise. It was thought that maybe, since the event, Zacharias had fallen ill, for indeed he had been absent from the temple for a while. Others speculated that maybe he had suffered a seizure whilst performing the incense offering. Whatever the case, his regular presence was not visible, and his younger brothers simply reported that he was weak but not frail, not at his best, but steadily recovering. The sudden whirlpool of gossip and assumption about Elizabeth was thus to some minds quite ill placed and somewhat inappropriate. No one quite knew the source of the conjecture, and none of the women from Ein Karem had noticed any sign of the priest's wife being with child.

Certain women who continued to fast and pray began to sense that something extraordinary had occurred. As months passed, they cried out for health and restoration to Zacharias. A few of these women were young mothers, friends of Jorah and Orpah. They were as daughters to the aged prophetess, their hearts innocent and recipient. As Anna interceded and reentered visions of the past, her eyes met once again with former images of ladders upon which angelic beings were ascending and descending. She saw again the angels of deliverance stepping down upon the land. The angels held scrolls, unravelling them as they descended. These were the same letters that had announced local and regional births. She saw the mantle of Elijah spread over the hills as an outstretched garment.

It was not long after these visions that Anna returned for a few days to the hill country. She was due to visit Bezalel and his family as well as brothers and other elderly relatives, and it was during this visit that the elderly widow received confirmation of the truth. Eliab, who was still alive though frail, had spoken to Japhlet and his sons regarding the extraordinary happenings of which only a handful of close friends were aware. Zacharias had remained unable to give utterance, even a slight whisper. It was still not quite understood by Japhlet and his sons whether the sudden dumbness that Zacharias had experienced had unfortunately now been prolonged by old age and by the shock of his wife becoming pregnant at such an advanced age. Clearly, the priest's soul was overwhelmed, yet again no one was sure whether this sudden extreme effect on his body was due to the terror or wonder that had obviously overwhelmed him in the vision that he had experienced or whether judgement had come upon him due to some possible failure or error in his priestly service that day. What was clear to all who knew him was that he and his wife Elizabeth were humble, righteous, God-fearing people of excellent moral stature and highly reverent in their walk. As such, this punishment could not have been the result of deliberate sin, conscious transgression of the law, or lack of prudence in service. The predicament thus remained a mystery, and the few acquaintances that knew of the pregnancy both from conversing with Elizabeth herself, and from the written messages of Zacharias, had vowed to keep the matter a secret. Evidently, some news had made its way to the temple, yet little was known for sure. Many assumed that it was all a fictitious explanation for why Elizabeth had not been seen for so long at the temple whilst others argued that her husband's requirement of physical care was a perfectly logical and natural reason for why she too would be in a season of retreat. As the weeks passed, little more was said. Temple gossip died down, or at least so it seemed. After all, Passover was imminent, and clearly there were more important affairs to be engaging with.

It was with great rejoicing that Anna later returned to the hills just prior to the feast. Jehovah had shown regard for the humble state of these true and righteous bond slaves. Generations ahead of Elizabeth and Zacharias would declare them blessed. This was a divine miracle, like that of Sarah and Hannah. The Mighty One had done great things, revealing the holiness of His name and mercy towards those who feared Him. His arm of provision was never too short. He was the faithful, all-sufficient one who exalted the meek and abased the proud. Yet for what great purpose was this child to be commissioned? Was this the restorer and forerunner of which the prophet Malachi had spoken? Messiah was to be born in Bethlehem, and Bethlehem was not far from Ein Karem. It was just across the hills.

Anna spent just a short time back in the hills before Jorah took her back down to the city, which was soon to flood with streams of pilgrims. They talked a lot during the journey. Jorah was the closest to his grandmother. He reminded her of her beloved Joash, his eyes ablaze with conviction, his obsession with the unseen Messiah, his desperation for his son Lazarus to carry the flame and demonstrate his allegiance to the new king within the coming reign of peace.

The descent from the hills back to the city was overshadowed with joy and anticipation. As they neared Jerusalem with the hills behind them, the purple light on the mountains of Moab was fast fading out. Across the city the sinking sun cast a rich glow over the pillared cloisters of the temple and the silent courts as they rose terrace by terrace. The hand of the Almighty was as powerful now as it always had been, and His promises were as sure as ever. No mystery, no torment, no darkness could shroud this truth. Light would always shine through darkness and expel the shadows from its path. The night would not be long.

Rumours and assumptions continued to circulate. Now that it was established as true that the Elizabeth at the centre of former rumours was not Elizabeth Ben Amzi but indeed Elizabeth, wife of Zacharias, the nature of conversations that dominated the outer courts radically changed. The doubt and incredulity that had originally surrounded the report, engaging inquisitive minds during the first five months of pregnancy and seclusion, were finally silenced. As the full story gradually unravelled, facts were recounted, and timings disclosed. This knowledge of the miracle, accompanied by indisputable physical evidence that Elizabeth was with child, led some to believe that she was carrying Messiah despite the fact that both parents were from Levi, not Judah. The people waited as calmly as possible and with certitude that the child's true identity would be revealed in time. There was a level of secrecy amongst close acquaintances, few of whom had spent any real length of time with Elizabeth since her seclusion. Even this inner circle was only partially enlightened to the fullness of the events that had taken place during the incense offering. After all, the father of the child still remained entirely mute.

Nevertheless, a few men who were close to Zacharias in the temple had been informed by him in writing of the encounter within the Holy Place. In his written correspondence, Zacharias had quoted words that had been uttered by the angel: 'The child was to be a prophet of repentance and a forerunner of Messiah.' This news injected fresh hope and absolute certainty that God had heard their cry. In times of trouble, He was not as distant as it had appeared. He was near. In fact, He was very near.

44

The Birth of the Forerunner

The child was finally born at the end of Passover, and the news swept rapidly across the hills of Judea. As was custom, the mohel had come to the house to perform the circumcision and the blessing. The parents named the child John, a name confirmed by the still-speechless father who had written the large unmistakable letters on a clay tablet. As he raised the tablet for all to see the chosen name that was not a family name, the trembling priest retrieved his voice. It had been nine months since Zacharias had uttered his last word before performing his duties for the incense offering. Upon hearing his own voice, he looked as astonished and relieved as those who stood and watched. His words of prophecy, declaration, and blessing resounded as a song, a song full of fresh promise, hitherto unheard. His cousin, Azarel, came and blessed the child as the entire house became pervaded by a curious presence and a holy hush. This sudden change in atmosphere was accompanied by an unusual silence, and those who had witnessed the event compared the radiant countenance of the priest to that of a celestial being. In muteness, he had birthed a voice. It was a voice that would resound throughout Judea.

From that moment onwards Zacharias was a different man, his wife a different woman. He was carried back to childhood experiences in the Jericho balsam plantations, a fresh fragrance suffused the very air he was breathing, and excitement consumed every part of his being. This moment was not a normal moment, and this child was not a normal child. Energy, boldness, divine breath, and holy desire consumed him and his wife. When they spoke, they sensed an intense, tangible presence that was not their own. It was the presence of the Holy Spirit, the divine breath of God. Elizabeth was radiant, her womb was empty, yet she was pregnant with other secrets.

As news and rumour circulated, fragments of information were either discarded or confirmed, and a reverent fear consumed certain families in the region. Though they understood little, there was a deep curiosity and interest regarding the divine destiny and identity of this child, John. The trees were rejoicing, and the hills had become a different place. They had become home to an appointed one. Exactly who this child really was and who he was to become was something of a mystery. However, to his parents, the child's destiny was certain. He would prepare the way for Messiah and announce the emergence of the sunrise from on high. He would stand as a prophet of the Most High and illuminate the multitudes with flames of truth and revelation. He would raise a banner heralding the Prince of Peace, the strong one who would defend the righteous, crush the enemy, and draw all men to His throne. They clung to the words of Micah: 'The daughter of Zion would arise and her horn would be made as iron.' This horn of strength was Messiah. It was the great horn of salvation.

All who had been present at the birth as well as those who had heard the reports continued to ask what would become of the child, for so evidently the hand of the Lord was upon him. Furthermore, the certainty with which this newborn's father had spoken suggested that he possessed secret knowledge and knew more about the timing of Messiah's arrival than others. Several truly wondered whether the child was in fact Messiah; others were not so sure. Evidently, Zacharias and Elizabeth had been richly blessed. There was no doubt about it. Discussion was lively and opinion diverse, yet common to all who listened and pondered was the revival of lost hope.

Anna reflected on the years passed. So much had happened since those childhood days when she had danced around the terraces imagining that she was Queen Salome. She had lived through eleven Shemitah years and two Yovel years in which Jubilee had been declared. The cycles of nature, seasons, and feasts had been as reliable as ever, yet political, social, and religious life had become so fragile, so desperately unpredictable. She had been a daughter, a sister, a wife, a mother, an aunt, a widow, and a grandmother. She had seen rulers come and go, Rome invade, and the empire birthed. She would refuse to meet her grave until Jerusalem met her redeemer. The great miracle granted to Zacharias and Elizabeth energised her to strengthen her grip on dreams and promised unfulfilled. Though apathy and fatigue overshadowed a people whose life and joy had been drained out of them and the land was enshrouded by dark mists of hopelessness, Anna's clarity of mind and spirit were as sharp as a knife blade.

Elizabeth too had increased in strength, and her countenance radiated a distinct glow. There had been a change in posture, and the two younger women to whom she was a close friend talked of how she seemed to be beholding a secret. They said that she talked of Messiah in a different tone, with a strange conviction and demeanour that was most difficult to describe. They said that her eyes glistened, and she talked as if Messiah was already there. They knew, though, that it was only natural for such an elated soul to now believe and expect anything. As such, they were not taking this air of mystique too seriously. They were simply rejoicing in the faithfulness of God.

The entire nation was being shaken by forces of darkness, and the majority of people were spiritually and morally destitute. The crushing weight of the tax system continued to take its toll on a fatigued and disillusioned population. The priesthood was corrupt and deceived, and the people had nowhere other than the stars to fix their gaze. Nevertheless, those who were proactive continued to partner with the God of promise—the living, steadfast God of

Abraham, Isaac, and Jacob. He was faithful and true, His word was sure, His promises eternal. These Heaven gazers were resolute in heart and had taken it upon themselves to remain in a position of alertness and readiness, eagerly contending and looking for the consolation of Jerusalem. One of the older known faces, Simeon Ben-Hillel, had announced to the house of Zacharias that he knew his soul would not be taken to rest until his eyes saw not only the forerunner, but Messiah himself. As for Zacharias, though not without voice, he was less vocal in the temple and had spoken very little since the birth of his beloved John. His face was full of joy, but it was a restless joy. His deep priestly eyes were pensive, contemplative, serious, yet assured, anxious, yet expectant.

Anna was standing for herself and for Joash. She was consumed with a double passion, ignited with a double flame. Blessed with children, grandchildren, and great-grandchildren, she cast her eyes over the generations, declaring over them, 'Ratzon Hashem' (Thy will be done). Like many of the older women she was known for gentle wisdom, like the peaceful and insightful Mother of Israel who in former times had called to the commander, Joab, and interceded for the lives of her people.

Massacres and sudden executions continued to add to the sacrificial blood flow of a land unforgiven. She cried out for justice and righteousness, compelled not just by faith and zeal but by the very force of Heaven. She wept the tears of the weeping prophet, Jeremiah. 'How lonely sits the city that was full of people! She has become like a widow who was once great among the nations. She weeps bitterly in the night and tears are on her cheeks.' Anna was a fiery intercessor, a weeping prophetess whose maker was her husband. She continued to declare that Jerusalem was not a widow and that her creator was not an unjust judge.

45

THE HEAVENS DECLARE HIS ROYALTY

Sept 3 BC Rosh Hashanah

Having returned from the evening sacrifice, Issachar surveyed the night sky with a close eye as there had been talk amongst a few of his elderly acquaintances that the previous night had been marked by unusual movement. As usual, he lay on his roof gazing up at the heavens, beholding a unique panorama. Within seconds, he fell into a deep sleep and was taken up into the heavens where he saw before him Sedeq, the king planet. This planet was known by the Romans as Jupiter, and they believed that it controlled the universe. Sedeq was a pale sphere ringed with bands that were the colour of desert sand. The king planet was moving closely to the king star known as Regulus Sharu to the Babylonians and Regulus Rex to the Romans. The two of them were moving purposefully and steadily towards each other within the great lion-like constellation of Arieh. Issacahar was well aware that every twelve years the king planet was known to glide past the king star as its orbit came close to the star. Indeed, on many nights he saw this planet rising in the east, and even in the daytime when the sun was low, it could be seen by the naked eye. As his dream merged with the drama of the sky that he had observed from the roof, Issachar witnessed a strange occurrence. He saw the king planet reverse its course and turn back three times to draw close to the king star—not once, not twice, but three times, he watched it turned back. This strange phenomenon he had never encountered either in observation or in dialogues with experts. It seemed that the planet was drawn to the star for some deep, significant reason. He knew from his studies that this sight of a triple pass was exceedingly rare, and he lay stunned and mystified. As he looked closer, he saw that the circular movements of the king planet had drawn a majestic golden crown over the king star. As it journeyed on through the constellation of the great lion, the king planet appeared to stop its eastwards drift and drift back westwards. Issachar found himself suspended between the heavens and the earth, and as he looked down, he saw the great light that had been caused by this conjunction, illuminating a small area of the hill country, just south of Jerusalem. He then heard a voice call his name, 'Issachar', and was transported by an angel to a different part of the sky. Here he observed the virgin constellation rising in the east steadily upwards behind Arieh, the lion constellation. As she rose up high, she was clothed in the glory of the sun. The crescent moon that had always so faithfully marked the sacred moment of Rosh Hashanah was positioned just at the virgin's feet.

When Issachar awoke, he was in the same position, staring upwards at the twilit sky. As he recorded the majestic panorama of the night, he recalled Jacob's prophecy over his son Judah and Micah's prophecy regarding the birthplace of Messiah being a small hill town. Could it be that this dream was a great sign, a confirmation that Messiah would come soon to establish his kingship in Israel? Had his relatives here and in Babylon witnessed anything similar either in the sky or in their dreams?

After Rosh Hashanah and the heralding of another new year, repentance was once again the keynote of the following ten days marked by fasting, prayer, and retreat leading up to Yom Kippur. These ten days were known as Yamin Noraim, the Days of Awe. If a man spoke simply of 'the day', it was understood by all people to which particular day he was referring. Pilgrims followed the rites with devotion as the burden of sin, the wretched condition of mankind, and the yoke of the law dominated the minds of the people.

46

Endless Need for Atonement

It was seven days before Yom Kippur, 'the day'. The high priest left his own house and took up his abode in the temple chambers. A substitute was appointed for him in case he died or became Levitically unfit for his duties. He was sprinkled twice with the ashes of the red heifer on the third and seventh day of this interval between Rosh Hashanah and Yom Kippur. During the whole of that week he performed various rites such as sprinkling blood, burning incense, lighting the lamp, and offering daily sacrifices. Every part of that day's services devolved on the high priest, and he was not permitted to make a single error. Various elders of the Sanhedrin were appointed to see to it that the high priest fully understood the procedure of the service and to instruct him if there were any areas of which he was unsure. On the eve of the day, the sacrifices were placed before him for preview, and he was bound by a solemn oath not to change or adapt anything relating to the services of the following day. He was not permitted to eat much for his evening meal, and throughout the night hours, he was to hear and expound the scriptures so that he would not fall asleep. He was to stay awake and not to submit to fatigue in any way. At midnight, the lot was cast for the removing of the ashes and the preparing of the altar. In order to distinguish the day from all others, four rather than three fires were arranged on the altar of burnt offering.

The services of the day began with the first streak of morning light, the people having already been admitted into the sanctuary.

Only a linen cloth excluded the high priest from public view when each time, before changing his garments, he bathed in a special place set aside from the usual bathing quarters. Throughout the day he changed his garments and washed his entire body five times and his feet ten times. In case of age or infirmity, the bath was allowed to be heated either by adding warm water or by putting hot irons into it.

The first dawn of morning was announced in the usual manner, and the high priest bathed and put on his golden vestments before proceeding to perform all the parts of the regular morning service. After the morning service, the high priest washed his hands and feet and removed his golden vestments, bathed again, and put on his white linen garments, washing again his hands and feet. The young bull used for his sin offering stood between the temple porch and the altar. The high priest stood eastwards facing the worshippers and turned the head of the sacrifice westwards to face the sanctuary. He then laid both of his hands upon the head of the animal and confessed as follows: "Ah, Jehovah, I have committed iniquity. I have sinned. I have transgressed. I and my house. Oh then, Jehovah, I entreat you, cover over the iniquities, transgressions, and sins that I have committed, transgressed, and sinned before you, I and my house, even as it is written in the law of Moses thy servant: 'For on that day will He cover over you to make you clean from all of your transgressions, before Jehovah you shall be cleansed.'" As he spoke, those who stood near cast themselves down with their faces on the ground and the multitudes responded, "Blessed be the name, the glory of His kingdom is eternal." The priests' instruments accompanied the benediction of the people.

The next part of the service was performed close to the worshipping people. In the eastern part of the Priests' Court, very close to the crowds of worshippers, the two goats stood with their backs to the people and faces towards the sanctuary. Two golden lots were drawn from the 'calpi', an urn that stood nearby.

They were placed by the high priest on the heads of each goat as he stood facing the people. One bore the inscription 'Jehovah' and the other 'Azazel', the scapegoat. The goats looked almost identical and were of similar value. A piece of scarlet cloth was tied to the horn of the goat to be cursed, and another was tied around the throat that was to be slain for Jehovah. The cursed goat was then turned around to face the people, which stood silently waiting for the sins of Israel to be laid upon it and to then be carried forth.

The third and most solemn part of the day then commenced. The high priest returned towards the sanctuary and a second time laid his hands on the bullock, which still stood between the porch and the altar, to confess over him his own personal sins, the sins of his household, and the sins of the priesthood. The young bull was then killed, its blood caught up in a vessel and given to an attendant to keep it stirring lest it coagulate. The high priest then advanced to the altar, filled the censer with burning coals, and arranged a handful of frankincense in the dish destined to hold it. Every eye of the crowd was strained towards the sanctuary whilst slowly bearing the censer and the incense, the figure of the white-robed priest faded away into the sacred place of His presence. After that, nothing could be seen of his movements. He stood alone, separated from the people, the Most Holy Place being lit only with the red glow of the coals in his censer. In the first temple where, within the veil, the Ark of the Covenant had stood with the mercy seat overshadowing it and the Shekinah above it. The outspread wings of the cherubim were either side of the mercy seat, and the high priest placed the censer between the staves of the ark. However, Herod's temple was void of both covenant and Shekinah. Most were ever conscious of this fact. This temple stood as dead as a cemetery waiting for glory to fill it.

The high priest proceeded to carefully empty the incense into his hand and throw it on the coals of the censer as far from himself as possible then waited until the smoke filled the Most

Holy Place. Retreating backward, he prayed outside of the veil for blessing, abundance of rain and sunshine, fruitfulness, and deliverance from captivity. He prayed this quickly so that his protracted absence did not cause the people to panic and lament for his safety. With the incense burning, the people withdrew from proximity to the veil and worshipped in silence. As they saw the high priest soon emerge from the sanctuary, they knew instantly that the sacrifice had been accepted. The high priest took the blood from the attendant who still stood stirring it and reentered the Most Holy Place, sprinkling with his finger towards where the mercy seat had been, once upwards and seven times downward, counting carefully each time.

Withdrawing again from the Most Holy Place, the high priest placed the bowl with the blood before the veil. He killed the goat that had been set apart for Jehovah, and entering the Most Holy place a third time, he sprinkled the blood of the goat. He then sprinkled blood from each bowl towards the veil outside the Most Holy Place. Finally he poured the blood of each into the same bowl and mingled the blood of the heifer and the goat, sprinkling it upon the altar of incense. Throughout this entire process, he was to ensure that his garments did not become spotted with sin-laden blood. The remainder of the blood was poured out in the west side of the altar of burnt offering.

As the worshippers looked on with awe, it was then time for their own personal guilt and sin to be removed from them as the high priest laid his hands upon the goat to be cursed and mediated for the people. As the prostrate multitude worshipped again at the name of Jehovah, the high priest turned his face towards them and uttered his last words: "You shall be cleansed."

After this, a strange scene was witnessed as the priests led the sin-burdened goat out through Solomon's porch and through the eastern gate, which opened upon the Mount of Olives. Here an arched bridge spanned the intervening valley, and over it they brought the goat to the mount where a man appointed for the purpose took charge of it. The distance between Jerusalem and the beginning of the wilderness was a five-day journey, and at the end of each day a person took over from a station en route in order to offer refreshment to the man leading the goat and to accompany him to the next station. When they reached the edge of the wilderness, the scarlet cloth was torn off and left on the edge of the cliff. Then the goat was led backwards and pushed over the projected ledge of rock. Though this rocky precipice had not been required in Mosaic Law, this finality of action had become the tradition throughout generations. There was a moment's pause and then the man, who was now defiled by contact with the sin-bearing goat, retraced his steps to the last of the ten stations where he spent the rest of the day and the night. Flags were waved from station to station to signal the completion of the task, and after a few minutes, it was announced back in the temple that the goat had borne upon itself all of their iniquities, which had been carried to an uninhabited land.

Whilst this had been taking place, the high priest had cut up the two animals with whose blood he had previously made atonement and had sent the carcasses to be burnt outside of the city in the place where temple ashes were usually deposited. Then still wearing his linen garments, he had entered the Women's Court to read a series of scriptures and prayer for mercy, grace, assistance, and protection. Washing his hands and feet, he had removed his linen garments and put on his golden vestments, proceeding with the festive burnt offerings of the day as well as the inner parts of the bullock and goat. This had been followed by the normal evening sacrifice, after which he had washed his hands and feet once again and changed back into his linen garments in order to reenter the Most Holy Place and collect the censer and incense dish that he had left there. He had then washed his hands and feet again, burnt the evening incense in the golden altar, lit the lamps on the candlestick for the night, washed again, and put on his ordinary dress ready to be escorted home.

The people formed a huge procession and escorted the high priest to his house. The whole evening closed with a feast. The maidens of Jerusalem adorned themselves in white garments that had been specially lent to them for this sacred day so that rich and poor could not be distinguished. They danced and sung in the vineyards close to the city. Not only had sin been atoned for, but also guilt had now been removed. However, although the people were not purged, they were not free. True mercy could not flow out to man. Though transgression had been removed, it had not been permanently blotted out. In accordance with the law, guilt had been displaced and deposited elsewhere, but only for another year. There was nothing permanent, and there never would be. A new and better solution was required.

47

Movement in Heaven – Movement on Earth

It soon became known that Caesar Augustus had decreed from Rome that an official census be taken of the entire empire. As instructions and stipulations circulated across the land, further agitation and unrest was stirred amongst the population. The costs of travel and road tax and the lack of any prepayments for the days of lost labour as well as the fact that Roman allegiance and 'ownership' was now becoming an increasingly personal matter was the cause of bitter resentment and uprising. In fact, many claimed that the census amounted to enslavement. Registering was not a simple process as the crowds were dense, the heat was heavy, and family records were often confused. The Romans were contentious, controlling, and often suspicious. The people, though, had no choice in the matter. The consequences of failing to register would be heavy.

During the period of weeks in which the census took place, key travel routes throughout the nation were busier than ever. Masses of pilgrims who had recently arrived prior to the start of Sukkot were steadily flowing in and out of the courts, animals bleating and lowing, money changers competing for business. The roads passing through the hill country were not only teeming with members of the Davidic tribe heading for Bethlehem in order to register families, but also with crowds of visitors who were staying in the hills overnight prior to entering the city—many of whom had relatives in the area, or many who had planned to build their sukkot in pastures overlooking the city.

Matthan and Jehosheba celebrated the return of their eldest grandson Joseph who had recently become engaged to a woman in Nazareth. He had been unable to visit regularly due to the demands of trade. There were many such families who made the most of such reunions, yet this did not sweeten the bitter reality of this census. It was a final symbol of oppression and foreign dominion. Registration simply affirmed the forced subjection of the populace to taxation. The whole census was no less than personal subscription to oppression. As the city filled with crowds, there were at least a few who pondered: Had the census been orchestrated by God in order to place the spotlight of Heaven on Bethlehem? Was it time for prophecy to be fulfilled?

It was some nights thereafter at the end of the agricultural year, on the second day of Sukkot, that Issachar, after lying on his roof, surveying the skies, dreamt another extraordinary dream. This night, he saw the king planet journey through the field of stars and join with Kokebet, the mother planet (known by the Romans as Venus). She was a fiery orange wonder, idolised by the Greeks as a love god. The king planet and the mother planet drew close to each other but did not block out each other's light. As Issachar gazed at the spectacle, he watched the two balls of light seemingly fuse so that one could not be distinguished from the other. Merged together, the two planets formed an intensely majestic spectacle, quite beyond description. Such was the phenomenon. Issachar awoke suddenly from his sleep with singed and burning eyes. He was certain that he had been sleeping, yet the pain in his eyes left him deeply perplexed. He knew for sure that this great sign must relate to a royal birth. Whether it related to Messiah or not, it was a sign of colossal significance that demanded prudent research. Hastily changing his garments, Issachar went straight to the temple to speak with friends, some of whom were sages. Clearly, he had no choice but to converse with the schooled. As soon as Sukkot ended, he would start to arrange and plan the first stages of a lengthy trip to Babylon. Aged and wise Jewish ancestors as well as other contacts of his father were still living. These learned astrologers influenced by the schools of Kidinnu and Zoroaster would surely be able to help him. Surely others had dreamt this dream. Surely this was a sign that would manifest visibly in the sky.

Shortly after passing through the Huldah Gates and weaving himself in and out of the steady flow of joyous pilgrims gathering materials to prepare their tents, Issachar entered an exceedingly great commotion. The great festival of nations as promised by Zechariah was always a time of lively discourse and vibrant interaction, but unusually, this latest drama was not caused by the entertaining exchanges of lavishly robed pilgrims. Rather, hundreds of curious eyes were on a group of unspectacular locals who had hurried through the Sheep Gate with their animals for sacrifice with unusual speed and urgency.

In the centre of the chaos stood a group of familiar shepherds whose flocks were used for temple sacrifices. They had arrived at the city by the usual route having passed by the Pool of Bethesda towards the sheep markets just outside the Sheep Gate. Some were owners of flocks; others hired labourers. Having washed their hands, the shepherds had uncharacteristically rushed into the Gentiles' Court in a state of atypical emotion. Amidst the usual groups of merchandisers, soldiers, pilgrims, and disabled beggars, sitting in the garments assigned to them by priests, a sizeable and prominent gathering had occurred. As Issachar approached the scene, he heard the group of men reporting an extraordinary occurrence. Urgently addressing as many who would listen, they relayed a terrifying experience that had taken place the previous night. Many had eagerly gathered to listen. The shepherds had been watching over their flocks as normal in the pastureland surrounding Bethlehem in the hill country. All of sudden, the night sky had been illuminated by a blazing light brighter than the noon day sun. The canopy of stars that decorated the night sky over their pastures had been swallowed up into an enormous ball of intense white light. Some of the shepherds had fallen to the ground in terror, and others had desperately gathered restless flocks in order to distance themselves from the shaft of light that was descending into the field. However, there had been literally no time to move. A giant angelic being had emerged from the blaze of flashing light, and the remaining shepherds had fallen to the ground in terror with the others. Some said that they had prayed anxiously for their life and mercy; others had been too paralysed to move, too terrified to make utterance.

This animated group of rough-looking shepherds continued their report. They claimed that the angel had commanded them not to fear and had announced a message of good news not just for Jerusalem by for all people, stating that Messiah had just been born in Bethlehem, the city of David. On hearing the news, many standing listening in the courts naturally assumed that the shepherds had been drinking excessively and that the drink had been sturdy. Their outrageous claims were dismissed with loud outbursts of laughter. After all, it was all quite entertaining. Others assumed that the shepherds had colluded in order to invent an imaginary drama and were behind the times in doing so, for it was common news that the priest Zacharias had finally been granted a son and that this birth had indeed brought good news to Judea. In the minds of the disapproving, not one word that any shepherd said could ever be taken literally; shepherds were poor, shoddy, simple, uneducated men. Many shepherds were also still young and naive. They knew the day and night sky for sure, and they regularly scrutinised patterns, colours and constellations; however, on this occasion, they had obviously been gazing for too long. It was assumed that even if the reports were true, the angel must have referred to the hill country generally and not specifically to Bethlehem, as the latter was not the home of Zacharias. At the most it had been an angelic affirmation of the divine promise embodied by the new child, John. Indeed Messiah would be born in the city of David as the prophet Micah had prophesied. Most rabbis and sages had taught this well. However, the time was clearly not now. Of course there were also those who discarded the words of Micah, insisting that Messiah would be born in Jerusalem. What was clear to all was that such holy, history-making news would certainly not be announced in a field to a mere group of shepherds.

Nevertheless, the shepherds were relentless, and the reports continued. As more people gathered, one of the older shepherds began to recount the story again from the beginning, his weathered face aglow, his wrinkled brow raised in awe, and tears streaming down his face into his long grey beard. As Issachar drew near he recognised the aged complexion as being that of Barzi, the father of Zibia who had never left the area. Barzi claimed that they had been directed by the angel to search for the baby in Bethlehem and that the sign for the exact location had been a feeding trough in a hillside cave. They had been told that here they would find a newborn child wrapped in strips of cloth. The shepherds in chorus, affirmed—their shouts competing with each other—that, as the angel's instruction had drawn to a close, they had suddenly found themselves surrounded in the field by hundreds of angelic beings. The great angelic symphony had physically elevated the shepherds from the ground, causing them to tremble with a mixture of terror, awe, and adoration. They described the sound as a divine serenade, a celestial melody unheard in nature and certainly more holy and spirit lifting than the Levites' worship. It had been a unique sound, indescribable with words, worship from elsewhere, an orchestra from Heaven that had resonated through their bodies at the speed of lightning yet with the fresh clarity of the spring rain. As the angels had sung, the rays of light emblazing the pastures had become even whiter, casting a glorious glow across the trees. The flocks had gathered close to the shepherds, these helpless animals, paralysed by fear of the volume, sight, and vibration of the spectacle. The host of voices had declared the glory of God and peace amongst all of mankind. In unity they had affirmed that this peace was an act of goodwill, motivated by divine pleasure.

The Quiet in the Land believed this report, receiving it as an affirmation of the great message of this feast. The eye of Jehovah was upon them. He would make his tabernacle amidst the praises of across the earth. Mercy would flood to every tribe and tongue. The eye of love was roaming to and fro over all nations. An endless flow of questions from curious adults, children, buyers, sellers, farmers, and other shepherds caused an even larger circle to gather as the crescendo of the tale brought timely entertainment as the shepherds claimed to have followed angelic guidance and located Messiah. In a city and a time when seemingly everyone was claiming to have birthed or located the new king, the majority laughed uncontrollably in jest, bidding old Barzi to share the strong liquor that caused his eyes to glow. Others stood by, mesmerised.

48

ANOTHER SUKKOT

As the feast drew near, the landscape became dotted with branched sukkot and the city continued to overflow with pilgrims. Festivity reached its usual crescendo with the torch dance and the lighting of the menorah. It was towards the end of this feast that Hiddai, having returned to Arimathea, had a powerful dream relating to the water libation. In his dream, the ground in the outer courts began to crumble and springs of water emerged from the ground. As they grew in power and height, the entire temple complex became engulfed in cascading fountains. Siloam and Bethsaida became crystal waterfalls, and as the torrents of fresh water flowed through the courts, he saw priests swimming though the courts using their robes as ropes.

Later in the month of Heshvan, the ploughing season commenced, and the wheat and barley were sown. The late grape and fig harvest had finally ended, the olives had been gathered, the dates were ripening, and the fattened sheep were ready to be slaughtered. The early rains had begun, and the dry ground was gradually regaining moisture.

The next great illumination of the temple would take place the following month during the Feast of Dedication. Until then, it was a time of intense labour and preparation of the soil. It was during this time of ploughing and seasonal change with the arrival of the former rains that those who prayed began to be overwhelmed with a fresh sense of expectancy. There was sustained hope that the temple would be illuminated once and for all by the light of the promised one. The recorded reports of angelic visitations and apparitions recounted by shepherds, prophets, intercessors, prophetesses, priests—as well as young Levite boys who gathered to record and discuss dreams—indicated that something was moving in Heaven and that Messiah was to born within the current era. It was said that the aged Simeon Ben Hillel had even declared to some that he would not see death until he had seen Messiah with his own eyes. Of course, even amongst the expectant, many were swayed by the winds of every new idea including the passionate assertions of the zealots. Equally there were those who possessed no faith in the fulfilment of ancient promises, but who knew that the revered Simeon had in the past described time frames for future events with notable accuracy.

Simeon was robust and youthful for his age, free from the fragility and frailty suffered by others who shared his number of days. He was a proud grandfather and a vivacious worshipper. Likewise his beloved wife Rizpah, though weak in sight, remained fervent in spirit. Simeon was one who lived with his mind-set on things above and occupied the heavens. Like the sages, he had an intricate insight into the divine oracles of the prophets, and he lived out his name as a great hearer. He was a man who literally abided within the voice of Jehovah and in the continuous flow of His enlightenment. Moreover, Simeon had many experiences in which he had physically felt the Ruach HaKodesh, the Spirit of the Holy One, breathing into him, encircling his body as a refreshing spring breeze. As he read the words of Isaiah concerning Messiah, he would see vapour arising from his scrolls. This vapour was often suffused with a tangible fragrance of incense and myrrh. Other times, when meditating alone and contemplating Messiah, he would feel a weighty presence on his shoulders causing him to sit for a while.

Since the start of Sukkot, Simeon had seen a sea of gold. The ocean was as golden as the sand on the shore. As he studied the landscape, he saw distant desert land that was more golden than ever. The sky was also a canopy of gold, and the horizon was barely visible. Colossal waves were rushing towards the shore, and again they were majestic waves of gold. There was nothing in these visions that was not golden. For days after Sukkot, Simeon reentered and studied these visions until he heard the words of the prophet Habakkuk: 'A day would come when, as the waters cover the sea, the whole earth would be filled with knowledge of the Jehovah's glory.' Simeon understood that this gold was knowledge. The Spirit of Knowledge that Isaiah saw resting upon Messiah would be released as a mantle across the expanse of universe, causing all nations to know of His glorious majesty. A new world consciousness would be released in the days to come. Messiah, the Wonderful Counsellor, would unleash this consciousness and bring revelation to the nations.

49

SIMEON
THE FULLNESS OF TIME

It was Simeon's constant desire to know and behold this glory. He believed that the Shekinah presence was the abode of Messiah and that He would carry this dimension with him when He came to rule. He lived in a sense of deep knowing that surpassed hope. It was absolute faith, absolute knowing.

Simeon heard and saw no vision of Messiah in person, yet he knew with absolute unshakeable certainty that his days would not end until he had witnessed His presence right there within the temple courts. He had heard the accounts of the shepherds forty days previously at the start of Sukkot. The exact details Simeon did not know, for stories had been adapted in passing. Nevertheless, he felt great certitude regarding the shepherds' integrity and sobriety. The illuminations and the water ceremonies that had marked the feast paled in comparison to the divine light and life that they must have witnessed. He spoke of his reflections and contemplations with only three people. One of them was his companion Ishvi, the youngest of Anna's brothers who, over the years, had been a faithful friend.

It was a normal busy day at the temple. The incense offering had just finished, and the crowd of worshippers were gradually leaving the Women's Court. The usual line of women were waiting at the Gate of Nicanor, approaching the top of the Levites' steps, which led up the immense court. They stood in line and witnessed all that passed in the sanctuary. Many priests had left after the completion of the morning sacrifice, several lingering behind whilst the offerings of purification were being made. As each woman approached the officiating priest, he received her offering of either a lamb and a turtle dove or two turtle doves in the case of poverty. These served one as burnt offering, one as a sin offering. The priest then proceeded to sprinkle the mother with sacrificial blood and declare her cleansed from all impurity. The firstborn sons were then redeemed with five shekels of silver. The rabbis had stated that redemption money was only to be paid for firstborn sons who were 'suitable for the priesthood', in so far as they did not possess any disqualifying blemishes. This requirement had been extended to all firstborns, not just those born of Levites. The women then joyfully descended the fifteen Levites' steps from where the Hallel was daily sung.

It was whilst watching the last women descend the steps that Simeon began to tremble and faint. Assuming this unforeseen occurrence indicated sudden weakness of heart, the men in the area carried him out to a place of calm. They insisted that a physician be summoned with haste, some muttering that the poor deluded man would sadly never see his blessed consoler after all. However, it soon became evident that the robust Simeon had been overshadowed by a divine being and not by death. He chose not to speak of what he had seen or heard, remaining silent as he regained strength.

The following day Simeon arrived unusually early at the temple—just after the priests had gathered in the Hall of Polished Stones for the first lot, before the morning offerings were prepared. Only the earliest faint glow of morning light streaked the eastern sky. He did not enter inside the temple until after sunrise. Until then, he sat outside of the Eastern Gate, his mind set on glory.

The following day as the sun rose over the eastern hills, Simeon felt a holy presence, this time more weighty and intense than ever before. Kneeling on the ground in the eastern portico, he became enveloped in translucent light, saturated in divine breath. His lungs filled with air untainted by the smoke of sacrifice or the spices of the previous day's markets. It was a clean air, indescribably pure. His body began to tremble once more, and as the holy Ruach of God became one with his own breath, his tearful eyes stared at the rainbow encircling him. He felt himself floating as a body without mass as the swirling rainbow began to lift him and raise him to his feet. As Simeon stood encircled by the rainbow, each band of coloured light ministered divine assurance to his soul. Each colour had a voice and imparted a specific piece of the same great divine secret that had hitherto been hidden within the archives of Heaven. Simeon was now being given the key to the ancient treasure box into which his dreams had previously allowed him to glimpse. The Spirit of the Lord breathed bold conviction into his being, anointing him with the very oil of Heaven. Through a series of short visions, the Spirit of Counsel gave him insight regarding the mother of Messiah and the future that would lie before her. The Spirit of Might infused his physical frame with inner fortitude. Knowledge revealed to him the exact details regarding the physical appearance of Messiah's parents— their stature, height, frame, and complexion. That which had been vague in dreams suddenly became clear and exact in his mind's eye. The Spirit of Understanding revealed the wider national and global implications of his visions for Israel and the nations of the world. The Spirit of Wisdom spoke to him of the glorious days when he had rested upon Solomon and of how once again the throne of Israel would be occupied by a wise ruler. The Fear of the Lord touched his eyes and revealed to him the interior of the Most Holy Place. Simeon's eyes streamed with tears as at once he felt the extreme urgency of the hour and the transforming peace of a Holy God.

With the morning sacrifices now over, the crowds dispersed and groups of people gathered to talk. Simeon walked slowly amidst the usual women and newborns speaking gentle words of blessing and peering into each tiny face. He proceeded to wander slowly through the Women's Court, and as he stopped in a certain place the rainbow dispersed, each colour dissolved and reformed itself into a majestic coloured flame, the height of a pillar. The seven flames formed a perfect circle around him, and nothing passed inside their radius. The radius in which Simeon stood was kept completely empty as if an angel were guarding it. Minutes later, it was into this sacred space that the young couple stepped. As the mother's deep, searching eyes penetrated his, Simeon gently took the child from her and held it in his arms, peering into its wide-open eyes. It was a glorious moment. It was the moment for which his entire life had been lived. Oh, the transcendent beauty, the profound holiness of this single moment, a thousand scrolls could not record.

The great scroll of history and eternity had taken on human form. The lion cub had been born and the obedience of the nations would be His. This child's stone was the deep crimson sardius stone that spoke of permanent atonement. Consolation no longer had to be searched for. The centuries of waiting had come to an end. The historical stage was being reset, and a new era of perpetual kingship had commenced. Heaven had generously released its beloved, the anointed ruler, the embodiment of peace, the wise counsellor who would guide the hearts and acts of men, drawing all nations to His love. Simeon's last words were 'Yovel'. As he later declared to a select few, this had been his day of Jubilee. Of course, Yovel did not just mean 'ram's horn'. It meant 'to be carried off to rest'.

50

AND AT THAT VERY MOMENT

Anna had watched intently as the young couple stood with the child, encompassed by the very vapour of Heaven and covered by the hand of the Most High. She had watched them stand before the longing gaze of Simeon as the familiar sounds of lively exchanges and priestly blessings continued to rise. As words, visions and ancestral promises streamed through her mind, she felt her heart rise within her. God would confirm His word through the presence of two witnesses. As Simeon had drawn in his breath and released a sob, unspeakable joy had consumed her being. Anna had moved calmly towards the four lives and three generations, her entire being consumed with glory and truth. There was no doubt, no possibility of error, no space for reflection or hesitation. Immense gratitude claimed every cell in her body and every space of her soul. Every emotion and thought was saturated with the purest, most profound gratitude and recognition of divine grace that a mortal soul could ever contain. Unable to stand upright and seemingly paralysed by expressible joy, Anna had lowered herself and knelt. She had wept and wept, her body trembling with awe, her eyes fixed upon her magnificent obsession, the promise of the ages to which her heart had been wedded.

After a short while, the aged prophetess had composed herself, and leaving the Women's Court, she had gathered and spoken to certain of her acquaintances as well as other widows for which she cared. Anna then journeyed to the hill country speaking with joy and certitude to relatives and all those who were actively looking and waiting for the redemption of Jerusalem. Every dream and vision documented and recorded in the scrolls of Joahaz by this small group of intercessors was being and would continue to be fulfilled. The fullness of time had arrived, and the words of the prophets were evidenced before the eyes of Israel.

From the temple courts to the hillside terraces, Anna faithfully carried the lamp of truth, its flame glowing brighter with every conversation, its oil self-replenishing. It was true. The days foreseen by Joel were upon them and would continue to be fulfilled throughout the generations. The mountains had started to drip with sweet wine, and the hills had started to flow with milk. Water was filling the streambeds of Judah, and a sovereign fountain had already begun to cascade from the temple.

Whether at markets, village wells, or at local synagogues, the announcement circulated rapidly, and amidst fields of suspicion and cynicism, fresh seeds of faith were scattered. Anna rose up and stood tall in Jerusalem in seamless robes of stature, dignity, and promise. Her spiritual magnitude was that of a cedar flourishing in the courts, yielding its fruit in old age, its sap greener than ever, its very presence an unwavering declaration of the uprightness of God. As she spoke to small faith-filled groups in the entrance to synagogues, Anna had visions of Messiah standing before them, anointed by the Spirit of the Lord declaring his mandate of liberation. Truth became her energy, gratitude her melody, redemption her testimony. She was not a widow, and He was not an unjust judge. She had wept endless tears and cried a thousand lamentations, yet her widow's garb had never defined her. It remained as black ashes buried beneath the soil of hope.

Overwhelmed by events, Anna meditated on the great hall of portraits where as children their minds had lived, dramatising its scenes in the fields. The magnitude and veracity flowing from the line of canvases painted by the prophets flooded her soul once again. On certain portraits, details had already been fulfilled. The great throne of justice and righteousness was about to be established, and the one into whose eyes she had gazed had finally been made visible. As she continued to survey the images, her eyes became transfixed on Isaiah's heart-wrenching canvas of the lamb without blemish, brutally torn and pierced, acquainted with sorrows, wounded for transgressions, and crushed for the iniquities of mankind. As she gazed again at Him into whose chest she had leaned for over half a century, and surveyed the blazing eyes of He who had removed her grief and torment, she stretched out her hands and reached into the atonement to come. She saw the mercy seat dripping with the crimson blood of a man. Simeon had spoken truly, the consolation of the nations and the enlightenment of the Gentiles would certainly come, but it would come at a very costly price. In fact it would be a horrific price.

51

THE CONSOLER

Against the dark backdrop of pernicious acts and beneath the crushing weight of injustice, hope had materialised into a reality far beyond human comprehension. The zealots continued to agitate the people, torturing those who they perceived to be in support of Roman rule. Disillusioned rebels continued to plan the destruction and assassination of Herod whilst others, such as the infamous Simon of Peraea, who had attacked the palace at Jericho, were said to be planning to usurp the throne and declare their own messianic identity as soon as the disease-ridden tyrant had finally been erased from existence. Amidst voices of revolution, self-righteousness, corruption, and disillusion, the voices of the wise were few.

Now in Israel amidst the grinding thuds of military horse hooves, the sharpening of swords, the reckless speeding of chariot wheels, the clamour of money changers, the menacing threats of tax collectors, and the inexhaustible blasts of the shofah, a new symphony was emerging. From within the chaos and noise, the song of all songs was being written, its composition perfect and its origin divine.

The departure of Simeon was greatly mourned. He had been an intrinsic part of temple life, as upright, reliable, and ever present as the very columns that sustained it. Life was not the same without Simeon. He was missed by young and old alike. This kind, charming old sage whose favourite words had been 'Ha-Melitz', the comforter, and 'Nacham', the consoler, had always voiced the thoughts of Anna's heart, and she had often sat in silence listening to every word. Like his companion Zacharias, Simeon's eyes had glistened with illumined revelation. He had talked of the consoler more often than he talked of Messiah yet always affirmed that they were one of the same. He was obsessed with the consoler, the comfort of Israel and every nation. He had quoted the words spoken to Abraham that all races would be blessed through the Jewish seed and the words of Tobit the elder who had confirmed the mission of making God's name known to every nation. He had spoken of Nineveh and the desire of God to grant pardon to entire populations, the promise of Jeremiah that, when Messiah came, all nations would be brothers, and the assurance of Malachi regarding universal salvation. Boundless mercy would stream from Heaven, and restoration would be total. Furthermore, as Rabbi Ben-Hillel had unrelentingly affirmed, the nations of the world would be the object of great love. Many rabbis could not conceive of this, disagreeing vehemently over whether one's neighbour could ever refer to a man outside of the twelve Jewish tribes.

Simeon's years had been marked by great intercession, and he had spent his days living for Nacham, longing for Nacham, searching for Nacham, waiting for Nacham. He had always affirmed that one day weeping would cease; the comforter would be a balm of healing that would pacify the nations. All those who beheld Him would rise on the promise of eternal peace, wonderful counsel, and unending consolation. This would be the fruit of fulfilled promise, and those who rejected the promise would fall. Certain younger men whose eagerness for learning was tempered with humility and peaceful zeal continued to draw upon the words of Simeon, opening their minds to the great legacy that lay before them. After all, this wise, old father had claimed to be an eyewitness of majesty.

52

HOPE IN HOPELESSNESS

Many did not believe it at first as it had been announced so many times before. It was the height of Passover and not a time for scandal and sensationalism. Nevertheless the latest news spread like fire throughout the land. Herod was dead. They reported that his body had become ridden with a wasting disease and that he had had himself carried to the waters of Calirrhoes near the Dead Sea in the hope that the heated salt baths would allay his pain. Rumour had it that he had died right there in the water having commanded that, after his death, all the most important men in the kingdom be executed. Such news was not surprising as many had revolted, secretly conspiring against him, well in advance of his death.

The massacre of young boys in Bethlehem had been his last and most horrific of rampages. It was a massacre that none would forget. Newborn babes had been torn from the arms of weeping mothers, toddlers had been snatched from the courtyards of houses, and baby girls, mistaken for boys, had been cast violently back to the ground, their tender limbs broken, tiny heads gushing with blood. The wielded swords of soldiers took their toll on incensed fathers and older brothers striving to defend the defenceless with whatever object they could find, as burning torrents of blood-red anger billowed through the palace gates. Horrific shrieks of agonised parents, the wailing of terrorised families, and the agonising screams of the young ascended relentlessly to the dark silence of the sky as the soil of this small hillside town absorbed the blood of its young. The tyrannical roar of this vile, envy-ridden beast had been finally muted. The news of his death was confirmed and Jerusalem, crushed and choking under the pounding hammer of terror and despair, gasped once again and drew sufficient air to breathe a sharp sigh of relief.

Augustus divided the kingdom between Herod's three sons. His oldest son, Archelaus, was named as successor to the throne with Antipas and Philip appointed as tetrarchs of Galilee and Bashan. The Jewish people continued to demand the abolition of the monarchy as young zealots—fervently driven by apocalyptic dreams of liberation and revenge—rapidly increased in number. Archelaus was as corrupt as his father and was scarcely on the throne before he was at odds with almost all of his subjects.

It was amidst this ongoing tension that the cry of Job took on a new significance and became for a small but bold minority the resounding anthem of the hour: "And as for us, we know that our Redeemer lives and at last He will take His stand on the earth." In the case of Anna, these were to be her final words and four generations would stand at her bedside to witness them. It was thus against this morbid, perilous backdrop of the Herodian Dynasty that a blazing flame of hope flickered brightly. It was fuelled by an effervescent furnace of love and revolution, a raging blaze of redemptive mercy radiating unquenchable rays of peace that beamed forth to every nation.

The political backdrop was thus deathly indeed, but Israel's stage had been rearranged. The decor of glamour and bloodshed remained unchanged though two crucial new faces were preparing to join the cast. The voice of reconciliation would soon resound throughout the nation, calling her people to repentance and baptising them in the Jordan. Meanwhile from Jerusalem and Arimathea, to Jericho and northwards to Galilee, the Quiet in the Land breathed an intense sigh of joyful relief and continued to join hands, sharpening their gaze on the kingdom to come. The night was still dark—yes, it was ever so dark—but soon they would see Him…the sunrise from on high.

"Oh Comfort My people," says your God.
"Speak kindly to Jerusalem;
And call out to her, that her warfare has ended,
That her iniquity has been removed,
That she has received of the Lord's hand
Double for all her sins."
A voice is calling,
"Clear the way for the Lord in the wilderness;
Make smooth in the desert a highway for our God.
Let every valley be lifted up,
And every mountain and hill be made low;
And let the rough ground become a plain,
And the rugged terrain a broad valley;
Then the glory of the Lord will be revealed,
And all flesh will see it together;
For the mouth of the Lord has spoken."
A voice says, "Call out."
Then he answered, "What shall I call out?"
All flesh is grass, and all its loveliness is like the flower of
the field.
The grass withers, the flower fades,
when the breath of the Lord blows upon it;
surely the people are grass.
The grass withers, the flower fades,
but the word of our God stands forever.
Get yourself up on a high mountain,
O Zion, bearer of good news,
Lift up your voice mightily,
O Jerusalem, bearer of good news;
Lift it up, do not fear.
Say to the cities of Judah,
"Here is your God!"

Behold, the Lord your God will come with might,
With His arm ruling for Him.
Behold, His reward is with Him
and His recompense before Him.

Appendix

'In prophetic intercession the burden of prophet and priest unite at the highest level. One of the most significant prophetic intercessors in the New Testament is the prophetess Anna. Anna was a prophetess of the secret place, interceding in keeping with the purposes of God for her generation. Her intercession was her prophetic ministry. Undoubtedly Anna's intercessory burden for years had been for a fulfilling of God's covenantal promises to the Patriarchs. She was one of the prophetic intercessors God had ordained to pray through those promises of a Messiah. God's entry into every generation has been through a line of faith such as is seen in Anna. The prophetic intercessor conspires with God to bring forth His glory in the church. The word "conspire" literally means "to breathe together." It expresses the most intimate joining of life. Prophetic intercession is our conspiring together with God, breathing violently into situations through prayer in order to bring life.'

—Bryn Jones
"Prophetic Intercessors in a Final Generation" in
The Restorer, 1997

"If I was to see what He was doing, I would have to have the heart of Simeon who could see in a mere infant the salvation of the world. Others could not recognise Him when He was doing all the things that it was prophesied that He would do. Here is a man who could see Him and perceive who He was when He was an infant. That is remarkable vision. Do we see things when they are just being born? The only ones who saw Jesus at His birth were those who were there by revelation. They had a revelation and according to that revelation, they came to worship Him [...] your level of worship is determined by your level of revelation."

—Rick Joyner
"Kingdom Breakthrough Outpouring" Conference
Knoxville, Tennessee
26 September 2008

"Jesus tied His hands to the prayers of His people. Jesus wouldn't come to earth Himself unless there were intercessors like Anna and Simeon in place to bring Him in. He chose for us to co-labour—such was His love for humanity."

—Bill Johnson
Holy Trinity
Brompton, London UK
23 May 2009

'Could it be that the hunger of a few simple people like Simeon, Anna and Mary attracted Heaven, bringing it to earth? Could it be that "at just the right time" is determined by our hunger for God and His kingdom? There was a four hundred year season of silence prior to Jesus' coming. Could it be that hunger broke the silence and released the good news?'

—Kevin Dedmon
Unlocking Heaven
(Destiny Image: Shippensburg, PA, 2009)
p.154

'Watchmen pray into the plans of God and at times watch them take place in their own lifetimes. Simeon and Anna were two watchmen who waited patiently for the one who would deliver Israel. There is a company of people God is grooming now. They are modern-day Simeons and Annas who are waiting on the Lord and watching for His movement in their midst.'

—Jamie Galloway
Supernatural Revolution
(Destiny Image: Shippensburg, PA, 2010)
pp.119, 121

'Prior to Christ's birth we find Anna, a prophetess, engaged in much prayer and fasting. In my opinion, it is quite possible that this woman was not alone in her intercession, but the leader of a prophetic prayer ministry that lived in anticipation of her times.'

—Francis Frangipane
This Day We Fight
(Baker Publishing: USA: MI, 2010)
p.95

'In our day, the Holy Spirit is looking for modern day Simeons and Annas who will minister in the temple and welcome the manifested presence of Jesus. "If they wait He will come" is a word that must be heard! The call for gatekeepers of His presence is going forth. Do you hear it? Will you be one?'

—James Goll
Gatekeepers of *His Presence*
"Elijah List," November 2013

'I would love for it be said of me that I was "like Anna," someone who focussed on nothing and nobody except

Jesus. In every prophetic word, long ones or short ones, in every vision, every dream, every inspired prayer, I want to be declaring the testimony of Jesus.'

—James Goll
Adventures in Prophetic Diversity
"Elijah List," May 2014